EXCLUDED

MAKING FEMINIST AND QUEER MOVEMENTS MORE INCLUSIVE

Julia Serano

SEAL PRESS

EXCLUDED

Making Feminism and Queer Movements More Inclusive

Published by
Seal Press
An imprint of Perseus Books, LLC, a subsidiary of Hachette Book Group, Inc.
1700 Fourth Street
Berkeley, California
www.sealpress.com

Library of Congress Cataloging-in-Publication Data

Serano, Julia.
 Excluded : making feminist and queer movements more inclusive / by Julia Serano.
    pages cm
 ISBN 978-1-58005-504-8
 1. Feminism. 2. Gay liberation movement. 3. Social isolation. 4. Discrimination.
 I. Title.
 HQ1101.S47 2013
 305.42—dc23
                                   2013016145

Cover design by FaceOut Studios
Interior design by Domini Dragoone

DEDICATION

In loving memory of my mother,
Kate Serano.
I miss your love and friendship.
I miss our long conversations on the phone
or up late at night keeping everyone else
in the house awake. As you always used to
say to me, "I miss your face."

CONTENTS

Part 2: New Ways of Speaking

INTRODUCTION

ll of us have been excluded at some point in our lives. Perhaps because of our size, or class, or age, or race, or nationality, or religion, or education, or interests, or ability. And of course, many of us are excluded because of different forms of sexism—that is, double standards based on one's sex, gender, or sexuality. Many of us are undermined and excluded by our culture's male/masculine-centrism—that is, the assumption that male and masculine people and perspectives are more legitimate than, and take precedence over, female and feminine ones. And those of us who are gender and sexual minorities are stigmatized and excluded by our culture's insistence that only "normal" bodies, and "straight" and "vanilla" expressions of gender and sexuality are valid. This sense of exclusion drives many of us to become involved in feminism and queer (i.e., LGBTQIA+) activism. We seek out like-minded people who share our goals to eliminate sex-, gender-, and sexuality-based hierarchies, and together, we work hard to build new movements and communities with the intent that they will be safe and empowering for those of us who have been shut out of the straight male-centric mainstream. And yet, somewhere along the way, despite our best intentions, the movements and communities that we create almost always end up marginalizing and excluding others who wish to participate.

Sometimes we are consciously aware that exclusion is a bad thing, and we may deny that it is taking place within our feminist or queer circles. We may even resort to tokenism—pointing to one or a few minority members in order to make the case that our movement or community is truly diverse. But in other cases, we are blatantly exclusive.

Some feminists vocally condemn other feminists for dressing too femininely, or because of the sexual partners or practices they take up. More mainstream gays decry the presence of drag queens and leather daddies in their pride parades, and there is a long history of lesbians and gay men who outright dismiss bisexual, asexual, and transgender identities. Within the transgender and bisexual umbrellas, there are constant accusations that certain individuals do not qualify as "real" members of the group, or that their identities or actions somehow reinforce "the gender binary" (i.e., the rigid division of all people into two mutually exclusive genders). And in most queer communities, regardless of one's sex or identity, people who are more masculine in gender expression are almost always viewed as more valid and attractive than their feminine counterparts.

The astonishing thing about these latter instances of exclusion is not merely their brazen, unapologetic nature, but the fact that they are all steeped in sexism—in each case, exclusion is based on the premise that certain ways of being gendered or sexual are more legitimate, natural, or righteous than others. The sad truth is that we always seem to create feminist and queer movements designed to challenge sexism on the one hand, while simultaneously policing gender and sexuality (sometimes just as fiercely as the straight male–centric mainstream does) on the other.

There have been many attempts to reconcile this problem. Newer feminist submovements have sprung up with the expressed purpose of accommodating more diverse expressions of gender and sexuality within feminism. More inclusive umbrella terms such as "queer" (meant to include all sexual and gender minorities) and "transgender" (meant to include all people who defy societal gender norms) have come into vogue in an attempt to move away from infighting over identity labels. And what were once simply called "lesbian and gay" organizations have since added B's, followed by T's, then a panoply of other letters at the ends of their acronyms in an attempt to foster inclusiveness. And while all of these measures have brought a modicum of success, sexism-based exclusion still runs rampant in feminist and queer movements.

As a transsexual woman, bisexual, and femme activist, I have spent much of the last ten years challenging various forms of sexism-based exclusion within feminist and queer settings. Over that time, I have come to the conclusion that we cannot Band-Aid over this problem by simply calling for more diversity in a general sense, or by petitioning for the inclusion of specific subgroups on a one-by-one basis. Nor do I think that we can blame this situation entirely on the human tendency to be tribal or cliquish (although admittedly, such us-versus-them mentalities do exacerbate the problem).

Rather, I believe that sexism-based exclusion within feminist and queer circles stems primarily from a handful of foundational, albeit incorrect, assumptions that we routinely make about gender and sexuality, and about sexism and marginalization. These false assumptions infect our theories, our activism, our organizations, and our communities. And they enable us to vigorously protest certain forms of sexism (especially sexisms that we personally face!) while simultaneously ignoring and/or perpetuating other forms of sexism. In short, the way we describe and set out to challenge sexism is irreparably broken. My main purpose in writing this book is to highlight these fallacies in our theory and activism, and to offer new and more accurate ways of thinking about gender and sexism that will avoid the pitfalls of the past.

This book is divided into two parts, the first chronicling instances of sexism-based exclusion within feminism and queer activism, and the second forwarding my proposed solutions to the problem.

The first section, entitled "On the Outside Looking In," is a collection of essays, spoken word pieces, and speeches that I have written over the course of an eight-year period (2005-2012), all of which, in one way or another, address the issue of sexism-based exclusion within feminist and queer settings, and offer my early formulations for how we might create more open and accepting movements and communities. It is a journey that begins with my activism fighting for trans woman–inclusion in lesbian and women's spaces, and my efforts to articulate trans women's experiences of sexism, both within these settings and in society at large. Later chapters grapple with femme and bisexual exclusion within various LGBTQIA+ settings. To be clear, this section is not meant to provide a comprehensive overview of the problem of exclusion. For one thing, the chapters are centered on practices of sexism-based exclusion—the hypocrisy of policing other people's gender and sexual identities and behaviors within spaces that were supposedly founded on anti-sexist principles. Furthermore, they focus rather exclusively on forms of exclusion that I have personally faced as a bisexual femme-tomboy transsexual woman. In addition to those identities, I also happen to be a white, middle-class, educated, able-bodied[1], normatively sized U.S. citizen—aspects of my person that are privileged in our culture, and which do not result in my exclusion. My focus on instances of trans, femme, and bisexual exclusion is not meant to suggest that these are the only, or most egregious, forms of exclusion— they most certainly are not, and I discuss other forms of exclusion in the second half of the book. Rather, trans, femme, and bisexual represent my vantage point onto the issue of exclusion within feminist and queer movements, and this is why I use them as my primary examples over the course of this book.

The second section of this book, "New Ways of Speaking," is a collection of previously unpublished essays that forward a new framework for thinking about gender, sexuality, sexism, and marginalization. Here, I explain why existing feminist and queer movements (much like their straight male–centric counterparts) always seem to create hierarchies, where certain gendered and sexual bodies, identities, and behaviors are deemed more legitimate than others. Of course, past feminist and queer activists have been concerned about these pecking orders, and they have often placed the blame squarely on identity politics, essentialism, classism, assimilationism, and/or reformist politics. However, such claims ignore the fact that sexism-based hierarchies are just as prevalent in radical, anti-capitalist, anti-essentialist, and anti-assimilationist circles as they are within so-called "liberal" feminist and single-issue "A-gay" activist circles.[2]

Rather than blaming the usual suspects, here I show how sexism-based exclusion within feminist and queer movements is typically driven by what Anne Koedt once called the *perversion of "the personal is political"*—that is, the assumption that we should all curtail or alter our genders and sexualities in order to better conform with feminist or queer politics.[3] This perversion of "the personal is political" can be seen in both reformist feminist and queer activist circles that seek to purge "less desirable" identities and behaviors from their movements in the name of political expediency, and among their more radical counterparts who denounce identities and behaviors that they perceive to be too "conservative," "conforming," or "heteronormative." In other words, both extremes share the expectation that their members will be relatively homogeneous and conform to certain norms of gender and sexuality. Such one-size-fits-all approaches ignore the fact that there is naturally occurring variation in sex, gender, and sexuality in human populations. We all differ somewhat in our desires, urges, and attractions, and in what identities, expressions, and interests resonate with us. Furthermore, each of us is uniquely socially situated: We each have different life histories, face different obstacles, and have different experiences with sexism and other forms of marginalization. So the assumption that we should conform to some uniform ideal with regards to gender and sexuality, or that we should all adhere to one single view of sexism and marginalization, is simply unrealistic.

One-size-fits-all approaches to gender and sexuality—whether they occur in the straight male–centric mainstream, or within feminist and queer subcultures—inevitably result in double standards, where bodies and behaviors can only ever be viewed as either right or wrong, natural or unnatural, normal or abnormal, righteous or immoral. And one-size-fits-all models for describing sexism and marginalization—whether in terms of patriarchy, or compulsory heterosexuality, or the gender binary—always account for certain forms of sexism and marginalization while ignoring others. As a result, such models validate some people's perspectives while leaving many of us behind. I believe that this pervasive insistence that we should all conform to some fixed and homogeneous view of sexism and marginalization, or of gender and sexuality, is the primary cause of sexism-based exclusion within feminist and queer movements.

In this book, I make the case that we should distance ourselves from these one-size-fits-all models, and instead embrace an alternative approach—what I call a *holistic approach to feminism*. I call this model "holistic" for a number of reasons. First, it moves away from the trite and overly simplistic "nature-versus-nurture" debates about gender and sexuality, and instead recognizes that biology, culture, and environment all interact in an unfathomably complex manner in order to generate the human diversity we see all around us. Second, this approach recognizes that each of us has a rather specific (and therefore, limited) view of gender and sexuality, and sexism and marginalization—a perspective largely shaped by our own life experiences and how we are socially situated. Therefore, the only way that we can thoroughly understand these complex phenomena is through a multiplicity of different perspectives. Third, this approach to feminism is holistic in that it provides a framework for challenging *all* forms of sexism and marginalization, rather than merely those that we personally experience or are already familiar with. I must admit that I was initially hesitant to describe this approach as "holistic," as the word often evokes "new age"- or "hippie"-esque connotations (whereas I am personally more agnostic- and punk rocker-identified). But despite these reservations, I feel that *holistic* best captures the totality of the approach that I will outline here.

A WORD ABOUT WORDS

CHAPTER ONE

Many disagreements within feminist and queer politics stem from language. So in order to avoid such confusion, in this chapter I will define many of the basic terms that I will use throughout this book, often with an accompanying explanation for why I have chosen certain words over others. While I cannot promise that all readers will agree on the terms I use or how I define them, I do believe that knowing where I am coming from, and what precisely I am trying to convey, is crucial to understanding many of the ideas that I forward in this book.

SEX, GENDER, AND SEXUALITY

Throughout this book, three particular terms will come up over and over again: sex, gender, and sexuality. The word *sex* is typically used to refer to a person's physical sex (e.g., their anatomy, genitals, reproductive capacity, hormones, sex chromosomes, secondary sexual characteristics, and so forth). *Sexuality* may refer to a person's sexual orientation, interests, acts, expressions, and/or experiences. The word *gender* is often used to refer to a number of different things, including a person's gender identity (e.g., whether they identify as a girl/woman, boy/man, or somewhere outside of those identities), their lived sex (whether they move through the world as female and/or male or other), or their gender expression (whether their dress, mannerisms, and interests are deemed to be feminine and/or masculine or other).

While it is often useful to distinguish between sex, gender, and sexuality, it is important to recognize that one cannot easily draw a sharp line dividing where each of these categories ends and another begins. For example, many aspects of physical sex (such as genitals) play an important role in acts of sexuality. Similarly, specific types of feminine or masculine clothing are sometimes considered to be sexually arousing. Gender expression more generally can play an important role in sexual attraction, as seen in conventionally straight people who prefer feminine female or masculine male partners, or queer people who may have a preference for either butch, or femme, or androgynous partners.

Along similar lines, some people try to make a sharp distinction between sex and gender by claiming that the former is exclusively biological in origin while the latter is exclusively social. This ignores the fact that biology likely plays some role in influencing gender identity and expression (discussed in Chapter 13, "Homogenizing Versus Holistic Views of Gender and Sexuality"), and that sex also has social components. For example, in our society, we are each assigned a "legal sex" based on certain sex characteristics (typically genitals) but not others (e.g., hormones, reproductive capabilities, etc.). Thus, the decision of which sex characteristics count (and which do not) is very much a social matter.

So while sex, gender, and sexuality are different from one another, they are also often connected or intertwined. (For this reason, on certain occasions in this book, I will use the word "gender" as shorthand for "sex, gender, and sexuality.") The fact that these three aspects are generally viewed as interconnected explains why most people typically assume that they should all "line up" in the same direction within any given person. In our society, most people routinely presume that all of an individual's sex attributes (e.g., their genitals, hormones, chromosomes) will all match up perfectly and fall within typical male or female parameters; that their gender identity and lived sex will align with their physical sex; that they will be gender conforming with regard to gender expression (i.e., feminine if female, masculine if male); that they will experience sexual attraction toward other people, and that this sexual attraction will be oriented toward members of one sex or the other, but not both; that their attractions and relationships will be exclusively heterosexual in nature; that the sexual acts they engage in will center around penile-vaginal penetration sex; and so on.

When a person lives up to all of these societal assumptions, they are often described as being "straight." Since straight mainstream values dominate in our culture, straight people can take their sexes, genders, and sexualities for granted, and are seen as "normal" in this regard. When a person defies one or some of these assumptions, straight mainstream society often deems that person to be not-straight, and therefore "queer." Throughout this book, I will be using the term *queer* to describe people who fall outside of straight mainstream expectations and assumptions (such as the ones listed in the previous paragraph) regarding sex, gender, and sexuality. Some people use the acronym (or part of the acronym) LGBTQIA+ (where L = lesbian, G = gay, B = bisexual, T = transgender, Q = queer and/or questioning, I = intersex, A = asexual, and + to recognize other identities and individuals not explicitly included) in the same way that I am using the word "queer" here. In addition, queer/LGBTQIA+ people may also be described as being *sexual and gender minorities*. Like other minorities, queer people are routinely delegitimized by society because of the fact that they are perceived to be different from the majority.

It should be noted that queer is one of many *reclaimed words*, that is, a derogatory term that targets a certain population which takes on a new life and meaning when that same population starts using it as a self-empowering term. The idea goes something like this: If people are going to use the term "queer" as a slur, I can either distance myself from the word and insist that others use more respectable language to describe me, or alternatively, I can embrace the word, in effect saying, "Yes, I am queer and proud of it!" Other examples might include women who reclaim the words "slut" or "bitch," sex workers who reclaim the word "whore," queer women who reclaim the word "dyke," gay men who reclaim the word "faggot," or trans women who reclaim the word "tranny." Reclaimed words tend to generate controversy, although sometimes (as in the case of "queer") the reclaimed word eventually evolves into a more acceptable term that is commonly used by everybody.

ESSENTIALISM, IDENTITY LABELS, AND UMBRELLA TERMS

It is impossible to talk about sex, gender, and sexuality—or any human trait for that matter—without using specific words or labels to describe differences that exist between people. There are at least three different ways in which such words or labels can be used. The first way is to view such words in terms of essentialist categories. *Essentialism* is the belief that all members of a particular category must share some particular characteristic or set of characteristics in order to be considered a legitimate member of that group. People often resort to essentialist thinking when considering categories they consider to be "natural"—i.e., ones that arise on their own, independent of any social context or influence. People who view sex, gender, and sexuality as entirely "natural" traits will often try to categorize differences between people in essentialist ways. An example of essentialism is when people claim that all women have a womb, are chromosomally XX, and/or are naturally nurturing. Feminists (including myself) typically reject essentialism for reasons I discuss in Chapter 13, "Homogenizing Versus Holistic Views of Gender and Sexuality." So when words like "woman" or "gay" or "transsexual" appear in this book, they are not meant to represent essentialist categories.

Another way to view such words is in terms of *identity labels*. For example, I identify as a woman, as transgender, as bisexual, and so forth. Identity labels are a highly personal way of conveying to others how we believe that we fit (or don't fit) into the world. Because they are so personal, often people who share the same trait or behavior may differ with regards to what identity labels they use to describe themselves. So unlike me, other people who are female-bodied may not identify with the word "woman," other trans people may not identify with the word "transgender," and other people who are sexual with members of more than one sex/gender may prefer the word "pansexual" over "bisexual," or they may choose not to label their sexuality at all. I am a big believer in the right of people to self-identify and to self-describe their own life experiences, and at no point in this book will I purposefully use a label to describe a specific person if I know that label runs contrary to how they self-identify.

It should be noted that people can use identity labels in either an essentialist or non-essentialist way. So, someone who believes that all women are chromosomally XX may identify as a woman on the basis that she shares that characteristic, and someone who believes that all transsexuals have a specific brain condition may identify as transsexual based on their belief that they have that supposed brain condition. In contrast, I call myself a woman and transsexual, not because I hold essentialist beliefs about those categories, but because I feel those words best describe some aspect of my person. Along similar lines, I also happen to identify as a musician (because I play musical instruments) and as a bird person (because I have parrots as animal companions, not because I identify as a bird!). I do not believe that there is some magical underlying quality that all musicians, or all bird people, or all women, or all transsexuals have in common. Rather, the only thing we have in common is that we loosely share some non-essentialist quality (e.g., we play musical instruments, we have birds as animal companions, we move through the world as women, we identify and live as members of the sex other than the one we were assigned at birth, respectively).

In the course of this book, I will occasionally use words like "woman", or "transsexual", or "bisexual" as identity labels, particularly when I am referring to a specific person. But more often than not, I will be using these words in the third manner: as *umbrella terms*. So for example, throughout this book, I will use the word "queer" as an umbrella term to describe people who (for one reason or another) are deemed by society to be "not-straight" because some aspect of their sex, gender, and/or sexuality falls outside of societal norms. I contend that one can use the word "queer" in this manner (i.e., as an umbrella term) while simultaneously recognizing that not all people who fall under the queer umbrella will necessarily identify with the term (i.e., they may not personally use "queer" as an identity label to describe themselves). Furthermore, one can use the word "queer" as an umbrella term without making any additional assumptions about individuals who fall under that umbrella. Indeed, I personally do not believe that any two given queer people necessarily have anything in common with one another other than the fact that they are both viewed by society to be "not-straight."

One might ask: "If some people don't identify with the term 'queer,' why not use a different word entirely?" Well, for one thing, there is about a twenty-year-long history of people using the word "queer" as an umbrella term in this way. And even if I were to invent a completely different word to describe this same group of people, there will always be some people who will choose not to identify with that term.

Others might ask, "If people who fall under the queer umbrella are all different from one another, and many of them do not personally prefer the term 'queer,' then why bother lumping them all into the same category in the first place?" My answer to this is simple: I am not the one lumping us all into the same category! It is society at large that makes a distinction between people who are deemed to be "normal" with regard to sex, gender, and sexuality (i.e., straight) and those who are deemed "abnormal" (i.e., queer). More importantly, those who are deemed straight are generally viewed as more natural and legitimate than those who are deemed queer. This double standard constitutes a form of sexism, one that routinely marginalizes and injures those of us who are queer. If we were to stop using words such as "queer" (on the basis that not all people who fall under that umbrella identify with the term), it would do nothing to stop society at large from deeming us to be queer and treating us inferiorly as a result. Indeed, *not* having a word to describe people who are marginalized by this double standard makes it difficult, if not impossible, for sexual and gender minorities to organize and carry out activism to challenge this double standard.

This point gets to the heart of the identity-labels-versus-umbrella-terms distinction: We use identity labels to tell our stories, to describe our experiences, to let people know how we see ourselves and how we believe we fit into the world. This is an important, albeit primarily personal, matter. In contrast, umbrella terms are primarily used in order to form alliances between disparate people who share some obstacle or form of discrimination in common. By saying that we both fall under the same umbrella term, I am not claiming that you and I are "alike" in some way, but rather that we are treated in similar ways by society, and that it is in our mutual interest to work together to challenge the negative meanings and presumptions that other people project onto us.

Since this book is about challenging societal double standards and norms, I will primarily be using words like "queer" (and other terms described below) as umbrella terms rather than identity labels.

SEXISM AND FEMINISM

Throughout this book, I will be using the word *sexism* to describe double standards based upon a person's sex, gender, and/or sexuality. The most commonly discussed form of sexism is what I call *traditional sexism*, which is the assumption that femaleness and femininity are inferior to, or less legitimate than, maleness and masculinity (i.e., what most people refer to as just plain "sexism"). This form of sexism primarily targets girls and women in our culture, although it also negatively impacts other people as well.[1] There are many other forms of sexism that exist, and which target specific sexual and gender minorities. People are probably most familiar with heterosexism—the assumption that same-sex attraction and relationships are less legitimate than their heterosexual counterparts. But there are many other forms of sexism out there, including monosexism/biphobia, cissexism/transphobia, and masculine-centrism/femmephobia, to name just a few. I will define less familiar forms of sexism when I first introduce them in the text, rather than overwhelming readers with a slew of definitions here. Note that labels describing sexism often take the form of an "ism" where the dominant majority is cited (e.g., heterosexism), or a "phobia" where the marginalized group is cited (e.g., homophobia). While some people use the "ism" and "phobia" variations differently, for simplicity's sake, I will use them interchangeably here.[2]

I will use the word *feminism* to describe various movements that work to challenge and eliminate sexism. There are many different strands of feminism, some of which are more narrowly focused on women's rights, issues, and liberation, while others are broader in scope and seek to challenge all forms of sexism. In other words, these latter strands of feminism are focused on challenging the marginalization of not only women, but of sexual and gender minorities (i.e., queer folks) as well. While I personally share this latter and broader perspective of feminism, I realize that not everyone does, so in the course of this book I will often refer to "feminism and queer activism" as though they are two different movements, even though they need not be. I will frequently refer to *intersectionality*, which is a concept that has come out of the work of feminists of color, and which examines how different forms of sexism, and other forms of marginalization (e.g., racism, classism, ableism, ageism, sizeism), can intersect with, and exacerbate, one another.[3] Thus, feminists who are coming from an intersectional perspective (such as myself) believe that feminism should be concerned not only with all forms of sexism, but with all forms of marginalization as well.

SEXUAL AND GENDER MINORITIES

Throughout this book, I will be using the word *gay* to describe men who are exclusively attracted to other men, and the word *lesbian* to describe women who are exclusively attracted to other women. Over the last two decades, the word *dyke* has come into vogue as a word to describe women who partner with other women, albeit not necessarily exclusively.

On a few occasions, I will collectively refer to gay and lesbian people as being *homosexual* to distinguish them from people who are *heterosexual* (i.e., individuals who are exclusively attracted to members of the other sex or gender) or *bisexual* (i.e., individuals who experience attraction to members of more than one sex or gender). There is no hard and fast line one can draw to definitively separate heterosexuals from bisexuals from homosexuals. Many people are bisexual in experience (e.g., they have been sexual with members of more than one sex) but identify strictly as heterosexual or homosexual, perhaps because they view some of their sexual experiences as inauthentic or merely experiments. Some people, both within and outside of the bisexual community, have issues with the word "bisexual," and instead prefer alternative labels such as pansexual or polysexual (this debate is discussed in more depth in Chapter 9, "Bisexuality and Binaries Revisted"). In any case, I will stick with the word "bisexual" for the same reason why I will use the terms "lesbian" and "gay" over other potentially synonymous labels: because they are the most commonly used and accepted labels for such people at this time and place.

Within lesbian, gay, and bisexual circles, people often use the term *butch* to refer to masculine individuals, and the word *femme* to refer to feminine individuals, regardless of the person's sex. Of course, in reality, gender expression is not a strictly dichotomous trait, and individuals may use variants such as androgynous, or soft butch, or stone butch, or high femme, or low femme, or (in my case) femme-tomboy, in order to communicate these differences. Many straight mainstream folks automatically assume that if a queer person is butch, then they must be attracted to femmes (and vice versa), but this is not necessarily the case. As a femme who prefers other femmes over butches, I can assure you that people are not necessarily attracted to their "opposites" in gender expression any more than they are necessarily attracted to the "opposite" sex.

There are at least two other sexual orientation categories: *Asexual* refers to people who do not experience sexual attraction toward other people, and *questioning*, which refers to people who are unsure of, or who are in the process of trying to figure out, their sexual orientation. (Note: This label is also sometimes used to describe people who are currently questioning some other aspect of their sex, gender, or sexuality.)

Outside of sexual orientation, there are other sexual practices or experiences that defy straight mainstream assumptions. One of these is *polyamory*, which refers to sexual relationships that are not monogamous. People unfamiliar with the term may mistakenly confuse it with polygamy, but the two terms are significantly different. Polygamy refers to relationships where a single man takes up more than one wife; such relationships are typically rooted in patriarchal ideas of men and women (e.g., that men are the head of the household, and that women are property and/or their primary duty is to bear their husbands' children). In contrast, polyamory refers to people (of any sex or gender) who have sexual relationships with more than one person (of any sex or gender). Such relationships may take place within or outside of the context of marriage. Polyamory is also sometimes described as *ethical non-monogamy* in order to stress that such relationships are consensual—that is, all parties involved are aware that their partners also have other partners.

Another sexual practice that also falls outside of straight mainstream presumptions is *BDSM*, a complex acronym meant to include bondage/discipline, dominance/submission, and sadism/masochism. Those who practice BDSM sometimes describe themselves as "kinky" and refer to sexual practices that fall outside the realm of BDSM as "vanilla." BDSM is also sometimes referred to as "role-play" or "power exchange" because the parties involved consensually take on roles where one party has power over another. Some people might mischaracterize BDSM as being equivalent to nonconsensual forms of abuse or rape, but this ignores the fact that BDSM practices are consensual—in fact, an often quoted tenet of BDSM relationships is that any act that occurs must be "safe, sane, and consensual."

While both BDSM and polyamory certainly fall outside of what the straight mainstream considers "normal," it is not generally accepted that people who engage in these sexual practices fall under the umbrella term "queer."[4] However, these groups are clearly sexual minorities who are unfairly marginalized for their consensual behaviors by mainstream society, and as such, I will consider them here.

There are a number of different gender minorities. The term *transgender* is typically used as an umbrella term to describe all people who defy straight mainstream notions regarding gender. The transgender umbrella may include (but is not necessarily limited to) people who are transsexual, crossdressers, drag artists, androgynous, two-spirit, genderqueer, agender, feminine men and/or masculine women. People who are *intersex*—that is, who are born with a reproductive or sexual anatomy that does not seem to fit the "standard" definitions for female or male—are sometimes included under the transgender umbrella as well (although some argue that intersex people differ with regards to their physical sex, not gender). As with all umbrella terms, many people who fall under the transgender umbrella do not identify with the term.[5] Some people use *trans** or *gender variant* as alternative umbrella terms to describe people on the transgender spectrum.

With regards to transgender trajectories, I will refer to people who were assigned a male sex at birth but who identify as female and/or are feminine in gender expression as being on the *MTF (male-to-female)* or *trans female/feminine spectrum.* And those assigned a female sex at birth but who identify as male and/or are masculine in gender expression will be described as being on the *FTM (female-to-male)* or *trans male/masculine spectrum.*[6]

Of the many transgender spectrum identities that exist, gender-queers and transsexuals are particularly common within contemporary queer communities, and as such, they are mentioned most frequently throughout this book. People who are *genderqueer* do not identify within the male/female binary, and instead may identify as being neither woman or man, or as a little bit of both, or as being gender-fluid (i.e., moving between different gendered states over the course of their lives). People who are *transsexual* identify and/or live as members of the sex other than the one they were assigned at birth. A *trans woman* (such as myself) is someone who has socially (and sometimes physically) transitioned from male to female, and a *trans man* is someone who has similarly transitioned from female to male. While the medical establishment and the mainstream media typically define "transsexual" in terms of the medical procedures that an individual might undergo (for example, hormones and surgeries), many trans people find such definitions to be objectifying (as they place undue focus on body parts rather than the person as a whole) and classist (as not all trans people can afford to physically transition). For these reasons, trans activists favor definitions based on self-identity or lived experience—i.e., whether one identifies and/or lives as a woman or man. It should be noted that "transsexual" and "genderqueer" are not mutually exclusive identities.

It is difficult to discuss trans people without also having language to describe the majority of people who are not trans. For this purpose, trans activists often use the word *cisgender* as a synonym for non-transgender, and *cissexual* as a synonym for non-transsexual.[7] In general, I tend to use the term cisgender when I am making a distinction between people on the transgender spectrum and those who are not, and I use the term cissexual if I am making a distinction between people who are transsexual and those who are not. And, in the same way that people often use "trans" as an abbreviation for transsexual and/or transgender, the term "cis" is routinely used as shorthand for cissexual and/or cisgender. Because I personally began using cis terminology around 2006, some of the earlier essays collected for this book use the more clunky phrase "non-trans" instead of "cis."

Finally, some people who pick up this book may be unfamiliar with and therefore curious (or perhaps even dubious) about transgender people. If you happen to fall into this camp, then I suggest that you check out my previous book, *Whipping Girl: A Transsexual Woman on Sexism and the Scapegoating of Femininity*, as I address most of the common questions, stereotypes, and assumptions about trans people there.[8] While I will often talk about trans people, politics, and issues here, it is mostly to highlight specific instances of exclusion and/or to draw parallels between how different forms of sexism function.

PART ONE

ON THE OUTSIDE
LOOKING IN

ON THE OUTSIDE LOOKING IN

CHAPTER TWO

AUGUST 2003.

When we hear story after story set in a landscape that we have never set foot in before, we can't help but create our own mental picture of that place. I realized only as my wife Dani and I turned off a dirt road and up to the welcome center that I always imagined that Camp Trans would resemble pictures I had seen of Woodstock, with tents strewn everywhere and people buzzing about busily with a sense of purpose and energy, with a sense that they were a part of history. But Camp Trans looked nothing like that. It was set on a modest-sized clearing in the middle of the woods. Cars were parked close to the entrance, tents tucked away just out of sight behind the trees. There was a main congregating area, where campers were slurping up the vegan miso soup that was being served for lunch. Everyone was way more mellow than I had imagined, perhaps because they had been baking in the ninety-degree heat for close to a week now.

Some of my straight friends thought it was hilarious when they heard that Dani and I were going to spend a long weekend at Camp Trans. They probably imagined something like summer camp meets *Priscilla Queen of the Desert*, only set in the Michigan wilderness. They seemed a bit disappointed when we told them that this was primarily a political, rather than social, event. We were there to protest the Michigan Womyn's Music Festival's "womyn-born-womyn-only" policy, which is a fancy way of saying that transsexual women like myself are not welcome.[1] My straight female friends were always the most offended on my behalf upon hearing this. These were women who welcomed me with open arms when I first started sharing women's restrooms with them, who made a point of inviting me along on their girls' nights out, who made it clear, even in those early days just after my transition, that they considered me to be one of them. When they asked me why the lesbian organizers who ran the festival were adamant about excluding trans women, I told them, "There's just a lot of really bad history there."

It all started during the '70s and '80s, when a number of influential lesbian feminists began to trash transsexuals in their writings and theories.[2] They argued that we propagated sexist stereotypes and objectified women by attempting to possess female bodies of our own. Eventually, this all became unquestionable dogma, and transsexuals, even those who identified as feminists and dykes, were conveniently banished from most lesbian and women's spaces. But things started to change by the mid-'90s, as a growing number of dykes began coming out as trans and referring to themselves as men. This caused many to question their views and, over the years, has led to a certain level of acceptance of trans men in the lesbian community. These days, it is not uncommon to find dykes who openly discuss lusting after trans guys. And many trans people who were assigned female at birth will still call themselves dykes long after they have asked their friends to refer to them with male names and pronouns.

So you may be asking where trans women fit in. Well, we don't really. Granted, there are some queer women who respect our female identities, many of whom now boycott Michigan because of the festival's trans woman–exclusion policy. And there are also quite a few lesbians who still view the identities of trans folks on both the MTF and FTM spectrums as somewhat dubious. But in between those two extremes lies a growing consensus of dykes who see female-assigned trans folks as their peers, as a part of the lesbian community, while viewing trans women with suspicion, disdain, or apathy.

Now an objective observer might suggest that this preference for trans men over trans women suspiciously resembles traditional sexism. As with most forms of prejudice, there is no shortage of theories one can use to rationalize their predilections. For instance, many lesbians believe that male-identified trans folks are more trustworthy because their ex-dyke status instills them with political enlightenment, whereas I, a trans woman who has lived as woman and a dyke for several years now, apparently can never truly understand what it means to be female because testosterone and male socialization have dumbed down my brain permanently.

These days, it is common to see the word "trans" used to welcome trans men (but not trans women) on everything from lesbian events to sex surveys and play parties. And even at Michigan, women are no longer defined based on their legal sex, appearance, or self-identification, but on whether or not they were born and raised as a girl. And while performers like Animal and Lynnee Breedlove, who identify as transgender and answer to male pronouns, are invited to take the festival stage each year, someone like myself who identifies one hundred percent as female isn't even allowed to stand in the audience.[3] As if that wasn't bad enough, many now use Michigan's tolerance of folks on the FTM spectrum to argue that the festival's policies are not transphobic. Well I'm sorry, but any person who considers trans men to be women and trans women to be men is not an ally of the transgender community!

Shortly after arriving, Dani and I met Sadie, a trans woman who is one of Camp Trans's main organizers. She tells me that she is excited to have another trans woman in attendance—I was the seventh one to make it so far. Virtually all of the remaining hundred or so campers were assigned female at birth: Some were dykes and bisexual women, some trans men, and the rest were genderqueers, who identify outside of the male/female gender binary. Apparently, the unbalanced demographics were a by-product of the more genderqueer-centric direction Camp Trans had taken a few years earlier. Many trans women, who felt they should be allowed into Michigan because they identified as female, felt abandoned by the cause when so many of its members seemed hell-bent on deconstructing their genders out of existence. I was told that this year's organizers were working hard to get Camp Trans back on track and to encourage more trans women to come to the event.

After Dani and I finished setting up our tent, we headed down to the main area and hung out by the campfire, starting up conversations with some of the other campers. Despite being so far from home, I almost felt like I knew a lot of these people. Demographically speaking, the mix was similar to the crowds who come out to the San Francisco trans and queer performance events I'm involved in. The campers were predominantly in their early twenties, white, and many either previously or currently identified as dykes. They shared similar political sensibilities: Many were anarchists and vegans, and many self-described as pansexuals and practitioners of BDSM and open relationships.

I always feel incredibly uncomfortable when people refer to this sort of crowd as "the trans community." The truth is, this is but a small segment of it. I've attended other trans gatherings where the crowd was predominantly made up of MTF crossdressers and transsexual women, plus their female partners. I've performed spoken word at events put on by the Tenderloin AIDS Resource Center, where many of the trans people in the audience were poor or homeless. I've been to San Francisco's

Transgender Day of Remembrance, where trans people of all races and ethnicities, all generations, and all economic classes come together to pay respects to those in our community who have been murdered.

No, this right here is not the trans community; it is merely a clique—a pro-sex, pro-trans faction of the dyke community borne out of the backlash against '80s-era Andrea Dworkinism.[4] And sometimes I feel like I'm a part of it and other times I feel like I'm on the outside looking in. I think about this as Dani passes me a small tin tray of salmon that we cooked at the foot of the campfire this evening, a much-anticipated meal as we were both unable to stomach the vegan beets and cabbage the camp offered for dinner. And I am grateful that none of the campers complain that our eating habits are triggering them. And as I enjoy this rare occasion of taking part in a trans-majority space, it occurs to me that I have never felt so old, so monogamous, so carnivorous, and so bourgeoisie in my life.

The following day, Dani and I sign up for a work shift at the Camp Trans welcome center. Part of the job involves briefly orienting incoming campers about the rules of the space, telling them where to park their cars, where to pitch their tents, and other such things. The hard part of the job is acting as an ambassador for Camp Trans if any festival folks come visiting us from just down the street.

In the middle of our shift, a woman from the festival makes her way over to our booth. She is carrying a pamphlet on trans woman–inclusion that Camp Trans had passed out earlier in the week. She told us she agreed with most of it, but that she was furious about one particular passage that read, "When members of the dominant group believe that they have the right to get rid of the minority group solely because of their own fear, such as when white aircraft passengers request Middle-Eastern passengers to be removed from a flight because the presence of Middle-Eastern people makes them feel uncomfortable or unsafe, it is called an undeserved sense of entitlement and it needs to be challenged."[5]

This festival woman (who happened to be white) proceeded to lecture us about how inappropriate it was for us to make any analogies with race. It didn't seem to faze her when I mentioned that the author of the pamphlet, Emi Koyama, is Asian. I find that the people who seem to get the most upset by comparisons between Michigan's anti–trans woman policy and instances of race-based exclusion are white women defending the festival's reputation. To me, it seems as though their primary motivation is not actually sticking up for people of color, but rather to thwart any attempt at comparing Michigan's policy to other historical examples of exclusion.

Dani, who has been a queer activist since she first came out as a dyke in the early '90s, does her best to reason with the woman. Eventually the woman calms down and brings up other issues that concern her. She asks if Camp Trans is fighting to let trans men into the festival, a common question since so many male-identified trans folks continue to attend the festival. We tell her no—Camp Trans supports the idea of women-only space, but believes it should be open to all self-identified women.

Next, the woman brings up her fear that trans women might bring "male energy" onto the land at Michigan. This is a classic argument that has been used time and time again to justify trans woman exclusion. So I ask the woman if she senses any male energy in me. She looks confused at first, but then I see the change in her eyes, a look I've seen hundreds of times before, the look that signifies that she is starting to see me differently, noticing clues of the boy that I used to be, processing this new realization that she is speaking with a trans person. She tells me that she is surprised, that she has never met a transsexual woman before. I tell her that every person I have ever met has met a transsexual woman, whether they realize it or not.

I go on to explain how Michigan, being the largest annual women-only event in the world, sets a dangerous precedent with its trans woman–exclusion policy, contributing to an environment in lesbian and women-only spaces where discriminating against trans women is considered the norm. I tell her about how trans women are routinely turned away from domestic violence shelters and rape crisis centers. I tell her about my own experiences dealing with lesbian bigots who have insulted me to my face once they discovered my trans status. And as I tell her this, it becomes apparent to me that my spiel doesn't really matter anymore. She is nodding her head up and down, agreeing with me. She gets it now, but it had nothing to do with my words or reasoning—it was my person that convinced her. Her senses told her that I was a woman and a dyke, not a "man in a dress" or some other stereotype. She now understands that if I am a transsexual, then any woman she meets could also be trans. And it's hard to justify discrimination when you are unable to find any distinguishing differences to begin with.

As the woman walks away smiling, Dani and I collapse in our chairs and squeeze each other's hands to celebrate the fact that we just changed someone's mind. But for me, the feeling is fleeting. I almost immediately begin second-guessing myself, wondering whether I took the easy way out, placating that woman's fears rather than challenging them. A part of me wishes that, instead of coming out to her, I had told her flat-out how anti-feminist the whole "male energy" argument is. By suggesting that trans women possess some mystical male energy as a result of being born and raised male, they are essentially making the case that men have abilities and aptitudes that women are not capable of.[6] It baffles me how anyone can argue this point without seeing how excruciatingly sexist it is.

Or maybe this just seems obvious to me because I am forced to deal with this sort of thing day in and day out. When you're a trans woman, you are made to walk this very fine line, where if you act feminine you are accused of being a parody, but if you act masculine, it is seen as a sign of your true male identity. And if you act sweet and demure, you're accused of reinforcing patriarchal ideals of female passivity, but if you stand up for your own rights and make your voice heard, then you are dismissed as wielding male privilege and entitlement. We trans women are made to teeter upon this tightrope, not because we are transsexuals, but because we are women. This is the same double bind that forces teenage girls to negotiate their way between virgin and whore, that forces female politicians and business women to be aggressive without being seen as a bitch and to be feminine enough so as not to emasculate their alpha-male colleagues, without being so girly as to undermine their own authority.

I find it disappointing that so many feminists seem oblivious to the ways in which anti–trans discrimination is rooted in traditional sexism. This is why the media powers-that-be systematically sensation-alize, sexualize, and ridicule trans women, while allowing trans men to remain largely invisible. It is why the "tranny" sex and porn industries catering to straight-identified men do not fetishize folks on the FTM spectrum for their XX chromosomes or their socialization as girls. No, they objectify trans women, because our bodies and our persons are female. Many female-assigned genderqueers and FTM trans folks go on and on about the gender binary system, as if trans people are only ever discriminated against for breaking gender norms. That's probably how it seems when the gender transgression in question is an expression of maleness or masculinity. But as someone on the MTF spectrum, I am not dismissed for merely failing to live up to binary gender norms, but also for expressing my own femaleness and femininity. And person-ally, I don't feel like I'm the victim of transphobia so much as I am the victim of trans-misogyny.[7]

The following day, two women from the festival came over to the main congregation area where a few of us were enjoying the shade. One carried a notebook and referred to herself as a graduate student. She asked us if we would like to be interviewed for her thesis project on the Michigan trans-inclusion debate. These days, it seems like everybody and their grandmother is getting advanced degrees in trans people. And while I can't help but feel insulted at the prospect of being somebody else's research subject, I usually agree to do these interviews in the off chance that my words may counteract some of the misinformation, appropriation, and exploitation of trans identities and experiences that have been propagated by academia.

The grad student introduces the other woman as her life partner. She says they have been coming to Michigan for years, but this is their first time visiting Camp Trans. The partner looks noticeably disturbed to be in our presence. When you're trans, you get used to not only the thesis interviews, but also having other people feel inexplicably awkward and uncomfortable around you.

The interview begins, and it is only a matter of time before the graduate student's line of questioning arrives at the "penis issue." This is a highly contentious matter, as many trans women (including myself) either cannot afford to have sex reassignment surgery or choose not to have it. The trans woman–exclusionists often take advantage of this situation, arguing that it would be a violation of women's space to have penises on the land and playing up how unsafe and uncomfortable some women would feel if they accidentally caught a glimpse of one of our dreaded, oppressive organs. Now granted, there are probably more dildos and strap-ons at Michigan than you would ever want to shake a stick at, many of them resembling anatomically correct penises. So I suppose phalluses in and of themselves are not so bad, just so long as they are not attached to a transsexual woman.

I answer the woman's question by stating the obvious: that it's ridiculous to believe that once trans women are allowed inside the festival that we would all go around flaunting our penises. I went on to talk about the societal shame that many of us have been made to feel about our bodies not living up to the cultural ideal, an issue which most women at Michigan should be able to relate with.

This was apparently the last straw for the graduate student's partner. After about fifteen minutes of fidgeting in silence, she suddenly burst out with questions of her own. While there were several of us being interviewed, she turned directly to me, and in a terse and condescending tone of voice, said: "How dare you! You have no idea what many of these women have been through. Don't you understand that many of them are abuse survivors who could be triggered by you? Can't you see why some women wouldn't feel safe having you and your penis around?"

I remember being dumbfounded, like a deer caught in the headlights, at the venom in her voice as she lashed out at me. And all of my well-thought-out trans-inclusive soundbites and anecdotes completely dissipated from my brain when confronted by this woman's anger for me. I'm not quite sure how I responded at the time. What I do recall are all of the things that I wish I had said to her after the moment had passed. How I wished I could go back in time, look her directly in the eye, and reply: Yes, I do know what those women have been through. I have had men force themselves upon me. Like you, we trans women are physically violated and abused for being women too. And there are no words in your second-wave feminist lexicon to adequately describe the way that we, young trans girls forced against our will into boyhood, have been raped by male culture. Every trans woman is a survivor, and we have triggers too. And my trigger is pseudo-feminists who hide their prejudices behind "womyn-born-womyn-only" euphemisms.

I wish I could have told her how hypocritical it is for any self-described feminist to buy into the male myth that men's power and domination arises from the penis. What's between my legs is not a phallic symbol, nor a tool of rape and oppression; it is merely my genitals. My penis is a woman's penis and she is made of flesh and blood, nothing more. And we have a word to describe the act of reducing a woman to her body parts, to her genitals: It is called objectification. And frankly, I am tired of being objectified by other lesbians!

Whenever I think about that woman's assertion that my penis would endanger safe women's space, I can't help but think of our daily trips to the lake. Piling up four to five people per car, waves of Camp Trans folks would take turns driving to a small, secluded beach to escape the humid August heat with an innocent skinny-dip. And as a trans person who has been on hormones but hasn't had any surgery, this is normally the sort of situation that I avoid like the plague. But here, it was okay for me to be my almost-naked self. This was a place where trans men felt comfortable enough to take off their T-shirts and unbind their breasts. Many of the trans women, dykes, and genderqueers would go topless too. And I remember how amazing it felt for the first time since my transition to strip down to nothing but my underpants, bulge be damned, in front of other people. And as we all soaked in the shallow water, laughing and talking with one another, I can't tell you how amazing it felt to have my body be absolutely no big deal to other people.

I realized right there at the lake what a mistake many women from Michigan make when they insist that trans women would threaten their safe space, destroying a rare place where they feel comfortable revealing their own bodies. Because there is never any safety in the erasing of difference, and no protection in the expectation that all women live up to certain physical criteria. The only truly safe space is one that respects each woman for her own individual uniqueness.

On our last night, there is a benefit show, and I am invited to perform spoken word. The event takes place shortly after a small procession of trans-inclusion supporters from Michigan march out of the festival gates and parade down the road to Camp Trans. Some of the campers had issues with the fact that these folks were being called "supporters," as each of them had spent about three hundred dollars for tickets to the very same festival we were protesting.

Some of these so-called supporters try to justify their attendance at Michigan by asserting that they are trying to change the festival's policy from within. But to me, that seems like a seriously flawed notion. If you look back at history, there has not been a single instance where people have overcome a deeply entrenched prejudice without first being forced to interact with the people they detest. Mere words cannot dispel bigoted stereotypes and fears, only personal experiences can.[8] Those who talk about changing the festival from the inside out often cite past instances where the festival has changed its ways, how it has overcome internal resistance to allowing BDSM, dildos, or drag kings on the land. But those policy changes did not occur because of discussions or debates—they happened because dykes were bringing those things into the festival with them, and there was nothing anyone could do to stop it. And once women at the festival had to live next to leather-dykes and drag kings, they began to realize that those women were not really so different from them.

The debate over trans woman–inclusion at Michigan has been going on for almost fifteen years now. And at this late date, anyone who still believes that they can change the festival from within is simply enabling lesbian prejudice against trans women.[9]

When the festival supporters finally arrive at the camp, they get a brief orientation at the welcome center. Some were apparently offended to find out that certain areas of the camp had been designated as "wristband-free" zones, a reference to the plastic bracelets they wore which allowed them to go in and out of the festival. They assumed that we were trying to teach them a lesson about exclusion, but that wasn't actually the case. The rule was put into place because the previous year there had been several incidents in which trans women were verbally attacked by festival visitors. The wristband-free zones were meant to offer trans women a safe space, just in case something similar happened again this year.

Eventually, the benefit show begins and there are a variety of acts: singers and spoken word artists, drag kings and queens, skits and puppets, even cheerleaders. My favorite performer of the night is Carolyn Connelly, a trans woman spoken word artist I hadn't met yet. In a thick Brooklyn accent, she belts out: "Fuck the lesbians who think I'm straight, I can't be femme/I'm not a girl/Fuck the gay men who out me at Pride every fucking year/Call me fabulous/Tell me to work it/And they're really girls too/Fuck the transsexual women who think I'm too butch/ Cause of my short spiked hair/Cause I drink beer or I'm a dyke . . . Fuck the genderqueer bois and grrrls/Who think they speak for me/Or dis me cause I support the gender binary . . . Fuck Post Modernism/Fuck Gender Studies/Fuck Judith Butler/Fuck theory that isn't by and for and speaks to real people . . ."[10]

When it is my turn to go on, I perform a poem called "Cocky," which I wrote to connect the dots between the uneasiness other people feel about me, the violent hate crimes that are committed against trans people, and the shame that I have been made to feel about my own body. "If I seem a bit cocky/that's because I refuse to make apologies for my body anymore/I refuse to be the human sacrifice offered up to appease other people's gender issues/Some women have a penis/Some men don't/ And the rest of the world is just going to have to get the fuck over it!"[11]

And as I recite these lines, four days worth of tension pours out of me. I perform my poem defiantly, my words fueled by a frustration that has finally boiled over after years of simmering on the backburner. I originally thought I could come to Michigan to intellectually fight for trans woman–inclusion. But coming to this place and having my body become the actual battleground upon which the trans revolution is being fought upon, well let's just say that it sobered me up a bit. And while other folks in my community may be content to simply celebrate their fabulous trans selves or take pride in living outside the gender binary, I am no longer satisfied with simply being allowed to exist as some third-sexed male-to-female trans-gender novelty. I maybe a transsexual, but I am also a woman. And my dyke community needs to realize that the anger that they feel when straight people try to dismiss the legitimacy of their same-sex relationships is what I feel when they try to dismiss my femaleness.

And later, after the show, I was told that several festival women left in the middle of the benefit because they were disturbed by the angry content of some of the acts. Well fuck them and their supporting-both-Michigan-and-Camp-Trans wussy fence-sitting politics! I am tired of lesbians and gay men who try to meet me halfway with fuzzy, pseudo trans–inclusive sentiments. Trans people are not merely a subplot within the dyke community, nor fascinating case studies for gender studies graduate theses. No, we trans people have our own issues, perspectives, and experiences. And non-trans queer people everywhere need to realize that they cannot call themselves "pro-trans" unless they fully respect our identities, and unless they are willing to call other queers out on their anti-trans bigotry.

And after releasing all of this pent-up tension and frustration, I had one of those rare moments of clarity. It happened just after my performance, when one of my new friends, Lauren, came over to give me a hug. She said, "Your piece made me proud to be a trans woman." And her words were so moving because I had never heard them spoken before. "Proud to be a trans woman." And as I looked around the camp at all of the female-assigned queer women and folks on the FTM spectrum, I realized that in some ways I am very different from them—not because of my biology or socialization, but because of the direction of my transition and the perspective it has given me.

I am a transsexual in a dyke community where most women have not had to fight for their right to be recognized as female—it is merely something they've taken for granted. And I am a woman in a segment of the trans community dominated by folks on the FTM spectrum who have never experienced the special social stigma that is reserved for feminine transgender expression and for those who transition to female. My experiences as a trans woman have given me a valid and unique understanding of what it means to be both female and feminine—a perspective that many women here at Michigan seem unable or unwilling to comprehend.

At Camp Trans, I learned to be proud that I am a trans woman. And when I describe myself with the word "trans," it does not necessarily signify that I transgress the gender binary, but that I straddle two identities—transsexual and woman—that others insist are in opposition to each other. And I will continue to work for trans woman–inclusion at Michigan, because this is my dyke community too. And I know that it will not be easy, and plenty of people will try to make me feel like an alien in my own community. But I will take on their prejudices with my own unique perspective because sometimes you see things more clearly when you've been made to feel like you are on the outside looking in.

ON BEING A WOMAN

CHAPTER THREE

A friend of mine was asked to write about being a femme for a queer women's event. She wasn't quite sure where to begin. "It's hard to write about being a girl," she said, and I knew exactly what she meant.

For some time, I've been trying to write my own poem about what it means to be a woman. But every time I pick up my pen, I'm afraid that I'll paint myself into a corner, betrayed by words forged from soft vowel sounds and weak, diminutive connotations. Words so delicate that they crumple under any further introspection. I'm afraid that I may lose a part of myself as I navigate my way through the landmines of other people's definitions and dogmas.

Pop culture tells us that a real woman knows how to use her body to get what she wants, wielding the power of attraction, seducing with her animal magnetism. But I ask, how much power is there in being a carrot on a stick that is dangled in front of someone? And I can't help but notice that when men try to flatter us, they often use words like "enchanting" and "mysterious." But to me, those words seem like a subconscious attempt by them to place some distance between us.

So it bothers me when I hear women buy into a similar mysticism, as they try to empower us by proclaiming that we are magical, that we are mother earth with the ability to give birth, bearing life cycles that follow the moon like the tides of the ocean. But don't they see the danger in buying into the idea that we are supernatural beings? For if we call ourselves "goddesses," then there is no need for anyone to treat us like human beings.

I believe that this is where second-wave feminism came to a grinding halt: When we got caught up in the myth that women are special because of our biology.[1] Because when we take pride in how fundamentally different we are from men, we unknowingly engage in a dangerous game of opposites. For if men are big, then women must be small. And if men are strong, then women must be soft. And it becomes impossible to write a loud and proud poem about what it means to be a woman without either ridiculing men or else pulling the rug out from under ourselves.

And being a woman is contradiction enough without being both a transsexual and a dyke like myself. I often feel like the monkey in the middle: On one side of me are older lesbians who insist that I am still a man, as if being born male was some awful disease that has infected my blood and my bones permanently. On the other side of me are younger dykes who are infatuated with trans men and tranny bois, yet secretly confess to friends that they are disturbed by trans women because we act so "effeminate."[2] I wonder how they can be so oblivious to their own arrogance, for anyone who admires trans men but dismisses trans women is simply practicing another form of sexism.

I used to think it was a contradiction that some dykes abhorred me for my masculinity while others hated me for my femininity, until I realized that being a woman means that everyone has a stake in seeing what they want to see in me.

My friend said, "It's hard to write about being a girl." I believe that's because the word "girl" doesn't really have a meaning of its own, as it is always defined in opposition to "boy." So when being butch is to make yourself rock solid, then being femme becomes allowing yourself to be malleable. And if being a man means taking control of your own situation, then being a woman becomes living up to other people's expectations.

Well, I refuse to believe in this myth of opposites. If we want to shatter the glass ceiling, we must first learn to move beyond biology and give ourselves permission to become anything we want to be. I say to set any standard that all women must meet is to commit an act of misogyny.

I refuse to believe in the myth that all women share a common bond. The truth is we are all very different from one another. We each live with a different set of privileges and life experiences. And once we acknowledge this fact, it will become obvious that when we try to place all women into the same box, we unintentionally suffocate ourselves.

Instead of pretending that all women share the same experience, that we are one and the same, let's make the word "woman" a perpetual agent of change. Instead of repeating history by chaining ourselves to one specific definition or concept, let's make the word "woman" a celebration of each of our uniqueness.

MARGINS

CHAPTER FOUR

NOVEMBER 2006.

T he nurse is pulling the stitches out of my face. I can tell that something is wrong because she doesn't offer any of the typical "it's-healing-nicely" affirmations that one usually expects. The doctor enters and tells me that the tumor exceeded three of the four margins of the diamond-shaped sliver of skin that he removed from my cheek one week ago. He explains that most basal cell carcinomas grow in one big lump, like a basketball, making them easy to remove in one fell swoop. But my tumor was a rarer, more aggressive type that grows unpredictably under the skin like an amoeba, sending out projections like tentacles.

He tells me that he won't know how far it has spread until the next surgery. Hopefully they won't have to remove too much more tissue. But he can't rule out the possibility that I might lose so much of my cheek that the plastic surgeon they will assign to me will have to resort to skin grafts.

Nobody wants skin cancer. And the very thought of skin grafts terrifies me. But in the three weeks prior to my scheduled surgery, what bothered me the most about the worst-case scenario was not just what I might look like afterward, but rather how it played into my trans issues.

Most people view transsexuals as constitutively artificial, as mere products of plastic surgeries and medical technologies. When I come out to people as trans, they often compulsively scan my body for any physical signs that my femaleness is fake. As a trans activist, I intellectually know that all of these attitudes are transphobic and complete bullshit. But I'd be lying if I said that I haven't internalized many of these very sentiments.

What frightened me most about the possibility of skin grafts was not my potential appearance, but rather the symbolism—my obviously stitched-together face being interpreted by others as a metaphor for the fakeness of my entire body, my gender. Whenever I shared this thought with cissexual friends, they always responded the same way, telling me that it was nonsense, that cancer-related skin grafts have nothing to do with transsexuality. And while that may be true in a logical sort of way, it seemed to me to be particularly convenient for them to say. Unlike them, I don't have the privilege of having my body viewed as inherently natural and congruent. My body is always betraying me, whether it was the male body that used to feel completely alien to me, or my current female state, which others view as inherently unnatural and illegitimate.

Eventually, I have surgery. The doctor ends up removing three square centimeters of my cheek—a big hole to be sure, but there is enough tissue left for the plastic surgeon to stitch me back up without requiring skin grafts. Afterwards, I am grateful, but I really feel the need to talk about my experience. I find out that the Women's Cancer Resource Center in Oakland has support groups, and at first I am excited. But then it hits me that I can't talk about my experience with skin cancer without also talking about transsexuality and the way that I've internalized other people's assumptions about my supposed artificiality. I realized not only that cissexual cancer survivors would not be able to relate to my experience, but also that because it was a support group for women, there was a distinct possibility that my presence might make others uncomfortable, that I may even have to face accusations of being an imposter or infiltrator. So instead of attending the meetings, I did what I always seem to do: I bottled up all of my anger, frustration, fears, anxiety, and sadness, and promised myself that I would write about it later.[1]

TRANS FEMINISM: THERE'S NO CONUNDRUM ABOUT IT

CHAPTER FIVE

n March of 2012, *Ms. Magazine*'s blog ran a month-long "Future of Feminism" series, which was billed as "celebrating organizations and ideas that represent the future of feminism." The author of the series covered a variety of topics, and portrayed them all—even those that have generated significant debate within feminism—in a generally positive light. The glaring exception to this was her article on trans feminism (ominously entitled "Transfeminism and Its Conundrums"), which framed the movement as a "controversy" that is fundamentally incompatible with certain basic tenets of feminism.[1] As far as I can tell, this was the only "Future of Feminism" article in which she gave equal space to arguments against the featured feminist submovement. I strongly disagreed with the article, as did a number of commenters, and *Ms.* blog graciously gave me the opportunity to post a rebuttal. Here's what I wrote[2]:

Trans feminism—that is, transgender perspectives on feminism, or feminist perspectives on transgender issues—is one of many so-called "third-wave" feminisms.[3] Its origins are closely linked with other feminist submovements—specifically, sex-positive feminism, postmodern/ poststructuralist feminism, queer theory, and intersectionality. These strands of feminism represent a move away from viewing sexism as an overly simplistic, unilateral form of oppression, where men are the oppressors and women are the oppressed, end of story.

Instead, these feminisms recognize that there are numerous forms of sexism—that is, numerous double standards based on a person's sex, gender, or sexuality. In addition to traditional sexism (where men are viewed as more legitimate than women), there is heterosexism (where heterosexuals are viewed as more legitimate than homosexuals), monosexism (where people who are exclusively attracted to members of a single gender or sex are viewed as more legitimate than bisexuals/pansexuals), masculine-centrism (where masculine gender expression is viewed as more legitimate than feminine gender expression), and so on.

There are also other forms of marginalization prevalent in our society, such as racism, classism, and ableism. As feminists of color have articulated, these do not act independently of one another, but rather intersect with and compound one another. A woman of color doesn't face racism and sexism separately; the sexism she faces is often racialized, and the racism she faces is often sexualized.[4] This concept of intersectionality is now very well accepted among many contemporary feminists (albeit not by those who continue to adhere to a unilateral men-oppress-women-end-of-story approach to feminism).

Trans feminism is rooted in this idea that there are multiple forms of sexism that often intersect with each other, and with other forms of oppression.

Although some feminists have historically framed sexism in terms of patriarchy, early trans feminists forwarded *the gender binary*—being nonconsensually assigned a female or male sex at birth—as a way to describe the myriad forms of sexism in our society. Those assigned a male sex are expected to grow up to identify as a man, to be masculine in gender expression, and to be exclusively attracted to women; those assigned a female sex are expected to grow up to identify as a woman, be feminine in gender expression, and be exclusively attracted to men. Anyone who fails to conform to the gender binary—whether an intersex child, a tomboyish girl, a gay man, a transgender person, etc.—is marginalized by society, albeit in different ways. The gender binary concept was an attempt to create a synthesis between feminist, queer, and transgender activism, and it has become quite popular among many feminists and LGBTQIA+ activists since its inception.

Trans feminists have also focused on how trans people are impacted by institutionalized *cissexism*—forms of sexism that construe trans people's gender identities and expressions as less legitimate than those of cis people (those who are not trans). Cissexism—or as some describe it, *transphobia*—can be seen in how individuals, organizations, and governments often refuse to respect trans people's lived experiences in our identified genders/sexes; in the discrimination we may face in employment or medical settings; and in how trans people are often targeted for harassment and violence.

While some examples of cissexism are quite trans-specific, others have strong parallels with what women face in a male-centric society. For instance, trans people and women are routinely objectified and deemed incompetent to make informed decisions about our own bodies, and our perspectives and lived experiences are often not taken seriously by cis people and men, respectively.

Of course, cissexism does not occur in a bubble. It occurs in a world where other forms of sexism and oppression exist. For instance, trans feminists such as myself have articulated the concept of *transmisogyny*—that is, the way cissexism and misogyny intersect in the lives of trans women and others on the trans female/feminine spectrum.[5] Transmisogyny explains why the lion's share of societal consternation, demonization, and sexualization of transgender people is concentrated on trans female/feminine individuals. Cissexism also intersects with other forms of marginalization—for instance, victims of transphobic violence are overwhelmingly trans people who are poor, who are of color, and/or who are on the trans female/feminine spectrum.[6]

So basically, that's it: Trans feminism is not a conundrum. Rather, it is simply one of numerous third-wave feminisms that take an intersectional approach to challenging sexism and oppression. The only thing different about trans feminism is that it extends this feminist analysis to transgender issues, which have been largely overlooked or misinterpreted by feminists in the past.

The article "Transfeminism and Its Conundrums" gave credence to those feminists who refuse to acknowledge cissexism or intersectionality, and who instead frame trans issues solely in terms of male privilege. In the past, such feminists have dismissed trans feminism, depicting trans men as being "female" traitors who transition to attain male privilege, and trans women as being entitled "men" who transition in order to infiltrate women's spaces. While this rhetoric has mellowed somewhat over the years, some feminists still argue that trans women have no right to participate in feminism because we were not socialized female, or because we may have benefited from male privilege in the past.

Of course, male privilege is a real phenomenon. In my book *Whipping Girl*, I discuss my own experience with male privilege—and losing it post-transition—at great length.[7] However, trans people's experiences of male privilege vary greatly depending upon the direction of one's gender transgression or transition, the age one transitions (during early childhood, as a teenager, or at various points in adulthood), one's sexual orientation, whether one "passes" as cisgender, one's race, and so on. For instance, many trans men of color say that whatever male privilege they have gained since transitioning has been very much offset by the increased visibility and the societal stereotypes of black men as predators that are constantly being projected onto them by others.[8] It's impossible to talk accurately about male privilege—or any aspect of sexism—without framing it in terms of intersectionality.

The myth that there is some kind of universal women's experience was debunked by women of color, among others, long ago.[9] All of us have different life histories; sexism impacts each of our lives somewhat differently, and each of us is privileged in some ways but not others. Some feminists may obstinately insist that cis women have it far worse than trans women, or that traditional sexism is far worse than cissexism, or heterosexism, but the point of feminism is not to engage in this kind of "oppression Olympics."[10] Rather, the point is to challenge societal sexism and other forms of marginalization. This is what trans feminists are focused on doing.

When trans feminism is reduced to a debate about whether trans women "count" as women or as feminists, it's a disservice not only to us, but to feminism as a whole.

RECLAIMING FEMININITY

CHAPTER SIX

O ver the last few years, my femme identity has very much informed the way that I relate to myself as a trans woman, as a queer woman, and as a feminist more generally. If you were to ask a hundred different femmes to define the word "femme," you would probably get a hundred different answers. Having said this, most femmes would no doubt agree that an important, if not central, aspect of femme identity involves reclaiming feminine gender expression, or "femininity." It is commonplace for people in both the straight mainstream as well as within our queer and feminist circles to presume that feminine gender expression is more frivolous, artificial, impractical, and manipulative than masculine gender expression, and that those of us who dress or act femininely are likely to be more tame, fragile, dependent, and immature than our masculine or "gender neutral" counterparts.[1] By reclaiming femininity, those of us who are femme are engaged in a constant process of challenging these negative assumptions that are routinely projected onto feminine gender expression.

While reclaiming femininity is an important part of our femme identities, the specific ways in which we engage in reclaiming, re-appropriating, and re-conceptualizing femininity differs from person to person based on our varied experiences, struggles, and histories. I have found that my life history as a transsexual woman has led to me having a somewhat different view of femininity and femme identity than that commonly held by the majority of cissexual femme women. In this chapter, I will explore some of these differences. My hope is that, rather than drawing a sharp distinction between trans femmes and cis femmes, what I have to say will make clear the many similarities that we share. And rather than dis-identifying with my trans experience, it is my hope that cis femmes (and other readers) will draw parallels between my struggles and experiences and their own.

Many of my thoughts regarding the similarities and differences between cis and trans femmes grew out of my experience at the Femme 2006 conference, which took place in San Francisco in August of that year. At the time, I was about three-quarters finished writing the book that would eventually become *Whipping Girl*. My main purpose in writing the book was to debunk many of the myths and misconceptions that people have—both in the mainstream and within feminist and queer communities—about trans women and femininity. Focusing simultaneously on both femininity and trans women was no accident. I had spent five years doing trans activism up to that point—conducting transgender 101 workshops, writing essays critiquing media depictions of trans people, and working to challenge trans woman exclusion from lesbian and women's spaces. And the one thing that came up over and over again was the way in which trans women and others on the trans female/feminine spectrum receive the bulk of society's fascination and demonization with regard to transgenderism. In contrast, people on the trans male/masculine spectrum have remained relatively invisible. This disparity in attention suggests that those of us on the trans female/feminine spectrum are culturally marked, not for failing to conform to gender norms per se, but because of the specific direction of our gender transgression—that is, because of our feminine gender expression and/or our female gender identities. And while it has become common for people to use the word "transphobia" as a catchall phrase to describe anti-trans sentiment, it is more accurate to view the discrimination and stigma faced by trans people on the trans female/feminine spectrum in terms of trans-misogyny.

I have found that many people who have not had a trans female or trans feminine experience often have trouble wrapping their brains around the concept of trans-misogyny, so I will offer the following two anecdotes to help illustrate what I mean by the term. Once, about two years ago, I was walking down the street in San Francisco, and a trans woman happened to be walking just ahead of me. She was dressed femininely, but not any more feminine than a typical cis woman. Two people, a man and a woman, were sitting on a doorstep, and as the trans woman walked by, the man turned to the woman he was sitting next to and said, "Look at all the shit he's wearing," and the woman he was with nodded in agreement. Now presumably the word "shit" was a reference to femininity—specifically, the feminine clothing and cosmetics the trans woman wore. I found this particular comment to be quite telling. After all, while cis women often receive harassing comments from strange men on the street, it is rather rare for those men to address those remarks to a female acquaintance and for her to apparently approve of his remarks. Furthermore, if this same man were to have harassed a cis woman, it is unlikely that he would do so by referring to her feminine clothing and makeup as "shit." Similarly, someone who is on the trans masculine spectrum could potentially be harassed, but it is unlikely that his masculine clothing would be referred to as "shit." Thus, trans-misogyny is both informed by, yet distinct from, transphobia and misogyny, in that it specifically targets transgender expressions of femaleness and femininity.

The second example of trans-misogyny that I'd like to share occurred at an Association for Women in Psychology conference I attended in 2007 (for those unfamiliar with that organization, it is essentially a feminist psychology conference). One psychologist gave a presentation on the ways in which feminism has informed her approach to therapy. During the course of her talk, she discussed two transgender clients of hers, one on the trans male/masculine spectrum, the other on the trans female/feminine spectrum. Their stories were very similar in that both had begun the process of physically transitioning but were having second thoughts about it. First, the therapist discussed the trans masculine spectrum person, whose gender presentation she described simply as being "very butch." She discussed this individual's transgender expressions and issues in a respectful and serious manner, and the audience listened attentively. However, when she turned her attention to the trans feminine client, she went into a very graphic and animated description of the trans person's appearance, detailing how the trans woman's hair was styled, the type of outfit and shoes she was wearing, the way her makeup was done, and so on. This description elicited a significant amount of giggling from the audience, which I found to be particularly disturbing given the fact that this was an explicitly feminist conference. Clearly, if a male psychologist gave a talk at this meeting in which he went into such explicit detail regarding what one of his cis female clients was wearing, most of these same audience members, as well as the presenter, would surely (and rightfully) be appalled and would view such remarks to be blatantly objectifying. In fact, in both of these incidents I have described, comments that would typically be considered extraordinarily misogynistic if they were directed at cis women are not considered beyond the pale when directed at trans women.

As both of these anecdotes demonstrate, expressions of trans-misogyny do not merely focus on trans women's female gender identities, but more often than not, they specifically target her feminine gender expression. Trans-misogyny is driven by the fact that in our culture, feminine appearances are more blatantly and routinely judged by society than masculine ones. It is also driven by the fact that connotations such as "artificial," "contrived," and "frivolous" are practically built into our cultural understanding of femininity—these same connotations allow masculinity to invariably come off as "natural," "sincere," and "practical" in comparison.

For example, when a woman wishes to charm or impress someone, she is often described as using her "feminine wiles." But when a man tries to charm or impress someone, nobody ever accuses him of using his "masculine wiles." Instead, he is simply seen as being himself. The word "wiles" is defined as "a trick, artifice, or stratagem meant to fool, trap, or entice; a device." This is the how people typically view feminine gender expression: as manipulative, insincere, and artificial.

There is a common, yet false, assumption that those feminists and queer women who favor trans woman exclusion are primarily concerned with the fact that trans women were born male, that we have experienced male privilege, that we have had or may still have penises, or that we may still have residual "male energy" (whatever the fuck that is). I would argue that the growing acceptance, and even celebration, of trans male and trans masculine folks within queer women's communities over the last decade demonstrates that this supposed fear of maleness and masculinity is largely a red herring. Rather, in my many encounters with cis feminists who are hesitant or resistant about including trans women's voices and issues within the feminist movement, almost invariably, the first thing they mention is what they consider to be our "over the top" or "exaggerated" feminine gender expression: the way we supposedly dress hyperfemininely and wear way too much makeup, that we turn ourselves into "caricatures" of "real" women. Janice Raymond chided trans women for the fact that we supposedly, "conform more to the feminine role than even the most feminine of natural-born women," and Robin Morgan claimed that by doing so we "parody female oppression and suffering."[2]

Anyone who knows multiple actual trans women knows that this monolithic image of trans women as "hyperfeminine" is nothing more than a ruse, one that typically grows out of an uncritical acceptance of media depictions of trans women, or out of stereotyping based on one or two actual trans women the person may have seen or met (and who were obvious as trans precisely because of their especially high femme presentation). Actual trans women differ greatly in our personal styles and gender expressions. Some are rather conventional in their femininity, while others are understated, and still others strive to be fabulously feminine. Some identify as femme dykes or femme tomboys. Other trans women are very androgynous in their manner of dress and gender expression, and still others dress and identify as butch. So what purpose does this monolithic image of trans women as hyperfeminine serve? Well, in a world where femininity is regularly disparaged as being manipulative and insincere, such images reinforce the popular cissexist assumption that our female gender identities are "fake" or "contrived," and therefore not to be taken seriously. Indeed, in the eyes of society, trans women are seen as doubly artificial, both because we are trans and because we are perceived as feminine.

As I became more and more aware of the ways in which anti-feminine sentiment is used to undermine and delegitimize trans women, I began to realize the ways in which I had unconsciously (and sometimes consciously) distanced myself from femininity in order to gain acceptance in the queer community. When I first began attending and performing spoken word at queer and feminist events back in 2002 and 2003, I definitely played down my femme side and played up my tomboy side. And you know what? It worked. I became relatively accepted in those circles. I honestly don't think that I would have been accepted so readily within San Francisco's queer and feminist communities if I attended those first events dressed in an especially feminine manner.

This, of course, is not just a trans woman issue; it is a femme issue. It's not just the heterosexist mainstream that promotes the idea that masculinity is strong and natural while femininity remains weak and artificial. In today's gay male communities, masculinity is praised while femininity remains suspect. In today's queer women's communities, masculinity is praised while femininity remains suspect. If one wants to be taken seriously in these communities, then they will inevitably feel a certain pressure to conform to the community's masculine-centric ideals. I can't tell you how many of my cis queer female friends have shared with me stories similar to my own, of how they really tried to butch it up when they first came out as lesbians or as dykes, because they really wanted to be accepted and to be taken seriously.

For me, as a trans woman, my attempt to distance myself from my own feminine expression was particularly poignant. After all, I had spent most of my life coming to terms with my feminine inclinations. As a kid, I repressed my feminine tendencies for fear of being called out as a sissy or fairy. As a young adult, I began to reclaim them, to feel empowered by them, and I lived openly as an unabashedly feminine boy for several years before I decided to transition. So it's sadly ironic that after my transition, I felt the need to play down femininity once again in order to be taken seriously as a queer woman and a feminist.

It was through conversations with my femme-identified friends— some who were trans, but many of whom were cis—and their sharing with me their own struggles with being feminine in a queer culture that is so masculine-centric, that I began to embrace my femme identity around 2005. So when the Femme Conference came to San Francisco in 2006, and when I was invited to do spoken word at one of the performance events, I was ecstatic. For me, it represented a sort of a publicly-coming-out-as-femme moment. It was also important for me because I was convinced that trans women and femmes were natural allies. I believed this not only because of the overlap between these two communities (for example, individuals such as myself who identify as both trans women and femmes), but because both groups share a history of being considered suspect in lesbian communities because of our feminine gender expression. My belief that trans women and femmes were natural allies also stemmed from my own experience in the San Francisco Bay Area, where I generally found that the cis queer women who were most willing to stand up for their trans sisters, and to call their peers out on trans-misogyny, were almost always femmes.

However, when I attended the conference, I found that my belief that trans women and femmes were natural allies was not shared by all of the attendees, not by a long shot. So for me, the conference was a bit of an emotional roller coaster ride. I want to share some of these moments, both the good and the bad. My purpose for doing so is not to call anyone out or to make people feel defensive. Neither is this a critique of the conference itself, because I feel the organizers sincerely intended the space to be inclusive and welcoming of trans feminine voices. Rather, I am sharing these moments with you in the hope that it might offer some insight into where trans women such as myself are coming from.

First, there was the love and appreciation I felt among the artists with whom I shared the stage at the performance—especially my friends Meliza and Celestina, with whom I performed. Their love gave me the strength to do something that I had never done before: to perform for a predominantly queer women's audience while wearing make-up, heels, and a dress. And a rather slinky dress at that. I'm sure this may not sound like such a big deal to many femmes, but anyone who has been on the receiving end of as many trans-women-are-caricatures-of-real-women comments as I have would surely understand.

After we performed our piece, I was on cloud nine, excited by how well it went and how well it was received. But I was brought back down to earth by a well-meaning audience member who stopped me to tell me that she enjoyed the piece. And before I could thank her, she added,

"And you look so real. I never would have guessed." On the outside I smiled, but on the inside all I wanted to do was cry.

Then, there were the events that occurred during a "Femininities, Feminism, and Femmes" panel that followed a film screening of the movie *FtF: Female to Femme* (and a number of other short films).[3] Many of the conference attendees seemed to love *FtF*, and I myself enjoyed much of the film—it included some excellent interviews, and I especially appreciated the fact that it depicted "femme" without automatically pairing it with "butch." But personally, I found it difficult to get around a recurring scene in the film (that was apparently meant to provide comic relief) that depicted a femme support group that was obviously meant to be parody of trans support groups. Having attended trans support groups myself, and having seen grown adults emotionally break down because for the first time in their life they were sharing their crossgender feelings with other people, or because they had lost their jobs or family after deciding to transition, I found those scenes to be disturbing. To draw what I feel is an apt analogy, as someone who has survived an attempted date rape, I would be offended if someone were to do a parody of a rape survivor's support group. Similarly, as someone who for much of my life would have rather been dead than have anyone else know about my transgender feelings, I found the parody of trans support groups to be offensive (despite the fact that it was probably not the filmmakers' intention to offend trans people).

Thankfully, the panel that followed the film was designed to present different perspectives within the femme community, and it included a trans woman, artist and activist Shawna Virago. Shawna brought up her similar feelings about the film, and how she felt that it invisibilized the cis privilege most of the conference attendees enjoy. I was grateful that that perspective (which I shared) was voiced. It made me feel like my own voice was included in the conversation.

But then, the first question immediately following the panelists' opening statements came from a cis woman who suggested that Shawna "didn't get" the film, that it was "just a spoof." She then added that she felt that Shawna's comments were "divisive." The word "divisive" is a red flag for me. I can't begin to tell you how many times I have heard trans women, or allies of trans women, called "divisive" when we call out people on their transphobia or trans-misogyny. In contrast, I have never once heard anyone use the word "divisive" to describe cis queer women who make trans-misogynistic comments, or who organize or attend queer women's spaces that exclude trans women. The fact that acts that marginalize trans women are not typically described as being "divisive" implies that there is a presumed and unspoken "one-ness" that exists in queer women's communities that implicitly precludes trans women.

The most difficult moment for me at Femme 2006 occurred during a keynote talk that I attended in which the speaker made three separate disparaging remarks about trans women. The first comment came out of the blue (as she was not discussing trans people or trans issues) when she referred to herself as a "bio-dyke" and defined that as someone who is born female and who is attracted to other women who are born female. (By the way, I am a biologist by trade. And I can assure you that I am 100% biological!) Anyway, I tried my best to ignore that remark. But then, a little later on in her talk, she made two more comments. The first was a rather confusing comment that seemed to legitimize queer women's fears of "accidentally" becoming attracted to a trans dyke—a sort of lesbian version of *The Crying Game* syndrome, I suppose. Shortly thereafter, she dusted off the thirty-year-old stereotype of the trans woman who "takes up too much space" at a lesbian meeting. This last comment was particularly infuriating for me given the fact that (like virtually all queer women's events these days) there was a significant turn out of trans male/masculine spectrum folks (even despite the fact that it was a femme-themed conference) yet there were hardly any trans women in attendance. So for the speaker to suggest that trans women "take up too much space" in a community where we have almost no voice and are often explicitly unwelcomed is both illogical and offensive.

My immediate impulse after hearing that comment—being the rabel rouser that I am—was to begin to craft a biting response for the question-and-answer session that was to follow. But then I realized how pointless that would be, as I would be playing right into her stereotype of me as "taking up too much space." She had placed me in a double bind. So, upset and without any other obvious recourse, I walked out of the session. I wasn't trying to make a statement or anything. I honestly just wanted to get as far away as possible. I wanted to go home.

During that long walk (as it was a large conference room), a couple things were going through my mind. First, I felt very alone. There was no evidence that the audience at large was bothered at all by these comments (although, after the fact, I found out that there were others who were also disturbed). Second, the phrase "trans woman exclusion"—which I had used countless times in my activism to change the policy at the Michigan Womyn's Music Festival and other women's events and spaces—suddenly popped into my head. For all of my work rallying against "exclusion," here I was leaving a queer women's event that I was explicitly invited to. In a sense, I was excluding myself, not because of any policy, but because I found the atmosphere and rhetoric in that room to be intolerable. I was leaving because I was made to feel like I didn't belong.

This latter form of trans woman exclusion, driven not by any formal policy, but by a more general sense of disregard or disrespect for trans women, typifies many queer women's events and spaces. Often, when trans women ask me when I'm performing next and I tell them that it is at a queer women's event, they will tell me that they'd rather not go because they do not feel comfortable or safe in those spaces, because they have been harassed or belittled at similar events before. In most cases, these women are sexually oriented toward women and identify as lesbian or bisexual themselves. But they want no part of queer women's events because of the unchecked trans-misogyny that is often pervasive there.

Anyway, I walked out of that talk, and it's very likely that I would not have come back to the conference if it weren't for the fact that an amazing cis woman named Tara followed me out. She stopped me in the lobby to tell me that she was embarrassed and disturbed by the speaker's comments, and she showed me much love and support in a discussion we shared just outside of the session. She let me rant for a couple minutes about how upset I was over those comments. And she listened. And that's really what I needed right then, to be listened to. To be reminded that my voice, my thoughts, my feelings still counted, at least to somebody.

In a way, what happened at that keynote talk and at the panel after the *FtF* film screening, while frustrating and difficult for me, also had a silver lining. These events provoked discussions about trans woman irrelevancy within queer women's communities—discussions that were long overdue. I don't think that such dialogue would have occurred at any other predominantly queer women's event. I believe it happened then and there precisely because it was a femme conference— because many femmes recognize trans women as being a vital part of the femme community.

Two years later, I was invited to give one of the keynote talks at the Femme 2008 Conference.[4] Because of my experience at the previous conference, I attended Femme 2008 with somewhat different expectations than I had before. For one thing, I no longer believe that femmes and trans women are "natural" allies. In fact, in retrospect, the very phrase "natural allies" strikes me as rather oxymoronic. Being an ally is not something that comes naturally. It requires work. To be an ally, you have to listen. You have to be willing to stand by your ally's side, even when it is not directly in your interest to do so.

I still believe that trans women and femmes make good potential allies, as we both face discrimination (both in the straight mainstream and within our own LGBTQIA+ communities) because of our feminine gender expression. And in similar (and sometimes different) ways, we are both working to reclaim femininity, to be empowered by our own feminine gender expression despite the negative and inferior connotations the rest of the world projects onto us for it. And trans women and femmes share another important attribute: We are survivors. The rest of the world may assume we are weak and fragile because of our feminine inclinations, but in reality, living with other people's relentless misogynistic bullshit has made us tenacious bad-asses.

While I feel that these shared experiences provide fertile ground for us to build an alliance upon, I also must recognize that there are many femme-identified folks who do not view trans women as potential allies and who do not see us as a part of their communities. Many femmes are indifferent toward trans women and our issues, and still others are downright antagonistic (as was evident at Femme 2006).

I have come to realize (and have written about this in *Whipping Girl*) that there tend to be two prevalent and very different attitudes regarding what queer communities should look like and who they should include.[5] The first—which is the one I favor—views queer community in terms of alliances built on shared experiences and interests. As a kinky femme-identified trans woman who just so happens to get it on with the ladies, I seek alliances with other women, with other femmes, with other transgender-spectrum folks, with others who engage in same-sex relationships or BDSM, and with fat, disabled, and intersex folks who share the experience of being made to feel that their bodies are unworthy and inferior to those of other people. Furthermore, as someone who experiences marginalization because of my queerness and transness, I also recognize the importance of creating and fostering alliances with people who are marginalized in other ways, for example, because of their race, class, and so on. For me, community is not so much about surrounding myself with people who are "just like me," but rather about learning from and supporting others who share issues and experiences that are similar (yet somewhat different) from my own.

This alliance model exists in sharp contrast to the second view of queer communities, which is centered on sameness rather than difference, on closed, insular communities rather than open ones. Many lesbian and gay communities are built according to this model, as are those segments of the queer community where one must constantly tout their über-queer credentials, lest they be accused of being "assimilationist," conformist, or simply passé. Queer people who prefer closed, insular communities typically insist that their own ideologies, values, expressions, and norms are not merely different, but superior to those who have more conventional genders and sexualities. And those gender and sexual minorities who don't quite conform to those community standards are typically seen as having no place within the community.

When I was first coming out as a dyke, I really wanted to fit in, to be accepted. I was really hoping that the dyke community would become a home for me. Unfortunately, it hasn't. While I've met a lot of really great, amazing, supportive women in those spaces, I've also had a lot of really sucky interactions with people who are either apathetic or antagonistic toward trans women. I've come to realize that I will never fully be accepted within lesbian or dyke circles because of the ways in which I differ from the majority: because I am a trans woman, because I am a femme, and also because I have recently come out as bisexual. In a world where many women define "lesbian" as being in opposition to maleness, in opposition to heterosexuality, and in opposition to femininity, I realize that I literally have three strikes against me. So I have instead decided to embrace the fact that I am lesbian kryptonite, as my existence blurs all of those distinctions, calls into question all of those oppositions. I no longer have any desire to try to gain inclusion or "acceptance" within lesbian- or dyke-centric spaces. Fuck insular communities that are centered around any identity. I'm no longer looking for a home; I'm looking to make alliances.

While many of us may call ourselves "femme," it is important for us to acknowledge that we are all socially situated in different ways, and this often results in each of us having our own perspectives on femininity and femme identity. Sometimes I find it difficult to talk about my very different history—specifically the fact that I was socialized male (or as I would put it, forced against my will into boyhood) because it is so often cited by trans-misogynistic women as evidence that I don't belong in lesbian or women's spaces, because I am not a "real" woman. But at the same time, I feel that often the most important conversations to engage in are also the ones that leave you most vulnerable. So in the last part of this chapter, I am going to throw all caution to the wind and talk about how my very different trans history has led to me having a very different perspective on femininity and femme identity than that held by many of my cis femme sisters.

It seems to me that for many cis femme dykes, a major issue that they must reconcile in their lives is the way their feminine expression seems to be at odds with their queer identity. This can lead to invisibility—that is, because they are feminine, they are often not read by others as queer. It can also result in having their queer and feminist credentials constantly called into question by those who view femininity as an artifact of compulsory heterosexuality and therefore, inherently conformist. In an apparent attempt to challenge accusations that they are conformists, or that they reinforce sexist stereotypes, many femmes have instead argued that their gender expression is subversive because it is employed toward queer ends, thus challenging heterosexism. Or they might argue that their gender expression is merely a performance, one that makes visible the ways in which gender itself is constructed. As Leah Lakshmi Piepzna-Samarasinha put it in her Femme 2008 keynote talk, this is the idea that femme gender expression is "ironic and campy."

Now I can certainly relate to the notion of feminine expression as performance. As someone who has to "dress down" for my day job, I know that when I do get the chance to dress up for an occasion, there is a definite sense of doing something different, of putting on a different exterior than I normally do. Having said that, even when I'm at my most outwardly feminine, the feeling that my gender expression is a "performance" does not even come close to how contrived and self-conscious I felt back before my transition, when I had to wear male-specific clothing (e.g., putting on a suit and tie when attending a wedding). So while you can make the case that both masculinity and femininity are "performances," for me, feminine expression feels way more natural. It resonates with my sense of self in a way that I don't really have words to describe. It just feels right to me, where as masculine expression always felt wrong.

What also strikes me is the fact that, while being dressed up as a guy felt very artificial and contrived to me, other people tended to read my masculine presentation as natural. In contrast, when I am wearing feminine clothing, it may feel natural to me, but other people tend to see me as being "all dolled up." This touches on what I said earlier about "feminine wiles" and femininity being seen as inherently artificial. In our culture, masculine expression seems to arise out of who one simply is, whereas feminine expression is always viewed as an act, as a performance.

This is why I recoil from this idea of femme gender expression as "ironic and campy," as a form of drag or performance, as it plays into the popular assumption that femininity is artificial. I am particularly sensitive about this because, as I mentioned earlier, others often view me as doubly artificial both because I am trans and because I am feminine. The assumption that my gender is artificial or a performance is regularly cited by those who wish to undermine or dismiss my female identity. I refuse to let anyone get away with the cissexist presumption that my gender must be a "performance" simply because I am a transsexual. And I similarly refuse to let anyone get away with the masculine-centric presumption that my gender must be a "performance" simply because I am feminine.

I also find the notion of femininity as performance to be somewhat disingenuous and oversimplistic. I mean, I can "perform" femininity. I can put on makeup, skirts, and heels. I can talk with my hands or twirl my hair if I want. But performance doesn't explain why certain behaviors and ways of being come to me more naturally than others. The idea that femininity is just a construct or merely a performance is incompatible with the countless young feminine boys who are not self-conscious about their gender expressions, who become confused as to why their parents become outraged at their behavior, or why the other children relentlessly tease them for being who they are. Many such children find their gender expression to be irrepressible, and they remain outwardly feminine throughout their lives despite all of the stigmatization and male socialization to the contrary. Other femininely-oriented male children learn to hide their feminine gender expression in order to survive, but at a great cost.

I was one of the latter children. I know that for many cis queer women, femininity is something that others foist upon them, an unwanted burden, an expectation that they are unable or unwilling to meet. This is perhaps why so many cis lesbian feminists have gone to such great lengths to argue that femininity is artificial, a mere artifact of patriarchy. But for me, femininity was like ether or air—it was always there, just waiting for the chance to leak out of me. When I think about gender expression as being a "performance," I think about myself as a kid, watching my S's when I spoke to make sure they didn't linger. "Performance" was me fighting back the urge to be more animated with my hands when I talked, or learning never to use words like "adorable" or "cute" nonsarcastically. "Performance" was going to the barber to get my hair cut short like my parents wanted it, when what I really wanted was to let my hair grow long. Like I said, for me, masculinity always felt artificial, while femininity felt natural.

Natural. The word natural has become super fucking taboo in queer and feminist circles. Usually when I utter the word "natural" in such settings, I feel as though the queer theory police will bust into the room at any minute and arrest me for being an essentialist. People are quick to toss around accusations of "essentialism" without really giving much thought to what that word actually means. An essentialist is someone who believes that all women are the same: that we are all naturally feminine, that we are all naturally attracted to men, and so forth. Essentialists view women who are not feminine, or not exclusively attracted to men, as unnatural. As artificial.

I am not an essentialist (despite the fact that some have accused me of that). I do not believe that all women are the same; I believe that all women are different. I believe that women naturally fall all over the map with regards to gender expression and sexual orientation. I believe that there are no wholly "artificial" genders or sexualities. I believe that many of us experience natural inclinations or predispositions toward certain gendered and sexual behaviors. But these inclinations do not exist in a vacuum—rather they arise in a culture where gender and sexuality are heavily policed, where they are defined according to heterosexist, cissexist, transphobic, and misogynistic assumptions, where they intersect with racism, classism, ableism, ageism, and other forms of oppression. I would argue that this view of gender and sexuality is not essentialist. It is holistic.

As I alluded to earlier, it is common for people to have somewhat varied opinions regarding what the word "femme" actually means. For me, having a holistic view of gender and sexuality, I would suggest that most of us who are femme share two things in common. First, we find that, for whatever reason, feminine gender expression resonates with us on a deep, profound level, in an inexplicable way that isn't easy to put into words. The second thing that we share is a sense of being different, perhaps because we are lesbian or bisexual. Perhaps because we are trans women or feminine men, or we fall somewhere else along the transgender spectrum. Or perhaps because our bodies fall outside of the norm in some way, because we are fat, or disabled, or intersex. Or perhaps we experience some combination of these, or maybe we are different in some other way. Because of our difference, we each have to make sense of what it means to be feminine in a world where we can never achieve the conventional feminine ideal, and in a world where feminine gender expression and sexualities are plagued by misogynistic connotations. For me, that's what femme is. It's a puzzle we each have to solve. And because we are all different, we will each come up with a different solution, a different way of making sense of, and expressing, our femme selves.

One reason why I forward holistic views of gender and sexuality is because they allow us to finally put to rest "the femme question."[6] People who dismiss femininity—who consider it frivolous, or vain, or a patriarchal trap, or a product of socialization, or an artifact of the gender binary, or whatever—have been fucking with femmes for far too long. Their attempts to try to artificialize or artifactualize our feminine gender expression (rather than accepting it as natural and legitimate) is the same sort of tactic that occurs when homophobes assume gay people are looking for an "alternative lifestyle," or just haven't met the "right person" yet. It's the same bullshit that occurs when bisexuals are accused of being "confused" or of "still having one foot in the closet," or when people assume that trans men transition to obtain male privilege, or assume that trans women transition in order to fulfill some sort of bizarre sex fantasy. We shouldn't have to explain why we are trans or why we are queer, and by the same reasoning, we shouldn't have to explain why we are feminine!

Once we accept that on some level feminine expression is natural, that for some of us—whether female, male, both, or neither—it resonates with us on a deep profound level . . . once we accept this, then we can tackle the real problem: the fact that femininity is seen as inferior to masculinity, both in straight settings and in queer and feminist circles. Once we accept the fact that femininity exists and it needs no explanation, then we can focus on debunking the countless double standards, like that masculinity is strong while femininity is weak, that masculinity is tough while femininity is fragile, that masculinity is practical while femininity is frivolous, that masculinity is active while femininity is passive, that masculinity is rational while femininity is overly emotional, and of course, that masculinity is natural while femininity is artificial. Once we get beyond having to account for why we are feminine, then we can finally make the case that all of the dismissive connotations and meanings that other people associate with feminine expression are merely misogynistic presumptions on their part.

This is why I also take issue with the notion of framing "femme" as transgressive or subversive because, unlike conventional femininity, it occurs within a queer context. This argument seems to buy into the assumption that expressions of femininity that do not occur in a queer context somehow reinforce the gender binary, or heterosexism, or the patriarchy, or what have you. And I think that is really fucked up! My mother is a heterosexual cis woman. My sisters are heterosexual cis women. As heterosexual cis women, they experience some privileges that I do not experience. They are accepted in the straight mainstream way more readily than I will ever be. But they are marginalized in their day-to-day lives because they are feminine. To argue that they are reinforcing the binary, or the patriarchy, or the hegemonic gender system, because they are conventionally feminine (as opposed to subversively feminine) essentially implies that they are enabling their own oppression. This is just another variation of the claim that rapists make when they insinuate that the woman in question was "asking for it" because of what she was wearing or how she behaved. I understand why male rapists try to blame the victim in this way, but for the life of me I cannot understand why we as feminists and queers buy into this same sort of mentality.

I'll be the first one to admit that the expectation that all girls and women are, or should be, conventionally feminine marginalizes and injures many people. Those who are androgynous, or tomboys, or butches, or on the trans masculine spectrum face disdain for their gender non-conformity. And many women who tend to be feminine are routinely made to feel embarrassed, ashamed, unworthy, and disempowered because they don't quite meet society's practically unattainable standards of beauty. But the problem here is not femininity, but expectations. What we as feminists should be challenging is *compulsory* femininity, rather than femininity itself.

If there is one thing that all of us femmes have in common, it is that we all have had to learn to embrace our own feminine expression while simultaneously rejecting other people's expectations of us. What makes femininity "femme" is not the fact that it is queer, or transgressive, or ironic, or performative, or the complement of butch. No. What makes our femininity "femme" is the fact that we do it for ourselves. It is for that reason that it is so empowering. And that is what makes us so powerful.

As femmes, we can do one of two things with our power: We can celebrate it in secret within our own insular queer communities, pat ourselves on the back for being so much smarter and more subversive than our straight feminine sisters. Or we can share that power with them. We can teach them that there is more than one way to be feminine, and that no style or expression of femininity is necessarily any better than anyone else's. We can teach them that the only thing fucked up about femininity is the dismissive connotations that other people project onto it. But in order to that, we have to give up the self-comfort of believing that our rendition of femme is more righteous, or more cool, or more subversive than anyone else's.

I don't think that my femme expression, or anyone else's femme expressions, are in and of themselves subversive. But I do believe that the ideas that femmes have been forwarding for decades—about reclaiming femininity, about each person taking the parts of femininity that resonate with them and leaving behind the rest, about being femme for ourselves rather than for other people, about the ways in which feminine expression can be tough and active and bad-ass and so on—these ideas are powerful and transformative.

I think that it's great to celebrate femme within our own queer communities, but we shouldn't merely stop there. We need to share with the rest of the world the idea of self-determined and self-empowered feminine expression, and the idea that feminine expression is just as legitimate and powerful as masculine expression. The idea that femininity is inferior and subservient to masculinity intersects with all forms of oppression, and is (I feel) the single most overlooked issue in feminism. We need to change that, not only for those of us who are queer femmes, but for our straight cis sisters who have been disempowered by society's unrealistic feminine ideals, for our gender-variant and gender-non-conforming siblings who face disdain for defying feminine expectations and/or who are victims of trans-misogyny, and also for our straight cis brothers, who've been socialized to avoid femininity like the plague, and whose misogyny, homophobia, transphobia, and so on, are driven primarily by their fear of being seen as feminine. While I don't think that my femme expression is subversive, I do believe that we together as femmes have the power to truly change the world.

THREE STRIKES AND I'M OUT

CHAPTER SEVEN

JUNE 2008.

In queer communities, we often talk about coming out. As far as I'm concerned, we should call it coming out again and again and again and again, because that's how life often feels. Sometimes I even find myself sort of "coming out" to people about aspects of my life that have nothing to do with gender or sexuality. For example, I might be at a queer or feminist event and mention offhand to an acquaintance that by day I'm a scientist, and they'll kind of freak out about it: "You're a scientist? No way, I never would have guessed!" Maybe they are surprised because they stereotype scientists as unapologetic heterosexists who delight in essentializing and pathologizing our genders and sexualities. Or maybe I "pass" as a nonscientist because I don't wear a lab coat, or because I don't have unruly Einstein hair. I'm not sure. All I really know is that when I come out to people, it's not really about me or my identity. It's about their assumptions, their expectations, their investment in who they think I am. If they didn't make any assumptions about me, then I couldn't possibly be "closeted" and I couldn't be accused of "passing" as anything. And if I told them something about myself, it wouldn't be a "coming out" because they wouldn't have already made their minds up about me in the first place.

Far and away, my biggest coming out occurred back in 2001, when I came out as transsexual. I just referred to that coming out in the past tense, which is weird, because I'm always still coming out to people as trans. (In fact, for anyone who has just picked up this book and randomly turned to this page, I have just come out to you as trans. Congratulations!)

But the coming out story that I wish to share with you now is not about me being or becoming transsexual. Rather, it's about my sexual orientation.

For most of my life—from puberty onward—I've been primarily attracted to women. Although pre-transition, I admittedly had fantasies about being with men, and I experimented with them to a certain extent, usually in the context of role-playing relationships. Sometimes those explorations were awkward or unpleasant, other times they were sexy and fun, but not one even came close to evoking the sexual or romantic intensity that I experienced when I was with women.

But then I transitioned. And things changed a little bit. Shifted, you might say. I'm still very attracted to women, but in addition, I find that men sometimes pique my interest. These are not the fantasies of being with faceless guys that I used to imagine. But rather, they'll often involve specific men. Sometimes I'll find myself appreciating the way a man looks or smells, and sometimes I'll think about fucking him.

I'm not sure what caused this shift. Maybe it's from me being on female hormones, or finally settling into my female body, or from years of interacting with the world as a woman, or perhaps some combination of all three.[1] Many people's sexual orientations shift for no apparent reason, so maybe that is what happened to me. I'm not sure. But the one thing that I do know is that my budding attraction to men kind of freaks me out a bit.

I've been running away from maleness and masculinity my whole life—especially with regards to my own male anatomy and history. For me, transitioning was not merely about physically becoming female—it was also about disassociating myself from the world of men more generally. And for years that felt like such a relief. So it's strange for me to find my mind wandering back to men, to ponder re-exploring them.

Another thing that makes this difficult for me is the fact that, frankly, men scare the shit out of me. During my transition, as soon as men started reading me as female, I was barraged by cat calls, sexual innuendos, come ons, occasional threats, and so on. A lot of it was the same bullshit that most women have to deal with, and other times it was the more hardcore, hypersexualizing remarks that I only ever seem to get when men know that I'm a trans woman.[2] I've survived by putting my guard up, by not letting any men get to me. So the idea of letting my defenses down, to allow myself to fool around with a man, is more than a little bit intimidating.

Anyway, while I first noticed this shift in my sexuality several years ago, I was not in a position to act on it, because for most of the last decade, I've been in a monogamous relationship—something else which I've found myself having to come out about on many an occasion, given the high frequency of polyamorous relationships in the queer circles I inhabit. Whenever I would mention being monogamous, I'd often feel the need to relieve the tension by reassuring people that it's okay, my monogamy is not "hegemonic," it's just a "me" thing, at which point they'd usually laugh, probably because I just used the word hegemonic, but anyway, I digress . . .

While my partner and I were together, and I was not acting on my latent desires, it just made sense to identify as a lesbian. After all, I was a woman who was in a relationship with another woman. But we have recently split up—which of course, is another coming out, with friends replying: "Oh My God?" "I'm stunned!" "I'm not sure what to say?" Anyway, now that I am on my own and beginning to explore my attraction to men, I've started using the word bisexual to describe myself. There. I said it. Bisexual. It only took me halfway through the piece to admit it!

For many gay men and lesbians, the word bisexual is the second most anxious-making word in the dictionary (just after bi-curious). When I told a queer friend that I was beginning to call myself bi, she jokingly replied, "No, don't do it!" And you know, I really don't have to do it. I could just call myself pansexual—that sounds hella queer. Or I could refuse to call myself bisexual on the grounds that the label "reinforces the gender binary" (a common soundbite that I debunk in Chapter 9, "Bisexuality and Binaries Revisited"). Hell, I know so many women partnered to trans guys who still identify as dykes—not to mention trans guys who also still identify as dykes—that I could easily just keep calling myself a dyke while dating guys, and it's likely that no one would even notice.

But I don't want to do that. My attraction to male-bodied/identified people feels very different from what I experience with female-bodied/identified individuals. The former occurs less frequently and feels more dangerous to me. So, at this time and place, bisexual feels like the best fit for me.

Maybe it's easier for me to identify as bi because of my ambivalence regarding the lesbian community. For many queer women, that community is where they first felt accepted, where they feel most empowered, the place they call home. I can understand why many bi-leaning queer women might feel reluctant to risk losing that. But I can't say the same is true for me. The lesbian community has not been a place where I have felt unconditionally accepted. It's a place where I am often explicitly disrespected or excluded. While some of my best friends and most loyal allies are dykes, I have found that the community in general expresses anything from apathy to antagonism toward trans women.

Furthermore, as a queer woman who is not ashamed about being feminine, I often find dyke spaces to be way too masculine-centric for my liking. Being a femme and a trans woman in the lesbian community, I've long felt that I already had two strikes against me. So I guess being bisexual is strike number three.

Most people I know who have come out as bisexual after identifying as a lesbian for many years only do so upon winding up in a serious relationship with a man. This makes me wonder whether I'm jumping the gun a bit. I mean, right now I am not dating a guy, so why come out as bi? Is it presumptuous for me to claim a bisexual identity if I've only ever had serious or committed relationships with women? Or did I become bisexual when I first started sexually experimenting with guys in the early '90s? Where does one draw the line?

Maybe this has more to do with the context of one's life than anything else. For cis queers, coming face-to-face with one's own bisexuality causes anxiety because it seems to signify a shifting back toward the heterosexual world they came from. But for me, a woman who was socialized male, with all the homophobic hysteria that that entails, the opposite is true. If I were with a guy, we might look pretty het on the outside, but on the inside, it would all feel really super fucking gay to me. And as out and proud to be queer as I am, I'd be lying if I said that I had completely worked through all of my own internalized bullshit. It took me years to become proud of being outwardly feminine, proud to call myself a woman and a transsexual. And now, to come out as transitioning from lesbian to bisexual is another step on that journey.

Lots of my friends consider themselves post-identity, shunning all labels related to sexuality. They see gay and lesbian and bisexual as boxes that people stuff themselves into—they find the words stifling and suffocating. But sometimes, for some of us, embracing a new identity isn't about boxing ourselves in, it's about setting ourselves free. At least that's how the word bisexual feels for me. It's about acknowledging a part of myself that I am honestly not completely comfortable with yet. It's about giving myself permission to be.

DATING

CHAPTER EIGHT

JUNE 2010.

I've spent much of the last decade writing about trans woman exclusion and trans woman irrelevancy in queer women's communities. You would think that by now, I would have little left to say about the subject, but this is not the case. In deciding what I would write about this time around, I wrestled with so many possible themes: for instance, discussing how my views on this issue have evolved over the years; critiquing the masculine-centrism of modern-day dyke communities; highlighting the need for heterogeneous queer spaces that are accepting of difference; explaining how trans male/masculine folks who claim a place in dyke spaces by emphasizing their lack of male genitals or their assigned-female-at-birth status royally screw over their trans sisters; or the misogyny inherent in the fact that the queer community loves it when trans female/feminine spectrum folks get all dragged up and lip sync along to some record, but when we speak in our own voices about issues that are important to us, nobody wants to take us seriously.

While these are all worthy topics, I couldn't make up my mind about what I most wanted to write about. So I decided to take a different approach. Instead of figuring out what I most wanted to say, I asked myself: What do I most want to hear? What topic would I most like to see addressed? And the answer to that question is easy: dating. Unfortunately for me, this also happens to be the topic that I least want to publicly share my thoughts about, in part because I like to keep some parts of my life relatively private, and in part because I know some people will not like what I have to say. But I suppose that neither of these reasons has ever stopped me from speaking my mind before.

About two years ago, my ex and I split up after being together for nearly a decade. She was a cis queer woman who was supportive when I transitioned a few years into our relationship, and we were monogamous during the lion's share of our time together. This meant that for the first time in a decade, I would be re-entering the dating scene. This could be somewhat disconcerting for any person, but there were a few compounding factors that made it especially . . . well, let's say "interesting" . . . for me. First, this would be the first time that I would be dating people as a woman. Furthermore, while I had dated queer women before my transition, this would be my first time formally dating within the queer women's community. On top of that, around this same time, after years of identifying as a lesbian, I came out as bisexual, so I also planned on dating men.

With regards to meeting queer women, it seems that traditionally much of this takes place in dyke bars and clubs. While I am sometimes in such spaces, I don't feel that they are very conducive for me to meet potential romantic or sexual partners. This is partly due to the fact that I am generally read as a cis woman. While I recognize this is a privilege, as it makes my life significantly easier in many ways, it also means that any flirting, making out, or heavy petting I engage in will eventually lead to a coming-out-as-trans moment, which often leaves me with an awful feeling in the pit of my stomach. While you would think that cis dykes (being more trans aware than the public at large) would take such coming outs in stride, this is not actually the case. Trans female friends of mine have had to suffer through cis dyke "freak out" moments, or even accusations of deception, that rival stereotypical reactions of straight people. For obvious reasons, I'd rather avoid this if I can.

The second reason why the bar and club scene doesn't work for me is that I fall outside of the butch/femme binary, which is a central part of the San Francisco Bay Area's dyke dating scene. While I identify as femme, I am not "high femme" or "sexy femme," which are the only kinds of femme that seem to get read as legitimately femme in dyke spaces. Several of my trans female friends have told me that cis dykes began to take way more interest in them once they cut their hair short and began to dress more androgynously. While I don't doubt that this is true, I have no desire to do this, as I am very happy with my gender expression the way that it is, thank you very much. Even if I did take that route, it wouldn't necessarily solve all of my problems. One trans woman friend told me about how she recently met a cis dyke, and they were really hitting it off, until she realized that this person was misreading her for a person on the trans masculine spectrum. When my friend told the cis dyke that she was in fact a trans woman, the cis dyke seemed to immediately lose interest.

So, given all this, I figured that I would have better luck with personal ads, which are often driven more by shared interests rather than appearance or dress, and in which I can disclose my trans status beforehand. On numerous occasions I have looked over the "w4w" section of Craigslist, but it inevitably leaves me traumatized.[1] There is so much trans hate speech on that site, and the very few ads that mention being open to trans are specifically looking for trans men or tranny bois, not trans women.

I had heard decent things about OkCupid, so I figured I'd give it a try. I listed myself as bisexual, and at the end of my profile, I explicitly mentioned that I was a trans woman. I got a significant number of responses from women as well as men. But in follow-up emails, it became clear that most of the women who responded hadn't read my entire profile. At some point, once we started chatting, I would usually ask if they had ever dated a trans woman before (just to see what I was getting myself into), and suddenly—surprise!—I wouldn't hear from them again.

So then I decided to try an experiment. I rearranged my profile to put the trans disclosure right at the top, and I changed my orientation from bisexual to "gay" (OkCupid's category for exclusively same-sex) to ensure that I'd only receive replies from women. Over a four-month period, I received only five responses: one from a cis bisexual woman, three from trans women, and one from a trans man. Now one possible explanation for this is that perhaps there are four times as many trans people on OkCupid than cis queer women. But a quick browsing of OkCupid listings will show that this is certainly not the case. Therefore, the inescapable conclusion is that while trans people and cis bisexual women are often open to dating trans women, the overwhelming majority of cis dykes are not.[2]

While cis dykes have generally shown little interest in me, my experiences with cis men have in comparison gone rather swimmingly. We have all heard stories about how the only cis men interested in trans women are "tranny chasers," who are creepy, closeted, and who wouldn't be caught dead being seen with an out trans woman in public. And certainly, those men do exist. But many of the cis men that I have met or chatted with on OkCupid and other sites do not fall into that stereotype. Lo and behold, some of them are even kind, intelligent, interesting, and fun to hang out with.

When I asked the cis men who responded to my ad if they had ever dated a trans woman before, they didn't disappear like the cis dykes usually did. Instead, most of them gave thoughtful answers. Some said that they found trans women more interesting, open-minded, and/or courageous than the average cis woman. Others said they had honestly not considered dating a trans woman before, but they really liked my profile, and they considered themselves to be queer-positive, so they didn't consider my transness to be a big deal. Still others put it quite simply: They are attracted to women, and while most of their past partners were cis women, a few were trans women, and it really makes no difference to them.

When cis men tell me these things, it honestly makes me a little sad. I mourn the fact that I have not heard similar sentiments from my own cis queer women's community. I also find it ironic that cis dykes—many of whom pride themselves on their progressive politics and subversive sexualities—tend to be far more conservative and conforming to our culture's yuck-dating-a-trans-woman-is-gross mindset than their cis male counterparts, at least here in the San Francisco Bay Area. I am also embarrassed as a queer for the fact that so many straight cis men have worked through, or are beginning to work through, their own issues regarding trans women, whereas most cis queer women refuse to even consider the possibility that they even have an issue.

I know first-hand that it can be difficult to confront such issues. I remember a time many years ago—I was either just about to transition, or I had just transitioned, I can't quite recall—when I saw a short documentary about two trans women who were life partners. And I am horribly embarrassed to say that, at the time, I was somewhat squicked by their relationship.[3] The irrationality of my reaction was not lost on me. After all, I *am* a trans woman. And I am also attracted to women. So what was it about the idea of being with a trans woman that bothered me so? Over time, I realized that on an unconscious level, I was still buying into the idea that trans women were somehow unattractive, defective, and illegitimate, and that being partnered to a cis woman was somehow inherently better, or more authentic. After much personal reflection, I had to admit that my reaction was profoundly antitrans. And I eventually got over my internalized transphobia, just as I had to get over my internalized homophobia the first time I sexually experimented with a man, and just as I had to overcome my own fatphobia the first time I dated a differently-sized woman.

Sexual attraction is a complex phenomenon, and of course there is lots of individual variation. I certainly do not expect every cis queer woman to swoon over me. And if it were only a small percentage of cis dykes who were not interested in trans women at all, I would write it off as simply a matter of personal preference. But this not a minor problem—it is systemic; it is a predominant sentiment in queer women's communities. And when the overwhelming majority of cis dykes date and fuck cis women, but are not open to, or are even turned off by, the idea of dating or fucking trans women, how is that not transphobic? And to those cis women who claim a dyke identity, yet consider trans men, but not trans women, to be a part of your dating pool, let me ask you this: How are you not a hypocrite?

I did not write this piece to vent about my dating life. I go out on plenty of dates, and I'm having lots of super-fucking-awesome sex, just not with cis women at the moment. My purpose in writing this piece is to highlight how cis dykes' unwillingness to consider trans women as legitimate partners translates directly into a lack of community for queer-identified trans women. After all, queer women's communities serve several purposes. They are places where we can build alliances to fight for our rights. They are places where we can find friendship and chosen family. But one of the most critical functions that queer women's communities serve is in providing a safe space outside of the heterocentric mainstream where women can express interest, attraction, and affection toward other women. In other words, queer women's spaces fulfill our need for sexual validation. Unless, of course, you are a trans woman. And personally, with each passing year, it becomes harder and harder for me to continue to take part in a community in which I am not seen as a legitimate object of desire.

BISEXUALITY AND BINARIES REVISITED

CHAPTER NINE

Over the last several years, it has become increasingly common to hear people in queer communities claim that the word bisexual "reinforces the gender binary." In October 2010, I wrote an Internet article (which I'll refer to here as the "reinforcing" essay) challenging these claims.[1] Specifically, the article illustrated how *the reinforcing trope* (i.e., the notion that certain genders, sexualities, or identities "reinforce" the gender binary, or heteronormativity, or the patriarchy, or the hegemonic-gender-system-of-your-choice) is selectively doled out in queer and feminist communities in order to police their borders. Since queer communities are dominated by non-feminine, cisgender, and exclusively gay and lesbian folks, these individuals are almost never accused of "reinforcing the gender binary." In contrast, more marginalized identities (e.g., bisexual, transgender, femme) are routinely subjected to the reinforcing trope. While my "reinforcing" essay received many positive responses, it also garnered some harsh criticism, particularly from within certain seg-ments of transgender and gender variant communities. All of the critiques that I heard or read pretty much ignored my primary point—namely, there are underlying forms of sexism that determine who gets accused of "reinforcing" shit and who does not—and instead focused solely on the rote assertion that the word "bisexual" (and, by association, anyone who identifies as bisexual) really does "reinforce the gender binary."

Since then, I have been considering writing a follow-up piece to discuss the numerous problems with such claims (aside from the obvious fact that they single out bisexuals for being attracted to "two" sexes, but not the overwhelming majority of gays and lesbians who view themselves as attracted to the "same" sex, but not to the "opposite" sex—a notion that appears to be just as binary). In addition, since my piece was pub-lished, I became aware of an excellent blog post by Shiri Eisner called "Words, binary and biphobia, or: why 'bi' is binary but 'FTM' is not."[2] Eisner's piece made a number of points similar to my own, but it also forwarded new arguments that had not occurred to me before and which led me to think about this debate in new ways. For all of these reasons, I felt that it would be worthwhile to pen a new essay (this very one here!) to revisit this subject.

Before delving into this topic, let me state for the record that I am writing this piece from the perspective of a bisexual-identified transsex-ual woman. Since some people paint bisexual-identified folks out to be "binarist" in our partner preferences, I will mention for the record that I date and am sexual with folks who are female and male, trans and cis, and non-binary- and binary-identified. I most certainly do not speak for all bisexual or all transgender people. My views on this subject are my own, and if you disagree with what I have to say, please consider the possibility that our disagreements may stem from our differing van-tage points. Finally, over the course of this chapter, I will sometimes use the word "we" to refer to transgender folks, and other times to refer to bisexual folks. Perhaps some may find this a bit confusing, but it is an unavoidable consequence when one straddles multiple identities.

SOME PRELIMINARIES: MONOSEXISM, BI-INVISIBILITY, AND BISEXUAL COMMUNITIES (OR THE LACK THEREOF)

In my previous essay, I used the word "bisexual" because (both histori-cally and currently) it is the term most commonly used and understood to denote people who do not limit their sexual experiences to members of a single sex or gender. Of course, "bisexual" is not a perfect word, but then again, neither is gay, lesbian, dyke, homosexual, heterosexual, straight, queer, asexual, or any other sexuality-related label. However, perhaps more so than with any of the other aforementioned labels, peo-ple who are bisexual in experience often fiercely disavow the "bisexual" label. For instance, many prefer the labels queer, pansexual, omnisex-ual, polysexual, multisexual, or even no label at all, over the term bisex-ual. Sometimes I use the phrase *experientially bisexual* to refer to people who, regardless of label choice, do not limit their sexual experiences to members of a single sex or gender. But alas, some folks may also reject experientially bisexual because it contains the word bisexual. So an alternative solution, taking a page from the LGBTQIA+ acronym, is to describe experientially bisexual folks as BMNOPPQ folks, where B = bisexual, M = multisexual, N = no label, O = omnisexual, P = pansexual, P = polysexual, and Q = experientially bisexual folks who primarily identify as queer (arranged alphabetically).

Am I advocating BMNOPPQ terminology? Not necessarily. I think that it is rather clunky and confusing. Personally, I would prefer it if we all simply accepted bisexual as an imperfect, albeit easily under-stood, umbrella term for people who share our experience. But since I don't expect that to happen any time soon, I will instead use BMNOPPQ here in the hopes that we can put aside the issue of label preference for a moment, and instead focus on what the bisexual-reinforces-the-binary accusation means for BMNOPPQ people.

Important disclaimer: Above, when I used the phrase "share our experience," I am not in any way insinuating that BMNOPPQ folks all share the same sexual histories, or experience their sexualities in the exact same way. We do not. We are all different. We are all attracted to different types of people, different types of bodies, different types of gender expressions. We all fall at somewhat different positions along the dreaded "Kinsey scale."[3] Some of us are more immersed in queer communities, while some of us primarily exist in straight communities, and many (if not most) of us find ourselves constantly navigating our way within (and between) both queer and straight communities.

So if we are all so different, then why even bother to try to label or lump together BMNOPPQ people? Well, because the one thing we *do* share is that we all face societal *monosexism*—i.e., the assumption that being exclusively attracted to members of a single sex or gender is somehow more natural, real, or legitimate than being attracted to members of more than one sex or gender.[4] Monosexism is also sometimes referred to as *biphobia*. While biphobia is clearly the more common term, I will use monosexism here, both because I am not a big fan of the use of the suffix "phobia" when discussing forms of sexism (as it seems to stress "fear" over marginalization), and also because monosexism avoids the pesky prefix "bi" that some BMNOPPQ folks seem to find objectionable (more on that in a minute).

Monosexism exists because most people, whether in the straight mainstream or in gay and lesbian communities, view sexual orientation as a rigid binary, where people can only ever be heterosexual or homosexual in orientation. This hetero/homo binary directly leads to *monosexual assumption*—that is, the assumption that all individuals are exclusively attracted to members of a single sex or gender. (Note: The hetero/homo binary also assumes that all people are sexually attracted to *somebody*—an assumption that marginalizes asexual folks.) Because of monosexual assumption, most people automatically assume that BMNOPPQ folks must be heterosexual if they perceive us to be in an "opposite"-sex pairing, or that we must be homosexual (i.e., lesbian or gay) if they perceive us to be in a same-sex pairing. This is a foundational predicament experienced by BMNOPPQ individuals.

If we BMNOPPQ folks outwardly claim to be bisexual (or pansexual, or polysexual, etc.), monosexual assumption leads many people to doubt the validity of our identities, and to project ulterior motives onto us. This is why people will often say, "You're not really bisexual (or pansexual, or polysexual, etc.), you're just confused about your sexuality," or ". . . it's just a phase," or ". . . you still have one foot in the closet," or ". . . you're *really* gay/lesbian, but seeking out heterosexual privilege," or ". . . you're *really* straight, but just sexually experimenting, or perhaps overly promiscuous," and/or ". . . you're just a fence sitter. Choose a side already!"

In other words, monosexual assumption leads to what has historically been called *bi-invisibility*: We are presumed not to exist, and any attempt to assert our existence is immediately thwarted by accusations that we are hiding, faking, or simply confused about our sexualities. Bi-invisibility is what leads many of us to simply blend into existing monosexual communities (whether straight, gay, or lesbian) rather than seek out or create BMNOPPQ communities. This lack of community has had a devastating effect on BMNOPPQ folks. For instance, even though we outnumber exclusively homosexual people, we have poorer health outcomes and higher poverty rates than gays and lesbians, and we are generally not acknowledged or served by LGBTQIA+ organizations, even the ones that have "B" in the name.[5] Our invisibility is what allows straight, gay, and lesbian folks to regularly get away with forwarding stereotypes about us—that we are mentally deranged, predatory, hypersexual, promiscuous, deceptive, and/or fickle—without being called out or challenged. But most poignantly, bi-invisibility leads many of us to identify more with the straight, lesbian, or gay communities we exist in (and rely upon) than with other BMNOPPQ folks. This lack of identification with other BMNOPPQ folks, in combination with the external pressure placed on us to blend in with the monosexual communities we exist in, is a major reason why BMNOPPQ folks have historically tended to avoid calling ourselves "bisexual," often by refusing to label our sexualities at all. In stark contrast, exclusively homosexual people do not tend to outright disavow the labels "lesbian" and "gay," nor do they tend to get bogged down in philosophical battles over whether or not they should label their sexualities at all, to nearly the same degree that BMNOPPQ folks do.

I have heard countless BMNOPPQ people ask, "Why do we have to label our sexualities?" I do agree that we should not be forced to reduce our complex sexual attractions and orientations down to a simple moniker. But as an activist, I would argue that the most persuasive argument for why BMNOPPQ folks should unite around some kind of umbrella label (whether "bisexual" or otherwise) is to challenge monosexism and bi-invisibility. In this scenario, said label would not blithely detail who we are sexual with, nor claim that we are somehow inherently different from hetero- or homo- or asexual folks (because I do not think we are), but rather point out that we (and we alone) are targeted by a particular sexist double standard, namely, monosexism. Doing this would enable us to raise awareness about, and to challenge, monosexism in our culture.

Given that I am more well known for my trans activism than my bisexual/BMNOPPQ activism, I should point out that the case that I am making here is identical in form and structure to the case I make in *Whipping Girl* regarding cissexism.[6] That argument goes as follows: We live in a world where trans people are unfairly targeted by a sexist double standard (i.e., cissexism, analogous with monosexism) where one group (i.e., trans people, analogous with BMNOPPQ people) is assumed to be less natural, real, or legitimate than a majority group that does not share that experience (i.e., cis people, analogous with monosexual people). As I once wrote in a blog post called "*Whipping Girl* FAQ on cissexual, cisgender, and cis privilege":

> *When I use the terms cis/trans, it is not to talk about *actual* differences between cis and trans bodies/identities/genders/ people, but rather *perceived* differences. In other words, while I don't think that my gender is inherently different from that of a cis woman, I am aware that most people tend to *view* my gender differently (i.e., as less natural/valid/authentic) than cis women's genders.*[7]

I would argue that the above paragraph also holds true if you were to substitute "mono" for "cis," "bisexual/BMNOPPQ" for "trans," and "sexual orientation" for "gender."

So to sum up, from this activist perspective, the primary reason why I call myself trans or bisexual is *not* to communicate things that I have done (e.g., aspects of my gender transition, people I sexually partner with). After all, it should not be incumbent upon me to have to reduce the complexities of my gender and sexuality down to a one-word label and provide it for other people at the drop of a hat. Nor am I insisting that I am "just like" other trans or BMNOPPQ people when I call myself "trans" or "bisexual," respectively. After all, it goes without saying that all trans people and all BMNOPPQ people are different from one another. Rather, I embrace these labels in order to be visible in a world where trans and BMNOPPQ people are constantly erased by the male/female and hetero/homo binaries, respectively, and to build alliances with people who are similarly marginalized in order to challenge societal cissexism and monosexism, respectively.

HOW MIGHT RELINQUISHING THE TERM "BISEXUAL" IMPACT BISEXUAL/BMNOPPQ PEOPLE?

With this background in mind, let's go back to the recurring claims that calling oneself bisexual "reinforces the gender binary." Mind you, this claim is not typically made against people who gravitate toward sexual identity labels such as gay, lesbian, dyke, homosexual, heterosexual, straight, queer, asexual, and so on. Just bisexual folks. And it puts us in the unenviable position of constantly having to defend our label choice.

For example, even though my "reinforcing" essay was focused on how the reinforcing trope has been used to delegitimize both trans and bisexual communities, I still felt compelled to begin the piece with an explanation as to why I call myself bisexual. To this end, I offered both a personal and political justification. The personal explanation related to the fact that, while I am sexual with both female- and male-bodied/ identified people, I tend to be more attracted to the former than the latter, and perhaps for this reason, being sexual with a woman feels very different to me on a visceral level than being with a man. For this reason, labels like pansexual and omnisexual (which imply attraction to everyone) do not personally resonate with me, because they seem to erase a difference that I experience. While this continues to be an accurate description of how I experience sexual attraction, I now realize that this comment is somewhat superfluous. After all, all BMNOPPQ folks experience our sexualities somewhat differently, and if we each had a unique word to precisely describe our internal experiences of attraction, that wouldn't necessarily help us challenge monosexism and bi-invisibility. So if I were writing the "reinforcing" essay today, I probably would have left that personal tidbit out.

It is worth noting that (perhaps unsurprisingly) a few people took this personal comment as evidence that I must hold essentialist and rigidly binarist views of gender, even though earlier in the essay I stressed that there is lots of variation among, and overlap between, female and male bodies (this includes the existence of intersex people, and trans people who physically transition). Elsewhere, I have made the case that one can acknowledge differences between female and male bodies without necessarily engaging in essentialism or binarism, so I won't bother to rehash that argument here.[8] Suffice it to say, if simply recognizing differences between female and male bodies is tantamount to essentialism and binarism, then that means that *all* heterosexual and homosexual people are essentialist and binarist, because they are sexually attracted to one sex but not the other. It also means that *all* transsexuals who physically transition are essentialist and binarist, on the basis that we choose to be one sex rather than the other. Once again, calling out a bisexual person's experience of sex differences as "essentialist" and "binarist," while paying no heed to gay, lesbian, and trans people's experiences of sex differences, can only be viewed as monosexist.

The political explanation that I gave for why I choose the bisexual label stems from the fact that societal monosexism invisibilizes bisexuality and ensures that we can only ever be read in one of two ways, namely, as homosexual or heterosexual:

> *The "bi" in bisexual does not merely refer to the types of people that I am sexual with, but to the fact that both the straight and queer worlds view me in two very different ways depending upon who I happen to be partnered with at any given moment.*[9]

I admit that this is a relatively novel way of viewing the word bisexual, but it is one that I personally fancy, and it is consistent with the theme of challenging monosexism, bi-invisibility, and the hetero/homo binary. Here is another potential interpretation of the word bisexual: The prefix "bi" can mean "two," but it can also mean "twice" (e.g., as in bimonthly). So while monosexual people limit their potential partners to members of only one sex, bisexual/BMNOPPQ folks challenge the hetero/homo binary by not limiting our attraction in this way, and are thereby open to roughly twice as many potential partners. My main point here is that the prefix "bi" has more than one meaning, and can have more than one referent. So claiming that people who use the term bisexual must be touting a rigid binary view of gender, or denying the existence of gender variant people, is as presumptuous as assuming that people who use the term "bicoastal" must be claiming that a continent can only ever have two coasts, or that they are somehow denying the existence of all interior, landlocked regions of that continent.

The truth is that there are many different ways one can interpret the word bisexual (or other sexuality labels, for that matter). The bisexual-reinforces-the-binary accusation is an attempt to fix bisexual to a single meaning, one that is an affront to how many bisexual-identified people understand and use that label. As an analogy, what if cis people suddenly started claiming that they do not like the label transgender because (in their minds) it seems to imply that all people should change their gender. (I actually have heard someone make this bizarre claim once before.) How would we, as transgender people, react to that accusation? Personally, I would respond by saying that transgender is *our* word: it's about transgender-identified people's experiences with gender and gender-based oppression, and it makes absolutely no claims at all about what other people are, or how they should be gendered. Similarly, my response to the bisexual-reinforces-the-binary accusation is that bisexual is *our* word (in this case, bisexual-identified people): It is about our experiences with sexuality and sexuality-based oppression, and it makes no claims whatsoever about what other people are, or how they should be sexual or gendered.

But upon looking back on my "reinforcing" essay, my main regret is that I failed to explicitly mention what is perhaps the most important political reason behind why I call myself bisexual. Namely, the word bisexual has a long history, and it was the word that the original BMNOPPQ activists embraced several decades ago when they fought for visibility and inclusion within (and beyond) lesbian, gay, and queer communities. This activism spurred the creation of now common terms such as "biphobia" and "bi-invisibility" that have played a crucial role in challenging societal monosexism since their inception. Finally, and perhaps most importantly, the word bisexual is familiar to most people, both in the straight mainstream and within LGBTQIA+ communities. Having a familiar umbrella term is critically important given that one of the biggest challenges that BMNOPPQ folks face is invisibility and societal erasure.

I appreciate the sentiments behind alternative labels such as pan-sexual, omnisexual, polysexual, and multisexual, and I respect the right of BMNOPPQ folks to choose any of these (or other) labels over bisexual. But from an activist standpoint, the notion that we should completely abandon the word bisexual in favor of some alternative label that is unfamiliar to most people does not seem to be a wise political move. Indeed, such a move would make it significantly harder for us to come out and gain visibility in our communities, and we would need to start from scratch with new activist terminology (panphobia? poly-invisibility?) to describe how we are marginalized.

Along similar lines, I respect the right of BMNOPPQ folks to choose to identify as queer rather than bisexual. (For the record, I identify as both bisexual and queer.) However, queer is a much broader umbrella term meant to include all LGBTQIA+ people, and as such, it does not seem to be the best position from which to challenge monosexism and bi-invisibility.

Now of course, language is constantly evolving. And if this mass fleeing from the word bisexual toward alternate identity labels was simply part of a natural progression—such as the historically recent shifts from the label "homosexual" to "gay," or from "lesbian" to "dyke"—then

I would not have any problem with it. However, it seems to me that the primary force driving these alternate label choices is not coming from within the BMNOPPQ community itself, but rather from external pressure exerted on us by other queer subgroups. As I've already discussed, there has always been pressure on BMNOPPQ folks to hide or subsume our identities in order to fit into existing gay, lesbian, and queer communities. But these days, there is additional pressure placed on us by certain transgender voices that insist that we must stop using the term bisexual because it supposedly "reinforces the gender binary."

Lots of folks these days (both transgender and BMNOPPQ) seem to be buying into this "reinforcing" allegation, which essentially accuses bisexual-identified people (such as myself) of propagating cissexism/transphobia. And yet, virtually no one is asking what should be a rather obvious question: Isn't this argument quite one-sided? Shouldn't we also be considering what affect relinquishing the label "bisexual" would have for BMNOPPQ folks and our efforts to challenge monosexism and bi-invisibility? Genderqueer-identified bisexual activist Shiri Eisner (in the aforementioned blog post) was the first person I heard make this crucial point:

> *A discussion focusing around bisexuality solely in relation to transgender politics performs structural bisexual erasure, as it prioritizes transgender politics over bisexual politics in a discussion about bisexual identity."* [emphasis Eisner's][10]

When put this way, it becomes clear just how brazen it is for transgender folks to claim that bisexuals should abandon an identity label that BMNOPPQ folks have been using for decades simply because it is supposedly incompatible with transgender politics. Why stop there? While we are at it, why don't we tell lesbians that they have to stop using that word? After all, few ideologies have spouted as much cissexism over the years as lesbian feminism has. Come to think of it, what about people who describe themselves as a "woman" or a "man"—those labels most certainly reinforce the binary! Shouldn't we be calling out anyone who uses those labels? Or what about trans people who self-identify as "MTF" and "FTM"—acronyms that imply that there are two sexes. Don't they reinforce the binary?

Or, what if we put the shoe on the other foot? Cisgender feminists have long argued that gender is a patriarchal invention designed to oppress women. Given this, what if cisgender feminists took a similar tactic and began accusing transgender people of "reinforcing the patriarchy" because the word "transgender" has the word "gender" in it? Isn't this argument structurally identical to the bisexual-reinforces-the-binary claim? If cisgender feminists made this claim, how might we react? Would we stop calling ourselves transgender (or genderqueer, or gender variant) as a result? What would that mean for us as a marginalized group that has only recently garnered visibility and a modicum of acceptance in our society? What would happen to all the policies that now include "transgender" people, or that prevent discrimination on the basis of "gender identity" (yes, that term also has that pesky word "gender" in it)? Would we, as a transgender community, really be willing to give up all that in order to accommodate cisgender feminist politics?

I didn't think so. So how can we, as a transgender community, expect bisexual/BMNOPPQ folks to give up the same in order to accommodate our politics?

THERE IS MORE THAN JUST ONE BINARY!

Nothing demonstrates the fact that the bisexual-reinforces-the-binary claim prioritizes transgender politics over bisexual politics more than the assumption that the "bi" in bisexual must automatically be referring to "the gender binary." This is a bold assertion given that BMNOPPQ folks have our own sexual orientation binary to contend with, and that bisexual activists have long argued that being "bi" subverts the hetero/ homo binary. So how is it that a debate about "bisexual" (a sexual orientation label) can wind up being solely centered on the gender binary, yet completely ignore the sexual orientation binary?

This seems to me to be a fairly new development. Back when bisexual and transgender activism were first gaining momentum in the 1990s, it was quite common for activists from both camps to point out the parallels between the way transgender folks challenge the male/female binary and how bisexuals challenge the hetero/homo binary. There was even an entire anthology (entitled *Bisexuality and Transgenderism: InterSEXions of the Others*) largely centered on this theme.[11] Around the time that I transitioned (back in 2001), trans people referred to "the male/female binary" (which seems to acknowledge the possibility that there are other binaries out there) about as frequently as they mentioned "the gender binary."

But over time, this perspective has shifted. These days, many transgender folks seem to be referring to an all "caps lock" version of THE GENDER BINARY, as if it were the one and only binary from which all gender and sexual oppression stems. This interpretation reminds me of the way many cisgender lesbian feminists talk about THE PATRIARCHY, using it as the single lens through which they view all aspects of gender and sexuality. Viewing all forms of sexism in terms of THE PATRIARCHY (i.e., men are the oppressors, women are the oppressed, end of story) is precisely what led many cisgender lesbian feminists to misinterpret trans men as "female" traitors who transition in order to obtain male privilege, and trans women as privileged "men" who attempt to appropriate women's oppressed status and/ or to infiltrate women-only spaces.

When we view the world through any one single lens, we are bound to overlook many things. Viewing all aspects of gender and sexuality through the lens of THE PATRIARCHY has led many cisgender lesbian feminists to condemn not only transgender people, but feminine and masculine gender expression, butch/femme relationships, BDSM, pornography, sex workers, sex toys that resemble phalluses, and so on. Similarly, viewing all gender and sexual oppression in terms of THE GENDER BINARY might seem to make sense to some transgender people, but it overlooks (and thus erases) numerous other gender and sexual hierarchies, such as trans-misogyny, masculine-centrism, subversivism, asexophobia, and of course, monosexism.[12]

So, in other words, if we are going to have a cross-community conversation between transgender and bisexual/BMNOPPQ folks, then we have to talk about the male/female binary and cissexism, *as well as the hetero/homo binary and monosexism*. If we are not taking both communities' issues and interests into account, then we are not having a conversation, we are merely engaging in one-sided slander.

One final note on this point: During the course of writing this piece, it struck me how strange it is that the bisexual-reinforces-the-binary debate, which prioritizes transgender politics over bisexual politics, has successfully proliferated for several years now, and has persuaded many BMNOPPQ folks to disavow the word bisexual without that much of a pushback. And I find it alarming that, even though the word monosexism was coined and used by bisexual activists at least a decade before the word cissexism was by trans activists, these days I find myself having to explain what the former means far more so than the latter. In other words, while the bisexual movement gained initial momentum prior to the transgender movement (which is why the B typically precedes the T in most queer acronyms), the transgender movement seems to have leap-frogged over the bisexual movement, at least within the context of queer communities. To be clear, I am not in any way insinuating that BMNOPPQ folks are "more oppressed" than transgender people (lord knows, there is nothing I loathe more than playing "oppression Olympics"). But I do think that transgender people have gelled more as a community than BMNOPPQ folks have. And this lack of cohesion among

BMNOPPQ folks (in combination with the single-minded THE GEN-DER BINARY perspective) has certainly contributed to the one-sided nature of the bisexual-reinforces-the-binary debate.

ONE FINAL OBSERVATION

Finally, it must be stressed that this bisexual-reinforces-the-binary debate is not raging uniformly throughout all LGBTQIA+ communities. It seems to be largely absent from gay men's communities, and among transgender and bisexual folks who spend most of their time in straight communities rather than queer ones. As far as I can tell, this debate is primarily occurring within queer women's communities and among trans folks who also inhabit those spaces. And I think this specificity offers some insight into why this debate has surfaced and gained traction at this particular place and time.

This connection occurred to me after, on a couple separate occasions, I heard trans men claim that, in their opinion, bisexuals (as a group) tend to be more transphobic than lesbians. Frankly, this claim astonished me. Historically, transgender and bisexual activists often saw themselves on the same side of challenging exclusion within greater gay and lesbian communities and organizations.[13] And in my own personal experience, I have found that the self-identified bisexuals in my queer community tend to be far more supportive of me (as a trans woman) than exclusively lesbian and gay folks. And while cisgender lesbians typically do not view trans women such as myself to be legitimate romantic or sexual partners, cisgender bisexual women often do. As a testament to this, *all* of my queer female sexual and romantic partners have been either bisexual and/or gender variant in some way. While I am definitely open to the idea of having a cisgender lesbian lover or partner, I have never once had a cisgender lesbian express interest in me in that way. And this experience is not specific to me—it is pervasive enough that trans women and allies often refer to it as "the cotton ceiling."[14]

Of course, things are different for trans men and trans masculine spectrum folks. They often feel relatively accepted (as both individuals and prospective lovers/partners) by cisgender lesbians these days. So it makes sense that, from their point of view, bisexuals might appear more transphobic than lesbians (indeed, Eisner makes this point as well).[15] In stark contrast, from my perspective as a trans woman, I find that cisgender lesbians tend to be way more likely to be trans-misogynistic than cisgender bisexual women. These are generalizations, of course, but they seem to account for our greatly differing perspectives on this matter.

Ironically, while lesbian feminism is largely considered to be passé these days, its foundational premise—that cisgender men are inherently oppressive, and that women who partner with them are traitors to the cause—still lives on in today's queer women's communities. Elsewhere, I have referred to this mindset as *FAAB-mentality*, as it describes the presumption that the only truly valid relationships are those between individuals who are female-assigned-at-birth (whether they be cis women or trans male/masculine folks).[16] Because of FAAB-mentality, trans women are seen as suspect because we are viewed as being "really cisgender men," and femmes are dismissed for too closely resembling heterosexual women in their gender expression. And of course, bisexual women are viewed as suspect because some of us choose to partner with cisgender men.

I believe that this FAAB-mentality is at work behind the scenes when trans male/masculine folks stress how different they are from cisgender men in order to be accepted in queer women's spaces, and when queer women who partner with trans men (and who therefore fall under the BMNOPPQ umbrella) go to great lengths to avoid identifying as bisexual. While I respect any person's right to choose pansexual, polysexual, queer, etc., over bisexual, I sometimes feel that these alternative labels function like code words in queer women's communities, as if to say, "I am sexual with everyone *except* cisgender men." While people are certainly free to choose not to partner with cisgender men, I am disturbed by a new binary that seems to be developing here, one that positions pansexual/polysexual/etc.-identified women as supposedly subversive and queer because they refuse to sleep with cisgender men, whereas bisexual-identified women are presumed to be conservative and straight-minded because they do sometimes partner with cisgender men. And it seems to me that the bisexual-reinforces-the-binary trope exacerbates this binary, which is probably why this accusation has become so prevalent in queer women's communities.

While it is true that some bisexuals are cissexist, it is also true that many lesbians and trans folks are monosexist.[17] As a bisexual trans woman who is very active in queer women's communities, I would like to see us all stop pitting ourselves against one another, and instead work together to challenge all binaries and all forms of sexism.

HOW TO BE AN ALLY
TO TRANS WOMEN

CHAPTER TEN

F or many years, a major focus of my activism has been challenging the way in which trans women are often excluded from, or made to feel irrelevant within, queer women's spaces. Because I have been so vocal about the subject, people sometimes ask me for advice on how they can make their space or organization more genuinely welcoming to trans women. Sometimes I'd offer suggestions that would pretty much apply to being a good ally to any minority or marginalized group: Educate yourself about trans women's issues, call out transphobic and transmisogynistic attitudes in your community, allow trans women to have more than just a token voice in the space, don't project your assumptions onto us, listen to what we have to say about our own lives and perspectives even if it differs from yours, and so on. Of course, these are all helpful suggestions, but the more that I thought about it, the more I've come to realize that they don't quite get to the root of the problem. So lately

I've tried to boil down my "how to be a trans woman ally" spiel into one simple point: Destroy the insider/outsider myth.

The myth is very simple: it assumes that cis women are perpetually on the inside of queer women's communities while trans women are perpetually on the outside trying to get in. This is why cis women who take issue with trans women in their communities tend to portray us as infiltrators, interlopers, or impersonators—essentially, entitled "men" who have the audacity to want to take part in a women's community that we supposedly do not understand. This ignores the fact that trans women have been a part of queer women's communities since at least the 1960s, and we're not going away any time soon. More importantly, the insider/outsider myth ignores the fact that virtually all of us— whether cis or trans—begin our lives *outside* of the queer community. Almost all of us grew up in straight families. Our formative years were spent navigating our way through predominantly straight schools and communities where we were made to feel shame and stigma about our gender and sexual desires.

Like many queer women, I spent my teenage years closeted, feeling isolated and scared. I didn't dare tell anyone about my earliest fantasies, which invariably involved me (as a girl) making out with some girl I was crushed out on from my junior high or high school. As a young adult, I experimented a bit with men, but the lion's share of my relationships were with queer-identified women. Eventually, I came out to everyone in my life as a woman who loves other women. These days, when I move through the world, people generally perceive and treat me as a queer woman, either because I openly identify as queer, I am with a female partner, and/or because of my tomboyish nature. In other words, my story isn't really that much different from that of the average cis queer woman, except for the fact that I (unlike her) had been forced against my will into boyhood. But like all self-empowered queer women, I did not meekly accept the future that others had laid out for me. Instead, I followed my own desires, created my own path, just like my cis queer sisters. And I believe that we share a vital, mutual goal: to find a support network outside of the hetero male–centric mainstream where we can finally feel empowered and affirmed as women who love other women.

Lots of people in our culture express negative attitudes toward trans women. They will remark or rant about how sick or dangerous or gross or confused or fake or pathetic or ridiculous we supposedly are. But honestly, when straight folks make those remarks, it bothers me, but it doesn't hurt me as much as it does when a queer woman says the same thing. The reason for this is simple: I long ago gave up on trying to fit into the straight majority. But queer women are my chosen community. So when straight people dis me, it feels like it's coming from a stranger. But when queer women do it, it feels like it's coming from family.

Unfortunately, the insider/outsider myth creates differences in how cis and trans women are treated within queer women's communities. I remember asking a cis queer friend about how she felt the first time she ventured into a queer women's space, and her response was similar to what most of us would probably say: She said she was both excited and nervous. Excited about the possibilities the space held, but nervous because, up until that point, she had been a complete outsider. She was worried that she might say the wrong thing, come off as clueless, that she might not be accepted or taken seriously. But she found that over time she was warmly embraced. Older dykes saw her as a younger version of themselves and took her under their wing. They called her a "baby dyke"—a pejorative admittedly, but one that implied that it was inevitable that she would eventually grow into her queer womanhood. The more established dykes were patient with her and gave her the benefit of doubt.

Trans women are rarely given the benefit of doubt. Sometimes we are explicitly excluded. More often these days, we are formally allowed to participate, but are never made to feel welcome. Sometimes it feels like we've been placed on double-secret probation—we are tolerated until we say or do anything wrong or that can be misinterpreted in any way. And as soon as we do, others will not attribute it to our naiveté or the fact that we simply have a different perspective, but rather they will view it as some vestigial ever-present manifestation of our male privilege, socialization, and/or our dreaded "male energy." In other words, they will use the incident to portray us as outsiders.

When trans women *are* openly accepted in queer women's spaces, it is generally despite our trans status rather than because of it. In other words, we are expected to play down or even hide our trans histories, perspectives, and bodies in order to blend in with the cis majority. This is in stark contrast to the way in which our counterparts on the FTM-spectrum are often embraced, even celebrated, *because* they are trans, for the difference they bring to queer women's spaces.

I have heard numerous trans men complain about how they are "fetishized" by some queer women. As someone who is often "fetishized" by men, I can relate to how annoying or invalidating that can be. Having said that, there are some things that are worse than being "fetishized" in queer women's spaces—for instance, being de-sexualized in those spaces—to *not* be considered a legitimate object of queer female desire. Sadly, this is how trans women are often viewed. And while there are countless support groups for cis queer women who are in relationships with trans guys, there are virtually no resources for, or even discussions about, cis queer women who are partnered with trans women. Sometimes others even treat our cis partners as though they have been infected with our "trans woman cooties."

Because trans women are viewed as perpetual outsiders, people often assume that we can never fully become women. For example, although I transitioned eight years ago, occasionally when I am talking to my mom, she'll ask me, "So how is your transgendering going?" as though being a woman is a goal I am always trying to reach for but can never fully achieve. While it admittedly sounds somewhat cute coming from my mother, this assumption can be endlessly frustrating for me in queer women's communities. It doesn't matter how long I've been living as a woman, or how many books about lesbianism or queer feminism I have read (or written), I still come across cis queer women who will speak down to me as though I don't know anything about our community at all. So when I complain about some transphobic or trans-misogynistic comment that a queer woman has made, I am often told that I must be mistaken, or perhaps I'm too sensitive. I may even be lectured about how I should just be patient with the woman in question because she has been oppressed by the patriarchy (as though I *haven't* been oppressed by the patriarchy!).

Sometimes I will joke with friends that I am but one bad experience away from becoming a trans woman separatist. People always laugh when I say that because of how absurdist it is. There are simply too few trans women in the world to create a viable separatist movement. And while I find trans women to be extremely hot, I have no desire to limit my dating pool to just trans women. And while I think trans women have crucial (and underappreciated) insights into gender and sexism, I do not believe that we (and we alone) have all of the answers. In fact, I don't believe that any one group can have all the answers, because each of us inhabits different bodies. We have different histories, different predispositions, and we each lie at the intersection of different privileges and forms of marginalization.

So when people ask me what they can do to be allies to trans women, I tell them that the most important thing they can do is to help work toward creating new queer women's communities: communities that celebrate difference rather than sameness; communities where all of us are listened to and valued for our unique perspectives; communities where every person is seen as a legitimate object of desire; communities where our gender expressions and presentations are not policed; communities where "gold star" lesbians[1] are not viewed as any better than devoutly bisexual women, and where trans women are not viewed as less legitimate than cis women; communities that acknowledge that women who love other women may take an infinite number of different life paths in order to get there. Let's work together to build new queer women's communities where all of us, despite superficial differences in our bodies and histories, are given the benefit of doubt.

PERFORMANCE PIECE

CHAPTER ELEVEN

I f one more person tells me that "all gender is performance," I think I am going to strangle them.[1] What's most annoying about that soundbite is how it is often recited in a somewhat snooty "I-took-a-gender-studies-class-and-you-didn't" sort of way, which is ironic given the way that phrase dumbs down gender. It is a crass oversimplification that is as ridiculous as saying all gender is genitals, all gender is chromosomes, or all gender is socialization. In reality, gender is all of these things and more. In fact, if there's one thing that all of us should be able to agree on, it's that gender is a confusing and complicated mess. It's like a junior high school mixer, where our bodies and our internal desires awkwardly dance with one another and with the external expectations that other people place on us.

Sure, I can perform gender: I can curtsy, or throw like a girl, or bat my eyelashes. But performance doesn't explain why certain behaviors and ways of being come to me more naturally than others. It offers no insight into the countless restless nights I spent as a pre-teen wrestling with the inexplicable feeling that I should be female. It doesn't capture the very real physical and emotional changes that I experienced when I hormonally transitioned from testosterone to estrogen. Performance doesn't even begin to address the fact that, during my transition, I acted the same—wore the same T-shirts, jeans, and sneakers that I always had—yet once other people started reading me as female, *they* began treating me very differently. When we talk about my gender as though it were a performance, we let the audience—with all of their expectations, prejudices, and presumptions—completely off the hook.

Look, I know that many contemporary queer folks and feminists embrace mantras like "all gender is performance," "all gender is drag," and "gender is just a construct."[2] They seem empowered by the way these sayings give the impression that gender is merely a fiction. A facade. A figment of our imaginations. And of course, this is a convenient strategy, provided that you're not a trans woman who lacks the means to change her legal sex to female, and who thus runs the very real risk of being locked up in an all-male jail cell. Provided that you're not a trans man who has to navigate the discrepancy between his male identity and female history during job interviews and first dates. Whenever I hear someone who has not had a transsexual experience say that gender is just a construct or merely a performance, it always reminds me of that Stephen Colbert gag where he insists that he doesn't see race.[3] It's easy to fictionalize an issue when you are not fully in touch with all of the ways in which you are privileged by it.

Almost every day of my life I deal with people who insist on seeing my femaleness as fake. People who make a point of calling me effeminate rather than feminine. People who slip up my pronouns, but only after they find out that I'm trans, never beforehand. People who insist on third-sexing me with labels like MTF, boy-girl, he-she, she-male, ze, hir,[4] it—anything but simply female. Because I'm transsexual, I am sometimes accused of impersonation or deception when I am simply being myself. So it seems to me that this strategy of fictionalizing gender will only ever serve to marginalize me further.

So I ask you: Can't we find new ways of speaking? Shouldn't we be championing new slogans that empower all of us, whether trans or non-trans, queer or straight, female and/or male and/or none of the above?

Instead of saying that all gender is this or all gender is that, let's recognize that the word gender has scores of meanings built into it. It's an amalgamation of bodies, identities, and life experiences, of subconscious urges, sensations, and behaviors, some of which develop organically, and others which are shaped by language and culture. Instead of saying that gender is any one single thing, let's start describing it as a holistic experience.

Instead of saying that all gender is performance, let's admit that sometimes gender is an act, and other times it isn't. And since we can't get inside of one another's minds, we have no way of knowing whether any given person's gender is sincere or contrived. Let's fess up to the fact that when we make judgments about other people's genders, we're typically basing it on our own assumptions (and we all know what happens when you assume, right?).

Let's stop claiming that certain genders and sexualities "reinforce the gender binary." In the past, that tactic has been used to dismiss butches and femmes, bisexuals, trans folks and our partners, and feminine people of every persuasion. Gender isn't simply some faucet that we can turn on and off in order to appease other people, whether they be heterosexist bigots or queerer-than-thou hipsters. How about this: Let's stop pretending that we have all the answers because when it comes to gender, none of us is fucking omniscient.

Instead of trying to fictionalize gender, let's talk about all of the moments in life when gender feels all too real. Because gender doesn't feel like drag when you're a young trans child begging your parents not to cut your hair or not to force you to wear that dress. And gender doesn't feel like a performance when, for the first time in your life, you feel safe and empowered enough to express yourself in ways that resonate with you, rather than remaining closeted for the benefit of others. And gender doesn't feel like a construct when you finally find that special person whose body, personality, identity, and energy feels like a perfect fit with yours. Let's stop trying to deconstruct gender into non-existence and instead start celebrating it as inexplicable, varied, profound, and intricate.

So don't dare dismiss my gender as a construct, drag, or a performance, because my gender is a work of non-fiction.

PART TWO

NEW WAYS OF SPEAKING

THE PERVERSION OF
"THE PERSONAL IS POLITICAL"

CHAPTER TWELVE

A s countless writers and activists have chronicled[1], and as my own essays in the previous section of this book attest to, exclusion is a recurring problem in feminist and queer movements, organizations, and spaces. Whether unconscious or overt, exclusion always leads to the same end result: Many individuals who wish to participate are left behind, and the few who remain often bask in the misconception that they are part of a unified, righteous movement. To put it another way, exclusion inevitably leads to far smaller movements with far more narrow and distorted agendas.

Those of us who face exclusion within feminism or queer activism will often focus our efforts on challenging the specific isms that we believe are driving our exclusion. In my case, this has led me to spend much of the last decade critiquing cissexism, trans-misogyny, masculine-centrism, and monosexism within the queer and feminist spaces I have participated in. Others have focused their efforts on challenging heterosexism, racism, classism, ableism, ageism, and sizeism within these movements. All of this is important work, to be sure. But honestly, sometimes I feel like we are all playing one giant game of Whac-A-Mole[2]—as soon as we make gains challenging a particular type of exclusion, another type arises or becomes apparent. So while we may make significant inroads in challenging certain isms, as a whole, the phenomenon of exclusion continues unabated.

For this reason, over the last several years, I have focused my attention on a more fundamental, underlying question: Why do feminist and queer movements, which would so clearly benefit from strength in numbers, always seem to exclude certain people who are committed to our overall goal of challenging sexism? And is there a way to eliminate, or at least mitigate, our tendency toward excluding people simply because they are different from us?

Many other feminists and queer activists have asked these very questions. And, almost without exception, they all seem to reach similar conclusions: Exclusion, they will claim, always stems from conservative forces or ideologies within our movements. And, according to these accounts, the only way that we can ever transcend exclusion is to adopt a more radical approach to feminism and queer activism. For example, people who forward this approach often claim that the exclusion of women of color and/or queer women from mainstream feminism is the result of essentialism. Such people will often advocate social constructionist perspectives (which attempt to destabilize gender and sexual categories rather than portraying them as natural) as an alternative. Others will point to how mainstream feminism and queer activism have largely ignored their most economically disadvantaged constituents, and will argue that these movements should therefore move away from previous liberal or reformist approaches, and instead take a more politically radical and/or anti-capitalist approach. Others will argue that the exclusion of gender variant and unconventionally sexual folks from feminism and queer activism is a sign that these movements have become too "assimilationist." Such people will often encourage us to be even more unconventional and revolutionary in our genders or sexualities as a way to subvert heteronormativity and mainstream society. And still others will claim that activists who portray gay people or trans people as oppressed minorities that require legal protection are merely clinging to an outdated "identity politics" approach, one that is inferior to more anti-identity strategies for bringing about change.

While there is some truth to all of these claims, I strongly believe that this overarching narrative—that exclusion is an inherently "conservative" tendency that can only be countered by taking more "radical" approaches—is severely shortsighted. After all, radical movements practice exclusion and police their own boundaries just as fiercely as conservative ones (as can be seen in many self-identified radicals' pronouncements that certain individuals or identities are not feminist or queer enough). Indeed, exclusion within feminist and queer movements is not a conservative, liberal, or radical phenomenon, but rather a systemic problem that stems from the way we conceptualize sex, gender, and sexuality, and the way we frame sexism and marginalization more generally. And in this second section of the book, I hope to thoroughly detail this problem as I see it, and to offer alternative ways of thinking about sexism that more accurately reflect the world, and that are more likely to give rise to inclusive movements.

In order to illustrate these fundamental problems that exist with how we currently view gender and sexism, I will spend this chapter focusing on one specific example of exclusion, namely, the exclusion of transsexuals within more radical strands of feminism. While transsexuals have also faced exclusion in liberal or reformist feminist circles, I want to focus specifically on more radical feminist perspectives in order to challenge the assumption that exclusion necessarily stems from conservatism.

My goal here is not to simply petition for transsexual inclusion in feminism (I'd like to think that by this point in the book readers are already convinced that we should be included!), but rather to point out the fatal flaws in how we conceptualize sexism, and how these flaws often lead to exclusion. So while this chapter will begin with a lot of talk about transsexuality, toward the end I will be making much broader points about feminism and queer activism.

PARALLELS BETWEEN CISSEXISM AND HETEROSEXISM

Throughout this book, I have been using the word *transsexual* to refer to people who are cross-gender–identified—that is, who identify and live as members of the sex other than the one they were assigned at birth.[3] I find that during cissexual discussions about transsexuality, there is one question that invariably sucks all of the proverbial oxygen out of the room: "Why do some people cross-gender identify?" Of course, an analogous question can be (and often is) asked with regards to sexual orientation: "Why do some people experience same-sex attraction?" Despite well over a century of medical, biological, psychological, and sociological inquiry into these phenomena, no clear, singular, undisputed cause for either cross-gender identity or same-sex attraction has been found. And the fact that cross-gender identity and same-sex attraction are both pancultural and transhistorical phenomena[4], and that individuals who experience these inclinations typically describe them as unconscious, inexplicable, persistent, and deeply felt, seems to indicate that these are complex traits—this is the term biologists sometimes use to refer to traits that arise from a complex interaction between numerous biological, social, and environmental factors, and which always results in a panoply of outcomes rather than specific, fixed outcomes. So to clarify, I am not suggesting that biology is the only, or even primary, factor that shapes gender and sexuality. I am simply saying that biology and biological variation do, on some level, influence our gender and sexuality. (I will explain precisely what I mean by this in the following chapter.)

Over the years, lesbian, gay, and bisexual (LGB) individuals have forcibly made the case that the actual challenge they face stems not from their same-sex attraction *per se*, but rather from *heterosexism*—the institutionalized belief that heterosexual attraction and relationships are considered valid and natural, whereas same-sex attraction and relationships are not.[5] Analogously, the major obstacle that transsexuals face is not simply the fact that we are born into the "wrong body" (as that dilemma can be resolved via transitioning and living as members of our identified gender), but rather that our gender identities, expressions, and sex embodiments are typically viewed as being less valid and natural than those of cissexuals. As I have discussed in previous chapters, this double standard is called *cissexism*.

Now, heterosexism and cissexism have much in common. They are both forms of *oppositional sexism*, in which certain attributes are viewed as natural, legitimate, and taken for granted in one sex, and unnatural, illegitimate, and questionable when expressed in the other.[6] In fact, upon closer inspection, it becomes clear that heterosexism and cissexism are enforced in almost identical ways. Over the next few paragraphs, I want to highlight some of these parallels, both because they are germane to this chapter's focus on transsexual exclusion within feminism, and also because they provide insight into how sexist double standards function more generally—a topic that I will delve into more thoroughly in subsequent chapters.

First, heterosexism and cissexism function by ensuring that same-sex desire and cross-gender identity, respectively, are viewed as being inherently *questionable*, while their heterosexual and cissexual counterparts remain unquestionable and taken for granted. As a result, LGB individuals are expected to account for, and provide details about, our sexualities and relationships that heterosexuals typically are not (typical questions may include, "How do you know that you're really gay?" or "How do you have sex?"). Rarely does anyone ask reciprocal questions (such as "How do you know that you're really straight?") to heterosexuals. Transsexuals are similarly expected to provide details about our childhood gender identity and expression, to describe what medical procedures we have undergone, and so on, in order to justify our gender identity. In addition, same-sex attraction and cross-gender identity are generally deemed more *remarkable*—that is, people constantly comment upon, and openly debate, these phenomena, whereas heterosexuality and cissexuality typically receive little attention or discussion.

Often, people who are unapologetically heterosexist or cissexist are not content with merely bringing LGB and transsexual identities into question, but rather they seek to assign *ulterior motives* to these groups in order to explain these phenomena. For example, those who engage in same-sex relationships are often assumed to be merely sexually confused, to not have met the "right" other-sex person yet, to be looking for an "alternative lifestyle," or to have been recruited by the "homosexual agenda." Likewise, transsexuals are presumed to have similarly dubious motives: We are often accused of transitioning in order to obtain certain gender privileges, to satisfy some sexual urge or perversion, to assimilate into straight society, or because we are mentally ill or merely confused about our gender.

Another way that heterosexism and cissexism operate is by portraying same-sex relationships and cross-gender identities as inferior copies of heterosexual and cissexual ones, respectively. (In *Whipping Girl*, I referred to this tactic as *facsimilation*.)[7] For example, straight-minded people often compulsively attempt to assess which member of a same-sex couple is the "boy" (butch) and which is the "girl" (femme) under the assumption that their relationship merely mimics heterosexuality. Similarly, upon finding out that someone is transsexual, cissexual-minded people will often compulsively scan the person for any evidence of their assigned (read: "real") sex and begin interpreting the transsexual's behaviors and presentation as an "imitation," "emulation," or "impersonation" of cissexual women or men. The assumption that transsexuals merely imitate cissexual genders is apparent in media depictions, which almost invariably forward scenes of trans women and men in the act of putting on gender-specific apparel and accoutrement, and practicing and affecting female or male mannerisms.[8] Such depictions reinforce cissexual "realness" and transsexual "fakeness."

Heterosexism and cissexism function not only by portraying same-sex attraction and cross-gender identities as artificial, but by invisibilizing them in day-to-day life. Just as *heterosexual assumption* (the assumption that all people are heterosexual unless evidence is provided to the contrary) often erases the existence of same-sex attraction and relationships, *cissexual assumption* erases the existence of transsexual people. Many of the most common tropes that plague LGB and transsexual people—that we are "closeted," that we "pass" (as heterosexual or cissexual, respectively), or that we "deceive" other people—would not exist if it were not for these assumptions.

Of course, heterosexism and cissexism are not merely abstract concepts, but rather institutionalized forms of marginalization: They ensure that same-sex relationships and cross-gender identities will be viewed as being less socially and legally valid than heterosexual and cissexual ones, respectively. Obvious examples include the lack of legal recognition of same-sex marriages and transsexuals' identified genders in many jurisdictions. As a result, heterosexuals and cissexuals experience privileges that are regularly denied to LGB and transsexual individuals, respectively. Just as heterosexuals often take their sexual orientations for granted, and are oblivious to the heterosexual privilege they enjoy, cissexuals are able to take their gender identities and sex embodiments for granted, and are oblivious to their own cissexual privilege.

So with that quick primer in mind, we can now turn to our case study: transsexual exclusion within radical strands of feminism.

THE "GENDER SYSTEM" AND GENDER ARTIFACTUALIST POLITICS

The issue of transsexuality has come up time and time again in cissexual feminist theory. In the trans, queer, and feminist circles that I inhabit, I find that there is a recurring narrative that is often told to describe the supposed evolution in feminist thought regarding transsexual issues and individuals. According to this narrative, the negative views of transsexuality held by many second-wave feminists (e.g., radical and lesbian feminists) are attributed to gender essentialism, whereas the acceptance, and sometimes even embrace, of the phenomenon by more recent feminists (e.g., queer theorists and poststructuralists) arises from their recognition that sex and gender are both socially constructed. I believe that this narrative both misrepresents the concerns of radical and lesbian feminists and overlooks the high degree of ambivalence that social constructionists have expressed toward transsexuality over the years. Here, instead, I will be making the case that the views of transsexuality forwarded by all of the aforementioned camps of feminist thought are actually more similar to one another than they are different. And the reason for this similarity stems from their shared belief in *gender artifactualization*—the tendency to conceptualize and depict gender as being primarily or entirely a cultural artifact. Cissexual feminist fascination with transsexuality (where it has occurred) has typically been motivated not by a concern for transsexual individuals but by an interest in how the existence of transsexuality might impact, or provide support for, gender artifactualist perspectives and politics.

It is important here to make a distinction between gender artifactualization and social constructionism. To have a social constructionist view of gender (by most standard definitions) simply means that one believes that gender does not arise in a direct and unadulterated manner from biology, but rather is shaped to some extent by culture—by socialization, gender norms, and the gender-related ideology, language, and labels that constrain and influence our understanding of the matter. By this definition, I am most certainly a social constructionist. Gender artifactualists, on the other hand, are typically not content to merely discuss the ways in which gender may be socially constructed, but rather they discount or purposefully ignore the possibility that biology and biological variation also play a role in constraining and shaping our genders. Sometimes, even the most nuanced and carefully qualified suggestions that biology may have *some* influence on gendered behaviors or desires will garner accusations of "essentialism" in gender artifactualist circles (I discuss this tendency at greater length in the next chapter).

There have been two major approaches to gender artifactualism. Some subscribe to a sex/gender distinction, where the primary focus is on "gender," which is associated with the mind and viewed as entirely social and learned, whereas "sex" (the biological) is relegated exclusively to the body and is assumed to play little to no role in gendered behavior. Other gender artifactualists instead make the case that "sex" is just as much of a cultural artifact as "gender."

It has been my experience that many (albeit certainly not all) feminists who describe themselves as social constructionists in fact forward gender artifactualist positions. This tendency is perhaps most blatantly obvious in the popular slogans that are often quoted in feminist or gender studies settings—"all gender is performance" or "gender is just a construct." Such phrases seem to intentionally deny any possible role for biology. Gender artifactualism tends to be embraced in more "radical" or "revolutionary" feminist traditions (e.g., radical feminism, lesbian feminism, poststructuralism, and queer theory) because it forcibly challenges biological determinist notions that dominate in the culture. More importantly, gender artifactualism allows one to view gender solely in terms of a hegemonic gender system that may be challenged, undermined, subverted, displaced, or overthrown. Of course, this hegemonic gender system goes by many names—the patriarchy, the sex/gender system, compulsory heterosexuality, the heterosexual matrix, the gender binary, kyriarchy[9], and so on. For simplicity, I will simply refer to it as *the gender system*.

The gender artifactualist belief that "woman" and "man" are entirely socially derived categories foisted upon us by an oppressive gender system automatically forecloses any possibility that there might be non-social or intrinsic factors that influence or predispose one to cross-gender identification. As a result, gender artifactualists have typically dismissed transsexuals' claims of having a deep, profound, subconscious self-understanding of which sex we belong to, and instead have presumed that transsexuality is a form of "false consciousness" that arises as a symptom or by-product of the gender system. For example, feminist psychologist Sandra Bem claimed that transsexuality was part of "the same process of gender polarization that also produces highly conventional males and females. In a less gender-polarizing culture, after all, it would matter much less if the individual's personality did not cohere into a tightly gender-polarized package that matched her or his biological sex."[10] In her book *Woman Hating*, Andrea Dworkin states that "'man' and 'woman' are fictions, caricatures, cultural constructs," and she forwards androgyny as a way of undermining the gender system.[11] According to her worldview, "community built on androgynous identity will mean the end of transsexuality as we know it. Either the transsexual will be able to expand his/her sexuality into a fluid androgyny, or, as roles disappear, the phenomenon of transsexuality will disappear."[12]

Further, because gender artifactualists believe that the categories of "woman" and "man" underpin the gender system, they often view transsexuals and/or transsexuality as enabling or "reinforcing" the gender system. The most hardline take on this view has been advocated by radical and lesbian-identified cissexual feminists such as Janice Raymond and Sheila Jeffreys. In her book *The Transsexual Empire*, Raymond argues that, "Within [a patriarchal] society, the transsexual only exchanges one stereotype for the other, thus reinforcing the fabric by which a sexist society is held together."[13] Similarly, Jeffreys views transsexuals and others on the transgender spectrum as "engaging in behaviour which is in opposition to the feminist project of the elimination of gender, thereby helping to maintain the currency of gender."[14]

Critics of Jeffreys and Raymond often dismiss their work on the grounds that it is rooted in gender essentialism. I would argue that such claims are somewhat off the mark. After all, the main point both authors make—that transsexuals buy into gender and reinforce the gender system—is not rooted in gender essentialism, but in gender artifactualism. Indeed, the force of their critiques rests entirely on the assumption that gender identity and expression are cultural artifacts that have no biological basis and that serve the sole purpose of maintaining the gender system.

Furthermore, conclusions that are very similar to Raymond's and Jeffreys's radical feminist perspectives have been forwarded by a variety of social constructionist and poststructuralist theorists. For example, Judith Lorber (who, according to promotion for her book *Paradoxes of Gender*, "argues that gender is wholly a product of socialization") has said that "transsexuals do not challenge the social construction of gender. Their goal is to be masculine men and feminine women."[15] Serena Nanda, an anthropologist who celebrates how so-called "third gender" categories in other cultures challenge Western notions of binary gender, claims that "[t]ranssexuals . . . far from being an example of gender diversity, both reflected and reinforced the dominant Euro-American sex/gender ideology in which one had to chose to be either a man or a (stereotypical) woman."[16] Other theorists who take psychoanalytic or poststructuralist approaches, such as Carol-Anne Tyler, Bernice Hausman, and Marjorie

Garber, have portrayed transsexuals as being semiotically-challenged individuals who take signifiers a little too seriously and therefore wind up "literalizing," "essentializing," and literally embodying aspects of the gender system at the same time that they simultaneously reveal gender's constructed nature.[17] While these critiques differ from one another, and from those of Jeffreys and Raymond, they all rely on a similar gender artifactualist logic: 1) Gender is a cultural artifact; 2) Transsexuals mistake gender to be something real (rather than recognizing it as artificial); 3) Therefore, transsexuals reify the gender system.

Now from a transsexual perspective, such claims that we reinforce or uphold the gender system seem rather odd. For one thing, I didn't transition in order to better fit into the gender system—as a bisexual femme-tomboy transsexual women, I am still regularly viewed as gender–non-conforming. For me, transitioning wasn't about conforming to society, but about self-actualization, about becoming the person I know myself to be. In fact, I would argue that changing one's sex is generally viewed by most people to be the most extreme act of gender non-conformity that one could possibly engage in. When I come out as transsexual to straight mainstream folks, I have never once had someone say, "Thank you Julia for reinforcing our gender binary! You're such an outstanding gendered citizen, thank you for being you!" In fact, quite the opposite happens: People often become bothered, or confused, or disturbed. So the notion that my gender somehow reinforces the gender system does not have any bearing on my everyday life.

But what strikes me even more about the reinforcing-the-gender-system claim is how selectively it is doled out. For example, I never hear cissexual feminists say, "My mom reinforces the gender binary," or "My next door neighbor upholds heterosexist gender norms," even though such things may be true. Even more to the point, if a cissexual feminist such as Janice Raymond or Bernice Hausman or Sandra Bem were to call themselves a woman, or to do something generally associated with women, would it spark great debates within feminist circles over whether these individuals reinforced the gender system? I think not. Therefore, the reinforcing-the-gender-system trope seems to represent a double standard in that it is routinely applied to transsexuals but not to most cissexuals. In other words, it represents a cissexist double standard.

Trans man Max Wolf Valerio provides an anecdote that illustrates just how inane this double standard is. He had the opportunity to speak with a class on transgender and transsexuality just after they viewed a short documentary on him. Some of the more critical questions Max fielded centered on the fact that, at one point in the film, he boxes the camera—some of the students interpreted this action as evidence that Max was reinforcing conventional gender roles. Max muses about how, had he engaged in the very same boxing gestures prior to his transition (when he was perceived as female), these students would likely have viewed his actions as "rebellious" and "charming" rather than as oppressively masculine. He then imagines asking the women in the class how they feel whenever they do anything stereotypically female, such as wearing "women's" clothing, or being nurturing or communicative. He hypothetically asks these cissexual women:

> Would you only be filmed doing things that women are never supposed to do, or haven't typically done? Do you . . . monitor your actions and thoughts to prevent slipping up and "buying into the bipolar gender system?" Probably not. Then why expect me or any other transsexual to?[18]

So the fact that transsexuals, but not cissexuals, are routinely accused of reinforcing the gender system is clearly just a by-product of cissexism: Our gender identities and sex embodiments are seen as less legitimate than those of cissexuals.

As I noted earlier, a major way in which cissexism is enforced is via the assumption that transsexual gender identities, expressions, and sex embodiments are inherently "fake" and therefore can be called into question, whereas their cissexual counterparts are "real" and therefore taken for granted. This discrepancy explains why transsexuals seem to garner more disdain and criticism for reinforcing the gender system than the gender-normative cissexual majority. Furthermore, because cissexism causes cissexual-minded people to constitutively view transsexuals as "fakes"—as mere imitations or impersonations of cissexual genders—such people are inclined to (mis)perceive and (mis)interpret transsexuals as actively and purposefully trying to fit themselves into female and male stereotypes even when they are not.

Granted, some transsexuals do purposefully emulate the behaviors of cissexual women and men in order to "pass" successfully as cissexual.[19] Cissexual feminist theorists seem to share the mainstream media's fascination with capturing transsexuals in the act of affecting, practicing, and performing femaleness and maleness. Most often, these depictions focus on transsexuals who are newly embarking on social and physical transition—that is, transsexuals who are at their most gender incongruous, their most visibly "fake." An investment in "fakeness" is evident in most cissexual feminist accounts of transsexuality, whether it's Raymond and Jeffreys, who rebuke transsexuals for acting like grossly exaggerated caricatures of feminine stereotypes, or Tyler, Hausman, and Garber, whose primary interests are in the ways that transsexuals make the artificial and constructed nature of gender appear visible.

Once we acknowledge this double standard with regards to "fakeness," then it becomes apparent that many feminist writings that are not blatantly anti-transsexual are nevertheless rooted in cissexism. For example, in Kessler and McKenna's classic book, *Gender: An Ethnomethodological Approach*, they dedicate an entire chapter to exploring "what transsexualism can illuminate about the day-to-day social construction of gender by all persons."[20] But one might ask, if all people's genders are constructed, then why focus on transsexuals? Their reasoning: "It is easier for us to see that transsexuals 'do' (accomplish) gender than it is to see this process in nontranssexuals."[21] Kessler and McKenna make this provocative claim, yet they never take the next obvious step and ask, "Why is that?" While they never explicitly spell out why, it seems rather clear that this is due to the fact that transsexual genders are already assumed to be "fake" *a priori*. Thus, their approach both relies upon, and also exacerbates, societal cissexism.

To understand why this is so problematic, consider the following analogy: What if a sociologist hoped to demonstrate the socially constructed nature of monogamy? And to make their case, they focused on same-sex, rather than heterosexual, couples because they felt that the former better illustrated the ways in which monogamous relationships are artificial and contrived. Clearly, such an approach would reinforce the heterosexist assumption that same-sex relationships are unnatural, illegitimate, and inferior copies of heterosexual relationships. It would also exploit those who cannot socially and legally take their desires and relationships for granted in the way that the heterosexual majority can. Similarly, using transsexuals to illuminate the artificial nature of gender exploits the fact that transsexuals are viewed as "fakes," and that we cannot socially or legally take our gender identities, expressions, and sex embodiments for granted in the way that cissexuals can. In other words, such approaches simultaneously exploit transsexuals and reinforce cissexism.

Given Kessler and McKenna's assertion that all people's genders are constructed, we should consider what the effect might be if, rather than focusing on transsexual subjects, they were to focus their deconstructive efforts on a cissexual person instead. Let's imagine, for instance, that they chose Judith Lorber or Carol-Anne Tyler or Sheila Jeffreys as their subject. And in their analysis, they highlighted and detailed all of the aspects of that person's body, personality, mannerisms, attitudes, actions, desires, and interests that seemed mannish, androgynous, or incongruent to them, and then used this information to argue that they are not "naturally" female, but rather that they "perform" or "achieve" femaleness. Would that be an effective way to demonstrate that gender is socially constructed? Probably not. Because these women are all cissexual, their female gender identities, expressions and sex embodiments are viewed as natural and unquestionable *a priori*. So any attempt to deconstruct their genders would yield limited results, as readers would no doubt have a difficult time overcoming the nagging feeling that these women are *really* female no matter what anyone were to say or do.

The reason why I chose to use actual people in this example is to illuminate a second point, namely, that nonconsensually deconstructing a person's gender can be highly objectifying, even degrading. Yet this is precisely what cissexual feminists have repeatedly done to transsexual subjects. The fact that cissexual feminists regularly get away with dissecting and deconstructing the genders of actual trans people—whether they be "Agnes," Jan Morris, Beth Elliot, Sandy Stone, Renée Richards, Venus Extravaganza, and countless others[22]—and not have it come off as utterly disrespectful, suggests that most readers view transsexuals not merely as "fakes," but as inhuman to some extent as well. The fact that cissexual-minded people are unlikely to sympathize or identify with transsexuals undoubtedly plays a major role in why transsexuals are so routinely depicted as specimens in such a broad variety of feminist, sociological, psychological, and other texts.

THE ARBITRARY NATURE OF THE GENDER SYSTEM

Gender artifactualist politics place an extraordinary burden on feminist-minded transsexuals. In order to gain inclusion within feminism, transsexuals must constantly address accusations that they reinforce the gender system. If they assert that they transitioned not to reinforce the gender system but because they experienced a deeply felt self-understanding that they should be the other sex, their response will likely be dismissed as "essentialist" and taken as a sign that they buy into the gender system. Seemingly, the only alternative other than abandoning feminism altogether is to reframe their cross-gender identity in political terms rather than personal terms, by arguing that their transsexual gender identities and sex embodiments call the gender system into question, thus subverting it. This is precisely the approach taken during the initial rise of the transgender movement in the 1990s, and it is perhaps most evident in the writings of Kate Bornstein, Leslie Feinberg, and Riki Wilchins.[23] These authors use their own gender incongruity to destabilize and deconstruct the male/female gender binary, and they regularly draw parallels between their own gender transgressions and those of cissexual gender non-conformists. The notion that transgender people subvert or "shatter" the gender binary was strengthened by the fact that these authors all explicitly identify outside the binary. In today's parlance, we would describe their identities as genderqueer, an umbrella term for people who see themselves as being neither a man nor a woman, or perhaps a little bit of both, and/or who move freely between genders.

In addition to having a huge positive impact on me as a young trans person many years ago, the writings of these and other activists made great strides toward convincing many cissexual feminists that transgender people could be allies in the fight against sexism. This is clearly a good thing. However, reframing trans bodies and identities in purely political terms has several drawbacks. First, it is somewhat disingenuous. After all, many trans folks experience an inexplicable feeling that there is something wrong with the gender we were assigned at birth long before being exposed to any sort of gender politics. So playing up our supposed political motives, while playing down our personal motives, essentially erases trans people's subjectivity.

Second, this approach has encouraged some cissexuals who have no history of cross-gender identity whatsoever to embrace a transgender or genderqueer identity out of their desire to shatter the gender binary. I often refer to such people as being "intellectually genderqueer." This is not meant to be a pejorative by any means—I believe that every person has the right to choose (or not choose) to identify with whatever gender feels like the best fit for them. However, this trend can become an issue because, in certain spaces, intellectually genderqueer voices dominate discussions about trans people and issues. This can be problematic, especially for transsexuals, as it once again casts "trans" solely as a political move to shatter the gender binary, while erasing the very real obstacles transsexuals face, namely, the fact that we are seen as "fakes" and as illegitimate members of our identified genders.

Third, the claim that trans people subvert the gender system has been routinely twisted by many cissexual feminists (as well as some transgender activists) into an expectation that trans people must actively refuse to identify within the male/female binary, and must constantly make our gender incongruity visible in order to be viewed as sufficiently feminist.[24] As a result, gender variant people who fail to meet such criteria (e.g., transsexuals who fully transition and identify unqualifiedly as women or men) still to this day remain subject to accusations that they reinforce the gender system. This expectation—which I often half-jokingly refer to as *compulsory genderqueerness*—is something that I have personally faced time and time again in feminist settings, and I find it both endlessly frustrating and utterly silly. After all, the aspects of my person that are most often called out as reinforcing the gender system—namely, the fact that my gender identity and presentation are unqualifiedly female—are traits that also apply to the overwhelming majority of cissexual feminist women. But of course, unlike me, they are never called out for identifying as women and wearing women's clothing.

So clearly, the tactic of politicizing transgender identities under the rubric of "we subvert the gender system" is a well-meaning attempt to gain legitimacy for trans folks, but in the end it fails because it does not challenge the core problem: cissexism. This failure is especially evident in feminist critiques of claims that trans people subvert the gender system. For example, Bernice Hausman dismisses transgender politics as being liberal or reformist because "transsexualism and transgenderism rely on maintaining gender as a category of experience and being."[25] In other words, trans people fail to recognize the gender artifactualist position that "gender itself exists *only* as a convention" (emphasis hers).[26] Raymond makes a similar point in her 1994 essay on the rise of transgender politics, when she argues that trans people, "rather than transcending, i.e. dismantling and going beyond gender roles, seek to combine aspects of traditional femininity with aspects of traditional masculinity."[27]

I cannot tell you how many times I have read and heard claims that feminists are trying to "move beyond gender," or to bring on the "end of gender," invoked in attempts to portray transsexuality and transgenderism as antithetical to feminism. Here is what I want to know: What exactly is the "end of gender"? What does it look like? Are there words to describe male and female bodies at the end of gender? Or do we purge all words that refer to male- or female-specific body parts and reproductive functions for fear that they will reinforce gender distinctions? Do we do away with activities such as sports, sewing, shaving, cooking, fixing cars, taking care of children, and of course, man-on-top-woman-on-bottom penetration sex, because these have been too closely associated with traditional masculine and feminine roles in the past? What clothes do we wear at the end of gender? Do we all wear pants? Or do we all wear skirts? Or do we have to come up with a completely different type of clothing altogether? Or perhaps we must go naked because, after all, clothing has a long and troubled history of conspiring with the gender system. Who gets to make these decisions? Who gets to decide what is gender and what is not? By what criteria does one determine whether any given behavior is a whole-some natural human trait or an abominable social artifact?

It seems clear to me that everybody has a somewhat different view of what is "in" gender (and therefore bad) and what is "outside" of gender (and therefore good). I have been in spaces that are predominantly genderqueer where I have heard someone claim that anyone who uses male and female pronouns necessarily reinforces the gender system. I have on more than one occasion heard people who identify as bisexual or pansexual suggest that people who are exclusively attracted to one sex or the other reinforce the gender binary. Apparently, reinforcing the gender system, like beauty, is truly in the eye of the beholder.

A few years back, I thought about writing a satirical manifesto mocking the "reinforcing" trope. I would begin by claiming that the gender system is rooted in the premise that if you are born a boy, you will grow up to be a man, and if you are born a girl, you will grow up to be a woman. And based on this premise, I would go on to argue that transsexuals are at the cutting edge—the vanguard, if you will—of the gender revolution, whereas cissexuals (by virtue of their refusal to change their sex) reinforce the gender system. I know I could have made a convincing case, and it would have been a lot of fun to write, but in the end I decided not to because I knew that, sadly, some people would probably have taken me seriously.

While transsexuals, or bisexuals, or pansexuals, or genderqueers may have their own ideas about what reinforces or subverts the gender system, such views are usually not taken seriously in feminist circles because these groups constitute such small minorities. However, majority opinions generally prevail. And in a world where most people (and this includes cissexual feminists) consciously or unconsciously view transsexuality as illegitimate, as fake, and as questionable, those of us who are transsexual are essentially marked, and our behaviors and life choices are placed under the microscope.

Now, if I wanted, I could end this chapter here by saying, "cissexism is bad, and transsexuals do not reinforce the gender system," and we could all go home feeling good about ourselves. But I think that there is a far greater lesson to be learned here if we follow this through to its logical conclusion. Since I have been making an analogy between cissexism and heterosexism throughout this chapter, one might ask: What if most feminists believed that same-sex relationships were inherently less natural and valid than their heterosexual counterparts? Might this possibly result in lesbians getting accused of reinforcing the gender system? Well, this question is not a hypothetical one—we can simply look back in history to the late 1960s, when the "gay rights" movement as we know it was still in its infancy. Now I'm not talking about reformist-minded feminists such as Betty Freidan, who once infamously described lesbian feminists as "the lavender menace." I'm talking about radical feminists, who forwarded a view of gender that we would nowadays describe as social construction-ist, or which I would call gender artifactualist. Radical feminists often referred to the gender system (as they saw it) as "male supremacy" or "the sex-class system."[28] So how did they react to lesbians within their ranks?

Well, according to Alice Echols's book *Daring to Be Bad: Radical Feminism in America 1967-1975*, early on, radical feminists often made accusations about lesbianism that were eerily similar to those that have subsequently be made regarding transsexuality. For instance, some radical feminists claimed that lesbians were "hypersexual and oppressively male" and "were too attached to sex roles."[29] Ti-Grace Aktinson, a radical feminist who would eventually undergo an evolution with regards to her views about lesbianism, once said, "Because lesbianism involves role-playing and, more important, because it is based on the primary assumption of male oppression, that is, sex, lesbianism *reinforces the sex class system*," (emphasis mine).[30]

So what did lesbians do in order to gain legitimacy? You guessed it: They claimed that lesbianism subverted, rather than reinforced, the gender system! One of the most significant expressions of this move is found in a manifesto entitled "The Woman-Identified Woman," written by a group called Radicalesbians, in which they argued that lesbians, rather than being (in Echols's words) "male-identified 'bogeywomen' out to exploit other women" (read: reinforcing the gender system), they were "woman-identified" (i.e., they subverted the gender system by choosing women as partners, rather than men).[31] As Echols explains, they "accomplished this by redefining lesbianism as a primarily political choice."[32] So essentially, this is the same approach taken by transgender activists in the 1990s—playing up their political motives (while downplaying their personal ones) and claiming that their identity subverts the gender system. And according to Echols, it worked to some extent in that it made heterosexual radical feminists more accepting of lesbianism.

But if lesbians are woman-identified, and if that subverts the gender system, then doesn't that seem to imply that heterosexual feminists are male-identified, and therefore reinforce that system? Well, that is exactly what some lesbian feminists eventually went on to argue. As Echols describes, one particularly influential lesbian feminist group, The Furies, viewed "heterosexuality as the cornerstone of male supremacy and lesbianism as 'the greatest threat' to its continued existence."[33] In an article in their newspaper, one of the Furies claimed, "Lesbianism is not a matter of sexual preference, but rather one of a political choice which every woman must make if she is to become woman-identified and thereby end male supremacy."[34] According to Echols, "The Furies portrayed heterosexual feminists as the movement's albatross."[35]

In a 1971 pamphlet entitled "Lesbianism and Feminism," radical feminist Anne Koedt (who is best known for her essay "The Myth of the Vaginal Orgasm") described how heterosexual feminists of the time often faced accusations such as, "'You're oppressing me if you don't sleep with women"; "You're not a radical feminist if you don't sleep with women".[36] Koedt also mentions that she witnessed feminist women's perspectives about totally different issues be entirely dismissed by lesbian feminists because the woman in question "was not having sexual relations with women."[37]

Koedt refers to this phenomenon as a "perversion of 'the personal is political' argument."[38] For those unfamiliar with the phrase "the personal is political," it refers to the practice of women examining their own personal lives in order to better understand societal sexism.[39] Koedt goes onto observe that the perversion of "the personal is political" argument didn't originate with lesbian feminists. Rather, personal attacks (such as challenging a woman's feminist credentials if she was married, had children, or wore miniskirts) had always been a part of the movement, and in her words, these accusations were always deployed "in the guise of radicalism."[40]

If we step back for a minute, the assumption that we can subvert or overthrow the gender system by simply engaging in certain gendered or sexual behaviors (but not others) seems pretty silly. There have been gender outlaws and sexual outlaws of one stripe or another since the dawn of history, yet our mere presence has never once simply made sexism vanish into thin air. I would have to be pretty full of myself to believe that I could undo the gender system simply by behaving in one way or another. Such notions may be self-reassuring, but they ignore the fact that acts of sexism occur, not by how we dress, or identify, or have sex, but through the way we see and treat other people. Sexism occurs when we assume that some people are less valid or natural than others because of their sex, gender, or sexuality; it occurs when we project our own expectations and assumptions about sex, gender, and sexuality onto other people, and police their behaviors accordingly; it occurs when we reduce another person to their sex, gender, or sexuality rather than seeing them as a whole, legitimate person. That is sexism. And a person is a *legitimate* feminist when they have made a commitment to challenging sexist double standards wherever and whenever they arise. An individual's personal style, mannerisms, identity, consensual sexual partners, and life choices simply shouldn't factor into it.

It is notable that the aforementioned instances of the perversion of "the personal is political" within radical feminist circles very much resemble the sexism-based exclusion that occurred in more reformist feminist settings during the same time period. As alluded to earlier, back in 1969, Betty Friedan of the National Organization of Women (NOW) called lesbian feminists the "lavender menace," and in a press release about the First Congress to Unite Women to be held that year, she purposely omitted the name of a lesbian organization that was one of the sponsors of the conference.[41] These statements and actions surely put pressure on lesbians within NOW to either remain closeted or else leave the organization (which some did).[42] This exclusion of lesbians was all done in the name of political expediency: Friedan was concerned that if feminism were to be associated with lesbianism (and perhaps more specifically, stereotypes of lesbians as "man-haters"), that it would undermine the women's movement.[43] So in other words, in both reformist and radical feminist circles, certain people were deemed to be politically righteous, while others were accused of undermining the movement because they engaged in supposedly suspect personal behaviors (e.g., being, or not being, lesbian, respectively). This dynamic of sexism-based exclusion being justified via political arguments has occurred over and over again in feminist and queer circles, whether it be reformists who condemn the more "unseemly" or less politically "palatable" minority groups within their ranks, or the radicals who condemn anyone whose gender or sexuality is deemed too "seemly" or "palatable" to mainstream society.

TRANSCENDING THE PERVERSION OF "THE PERSONAL IS POLITICAL"

So how do we finally move beyond this perversion of "the personal is political" that has repeatedly created rifts and splits within feminism and queer activism? Well, I would like to make the following three suggestions:

First, whenever we come across a debate about whether some behavior "reinforces" or "subverts" the gender system, rather than engaging in that debate, we should instead ask ourselves which behaviors are marked (i.e., deemed questionable, remarkable, and therefore susceptible to the reinforcing-versus-subverting argument) and which are not, as this will usually expose some underlying double standard at work. For instance, if someone says that women who wear miniskirts reinforce the gender system, we should ask why women who wear pants are never called out. Isn't this because feminine clothing is marked in our culture (and thus open to attention, interpretation, commentary, and critique) whereas masculine clothing remains unmarked and taken for granted?

Second, we should stop forwarding gender artifactualist theories and arguments. First, gender artifactualism is incorrect—as I will explain in more detail in the next chapter, there is substantial evidence that biology does influence gender and sexuality on some level, albeit not in the ways, nor to the extent, that many people believe it does. Furthermore, gender artifactualism is inexorably linked to the perversion of "the personal is political." After all, if gender and sexuality are entirely social artifacts, and we have no intrinsic desires or individual differences, this implies that every person can (and should) change their gender and sexual behaviors at the drop of a hat in order to accommodate their own (or perhaps other people's) politics. This assumption denies human diversity and, as I have shown, often leads to the further marginalization of minority and marked groups.

For decades now, we as feminists have been touting the fact that gender and sexuality are socially constructed. I realize that people within certain academic and activist circles may have a nuanced understanding of what "constructed" means. But as someone who has been involved in front-line activism over the last decade, I can tell you that most people equate "gender is socially constructed" with "gender is just a construct"—that is to say, they assume that gender is entirely an artificial system that we can challenge by simply behaving in one way or another. For this reason, instead of constantly saying that gender and sexuality are socially constructed, I propose that we forward a somewhat different model, what I would call a *holistic view of gender and sexuality* (which I will explain more in depth in the next chapter). According to this holistic view, our genders and sexualities arise from an unfathomably complex interaction between a variety of biological, social, and environmental factors. Because there is such a vast amount of biological variation, and because each of us is uniquely socially situated, we will invariably fall all over the map with regards to what gender and sexual behaviors resonate with us personally. This is why some of us grow up with profound, inexplicable desires to express our genders and sexualities in ways that do not conform to cultural norms, and it is also why the perversion of "the personal is political"—that is, requiring people to alter their genders and sexualities in order to accommodate someone else's political agenda—is always a futile endeavor.

Third, and perhaps most controversially, we need to stop pretending that there really is a gender system. Certainly, for those of us who are deemed by society to be gender outlaws or sexual outlaws, sometimes it sure does feel like we are up against a massive monolithic gender system, one that is institutionalized and which seems to permeate every facet of life. Conceptualizing sexism in terms of a gender system does provide a fairly decent first approximation of how sexism functions. But like most models, it begins to fail when we look at exceptional circumstances— for instance, the way in which heterosexual women were sometimes marginalized in particular radical feminist circles, or the way in which certain genderqueer individuals look down upon people who identify as women or men. These more atypical forms of sexism cannot adequately be explained via the concepts of patriarchy, or heteronormativity, or the gender binary, and so on.

But more importantly, when we start buying into the existence of a hegemonic gender system, it becomes all too easy for us to get caught up in the illusion that we are infallible warriors in the fight to bring down that system. Suddenly we start seeing the world in black-and-white, cut-and-dried terms, where everybody is either with us or against us. When we get caught up in that illusion, it is easy to assume that any person who engages in a behavior that does not personally resonate with us must somehow be reinforcing, or conspiring with, that system. And when we accuse someone of reinforcing the gender system, it is always a dehumanizing act—it allows us to ignore that person's experience or perspective because after all, they are colluding with our enemy.

The truth is, there is no actual gender system, but rather just countless different sexist double standards. Some of these double standards are pervasive, even institutionalized, while others are fleeting, temporary, or loosely held. Some double standards change or disappear over time while others remain entrenched for century upon century. Some double standards are obvious to us while others may remain beyond our awareness. We may fight with all our might to overturn certain double standards, yet at the same time we may consciously or unconsciously hold or enforce other double standards.

Viewing gender and sexual oppression in terms of myriad double standards rather than as a singular hegemonic gender system is admittedly a lot messier, and it sounds way less sexy, and it cannot easily be summed up in a single witty catchphrase. But I do believe that it is more accurate. It is also humbling, as it acknowledges that even though we may righteously challenge certain double standards, we nevertheless might hold or enforce other double standards without realizing it. In fact, it challenges us to look for, and root out, all double standards, rather than viewing the world through a distorting single-issue lens (e.g., as cissexual feminists do when they view transsexuality solely in terms of male privilege, and as cissexual gays and lesbians have done when they view transsexuality solely in terms of heterosexual privilege).

And finally, as feminists, our goal should not be to "move beyond gender" or to bring on the "end of gender," as if such a thing were actually possible. Instead, we should envision ourselves as working to bring an end to all double standards based on sex, gender, and sexuality, as well as any other double standard that is unjustly used to demonize, delegitimize, and dehumanize other human beings.

HOMOGENIZING VERSUS HOLISTIC VIEWS OF GENDER AND SEXUALITY

CHAPTER THIRTEEN

I n the last chapter, I argued that we should abandon gender artifactualist theories because they inevitably lead people to presume that one can (and should) alter their gender and sexuality in order to conform to other people's political views. I believe that this perversion of "the personal is political" is a major (if not *the* major) tactic used to justify sexism-based exclusion within feminist and queer movements. Of course, the idea that gender and sexuality are entirely socially constructed is a central and cherished belief held by many in feminist and queer circles, so I doubt that those who are devoted to this gender artifactualist perspective will relinquish it simply because it promotes exclusion. So here, I will show that, in addition to disenfranchising many people from queer and feminist movements, gender artifactualism also happens to be flat-out incorrect as a theory to explain how gender and sexuality arise. I will also flesh out the details of my holistic view of gender and sexuality, which I believe has far more explanatory power than gender artifactualism, and which has the crucial benefit of fostering inclusiveness rather than exclusivity.

THE DREADED "NATURE VERSUS NURTURE" DEBATE

Gender artifactualism does not exist in a vacuum. Many feminists and queer activists embrace gender artifactualism because it seems to counter *gender determinism*—the belief that women and men are born with predetermined sex-specific behaviors and desires. Gender determinists typically believe that women are programmed to be feminine and men to be masculine; that women are naturally attracted to men, and men to women; and so on. So what force is supposedly at work behind the scenes doing all of this "programming" or "determining"? Some might claim that it is the hand of God. But in contemporary Western societies, gender determinists usually rely on biology to make their case. According to this account, women are chromosomally XX and men XY, and this genetic difference leads to differences in sex hormone production (e.g., estrogen and testosterone), and these hormonal differences lead to differences in brain development, which in turn supposedly leads to distinct and dramatic differences in women's and men's behaviors and desires. This gender determinist narrative is entrenched in our society. Rarely a day goes by where one does not come across some news report, magazine article, or pop science book claiming that our genes, hormones, brains, and evolutionary history all conspire to turn us all into perfect little heterosexual feminine women and masculine men.

Feminists and queer activists have good reason to be suspicious of gender determinism. There is a long history, going all the way back to Aristotle, of men pointing to supposed scientific facts to argue that women are less rational, mature, and intelligent than men.[1] Even today, the belief that men are naturally more competitive and technically oriented than women is often cited to justify inequities in the workplace, and the belief that men are naturally programmed to be sexually aggressive is sometimes used to excuse the nonconsensual sexualization of women (after all, "boys will be boys" and "she should have known better"). Along similar lines, the idea that people are simply programmed to become heterosexual and cisgender implies that those who are typically gendered and sexual are natural and normal, whereas those of us who are exceptional in one way or another (e.g., LGBTQIA+) must be viewed as unnatural and abnormal. As a result, exceptional gender and sexual traits are marked—they are seen as questionable, illegitimate, and subjected to undue scrutiny. So in other words, gender determinism seems to create and uphold many sexist double standards.

One way to challenge gender determinism is to critically examine the scientific research that is cited to support claims that biology-equals-gender-and-sexual-destiny. The scientific method can be a powerful tool to gain insight into the world around us, but it relies on several important criteria. For starters, one must have a hypothesis that is falsifiable—i.e., that has the potential to be proved incorrect. From there, one must design experiments that can yield evidence to either support or refute the hypothesis. It is crucial that such experiments are well controlled, to ensure that only one variable is being tested at a time; if there is more than one variable in play, it may generate misleading results that can lead to false conclusions. A scientist must also be aware of any unquestioned assumptions they may harbor. Historically, there are many examples of scientists who came to erroneous conclusions because they were unconsciously trying to make their data fit their assumptions, rather than allowing the data to challenge their assumptions. And finally, one must take exceptional results (i.e., those that do not fit the hypothesis) seriously, as they generally signal that the starting hypothesis is oversimplified, incomplete, or downright incorrect.

As many writers and researchers have chronicled, the lion's share of the research investigating biology's influence on human gender and sexuality fails to meet some of these basic standards of the scientific method.[2] As an example, let's take the common gender determinist claims that women are biologically programmed to be nurturing, and that men are biologically programmed to be aggressive. Now, the idea that women are naturally nurturing and men naturally aggressive pre-dates modern science—indeed, most people consider these to be "common sense" truths about gender. As a result, these ideas often become unquestioned assumptions that many scientists hold, which may unwittingly influence how they design their experiments or how they interpret their results. Furthermore, as with many traits associated with gender and sexuality, qualities like being "nurturing" or "aggressive" are situational and fairly complex. One can be more nurturing to some people, or in some situations, but not others. And one can express aggression in a number of different ways: through violence, verbal barbs, humiliation, passive aggressiveness, and so on. In fact, just about everyone expresses some degree of nurturing and aggressiveness in their lives. So how does one measure such complex phenomena? Generally, measuring multifaceted behaviors involves dumbing them down or oversimplifying them, for example, through a one-dimensional Kinsey-esque scale or a multiple-choice survey. Because many researchers unconsciously view aggressiveness as a masculine trait, and nurturing as a feminine trait, these assumptions are likely to bias how they define and measure these behaviors.

Despite such biases and the exaggerating effect they can have, virtually all measurements of *sexually dimorphic behaviors* (i.e., behaviors that tend to be more common in one sex than the other) reveal a large amount of variation within each sex and significant overlap between the sexes. So even if being nurturing or aggressive turns out to exhibit real, reproducible gender differences, we would still expect to find plenty of nurturing men and aggressive women out there. An astute scientist would pay heed to these exceptional results, as they indicate that the starting hypothesis (i.e., that men are programmed to be aggressive and women nurturing) is incorrect or incomplete in some way. Unfortunately, many scientists who study gender differences tend to play down or invisibilize these exceptions through various statistical methods—such as comparing men's average result to women's—thus giving the false impression that gender differences are discrete, when in fact they are not.

Another problem is that, starting at birth, we actively socialize girls to be feminine and boys to be masculine. Given that aggressiveness is considered to be a masculine trait, and nurturing a feminine one, boys are generally encouraged to express the former and not the latter (and vice versa for girls). Girls/women and boys/men who do not conform to these gender norms may face a significant amount of social stigma that may lead them to alter their behaviors somewhat in order to fit in. It is well accepted that the way that we are socialized, and our cultural beliefs, influence our brain development, and therefore our behaviors.[3] So while biology is one possible source of gender differences, so is socialization. In other words, research investigating gender differences is always dealing with two possible variables: biology and socialization. Despite this obvious problem, many researchers automatically presume that the gender differences they observed must stem from biology, and they discount socialization altogether. Such conclusions are generally not justified by the science. Some researchers (particularly those in a field called Evolutionary Psychology[4]) go even farther by assuming that these supposed biological differences represent adaptations that were selected for during human evolution, and from there, they will invent hypothetical evolutionary scenarios to explain why male aggressiveness and female nurturing came to be. Of course, many of these evolutionary tales are not falsifiable, and therefore fall outside the realm of science.

The prevalence of such shoddy gender-related research is exacerbated by two institutional factors. First, scientific journals rarely publish research articles that only provide "negative results"—that is, results that do not confirm the hypothesis.[5] So if a researcher were to carry out tests looking for differences in aggression or nurturing between women and men, and if they did not find any significant differences, their work would likely not ever get published. However, if they were to find such a difference, it is much likelier that such results would get published. Second, most people (whether they be researchers, journal editors, or media reporters) like to have their beliefs (e.g., about gender differences) confirmed—a phenomenon known as *confirmation bias*.[6] Therefore, research articles that claim to find a biological cause or source for gender differences tend to garner lots of attention, especially with the lay media.

While there is certainly plenty of sloppy science carried out with regards to human genders and sexualities, it must be stressed that not all biologists or scientists promote gender determinism. Indeed, it is often biologists and other scientists who have challenged gender determinist research for its lack of scientific rigor.[7] In addition, over the last two decades, there has been a lot of amazing research examining sexual diversity, and biological variation more generally, much of which either directly or indirectly challenges gender determinist accounts (some of this work is discussed in the last section of this chapter). Unfortunately, much of this research does not make it into biology textbooks or garner media attention, most likely because it complicates or outright contradicts gender determinist and other deeply held beliefs that predominate in our society.

While many biologists and other scientists challenge gender determinism by critiquing the science (or lack thereof) behind it, this has not been the main strategy taken by feminists and queer academics and activists. Rather, the overwhelming sentiment within these latter circles has been to challenge gender determinism by promoting gender artifactualism as an alternative. Feminist and queer researchers generally set out to show how gender and sexuality are socially constructed, merely the product of socialization and social norms. They discuss how categories and ideologies regarding gender and sexuality vary significantly between cultures and throughout history. They use transgender and intersex people as examples to prove that our culture's binary view of gender is neither natural nor accurate.[8] They stress that gender and sexuality are not something natural that stem from our biology, but rather they are something that we actively "do" or "perform."

In other words, just as gender determinists dismiss or ignore the possibility that social forces shape our genders and sexualities, gender artifactualists reciprocally ignore or dismiss any possible role for biology. In fact, gender artifactualists tend to portray biology, and science more generally, in a monolithic way, for instance, by insisting that it is an inherently patriarchal institution that seems to only exist in order to subjugate women and to pathologize queer people. This demonization of science, and of biology in particular, creates an atmosphere within gender artifactualist circles where anyone who suggests that biology might play *some* role in influencing our genders or sexualities will likely be accused of being an "essentialist" (I should know, as this has happened to me quite a number of times). Such stubborn responses ultimately lead to a philosophical battle between the gender determinists (who dismiss social influence) and the gender artifactualists (who dismiss biology). And of course, this battle has a very snazzy nickname: the "nature-versus-nurture debate."

Now, I understand why many feminists and queer activists are drawn to gender artifactualism. Gender determinists have mischaracterized biology as "programming" us and "predetermining" our behaviors, and this misconception has often been used to justify the marginalization of women, and of gender and sexual minorities. In contrast, the idea that gender is a simple matter of socialization, or that it is all a performance, seems to allow us to intervene, to overturn this regime, and to replace oppressive genders and sexualities with more liberated ways of being. In other words, gender artifactualism appears to be a force of good to counter the pure evil that is gender determinism. However, I believe that this good-versus-evil narrative is highly dubious. For one thing, it is possible to challenge sexism and the policing of genders and sexualities from a gender determinist perspective. An example of this is the idea that LGBTQIA+ people are simply "born that way," and therefore, we deserve the same rights and respect as heterosexual and cisgender folks. While such arguments tend to make gender artifactualists cringe, it is hard to dispute the fact that mainstream acceptance of this idea has helped make it far easier to move through the world as an openly queer person than it was twenty or thirty years ago.

But more to the point, as I demonstrated in the last chapter, gender artifactualism can also be used to promote sexist beliefs, and to police other people's genders and sexualities (e.g., via claims that certain gender and sexual behaviors "reinforce the gender system" whereas others do not). Many cis feminists, and cis gays and lesbians, seem to feel empowered and welcome in gender artifactualist circles, but as someone who faces the reinforcing trope for being transsexual, bisexual, and feminine, I can tell you that I often feel just as marginalized in gender artifactualist circles as I do in gender determinist ones.

The truth of the matter is that gender artifactualism can be used to promote sexist beliefs just as readily as gender determinism can. For much of the twentieth century, Sigmund Freud's hardline gender artifactualist theories were used to pathologize queer people and to portray girls and women as inferior to their male counterparts. Similarly, contemporary feminists and queer activists are outraged by stories of intersex children being subjected to nonconsensual genital surgeries, or gender–non-conforming children being subjected to rigid behavior modification regimes, yet the justification for these procedures is founded in the gender artifactualist theories of psychologists like John Money and Kenneth Zucker, respectively.[9] Indeed, people who promote sexist beliefs often use a strange mix of gender artifactualism and determinism to make their case. One example of this can be found among religious fundamentalists who claim that we are all naturally heterosexual (after all, "God made Adam and Eve, not Adam and Steve"), yet who also hold the seemingly contradictory view that their children can be easily swayed into adopting a "gay lifestyle" as the result of having a gay teacher, or legalizing same-sex marriage.

As feminists and queer activists, we should not waste our time promoting gender artifactualism. Instead, our top priority should be challenging all forms of sexism. Period. And we should recognize both gender artifactualism and determinism for what they really are, namely, concepts that are highly susceptible to being exploited by people with sexist agendas. Why are they so susceptible to such appropriation? I believe that it is because they are both overly simplistic models for how gender and sexuality arise. When gender and sexuality are imagined to arise in a straightforward, overly simplistic manner (i.e., from biology, or from culture), it enables people to falsely conclude that there must be right ways and wrong ways, good ways and bad ways, to be gendered and sexual. Such misconceptions deny sexual and gender diversity, and thus ultimately lead to gender policing and sexism, whether it be in straight mainstream society, or within feminist and queer movements.

I am sure that some readers may object to my assertion that gender artifactualism is overly simplistic. In response, they may point to numerous ways in which certain gender artifactualist theories are, in their eyes, nuanced and comprehensive. To be clear, I am not claiming that gender artifactualism is "not complicated enough," but rather that it's overly simplistic with regards to its exclusive reliance on social explanations, and its inability to explain how exceptional genders and sexualities arise. In the next section, I will show exactly what I mean by this.

HOMOGENIZING VERSUS HOLISTIC MODELS

As they are most commonly practiced, both gender artifactualism and determinism are *homogenizing* models, in that they attempt to explain why the majority of people tend to gravitate toward typical genders and sexualities: Gender determinists claim that we are all biologically programmed to be heterosexual and cisgender, whereas gender artifactualists claim that we live under a hegemonic gender system that socializes and coerces us into becoming heterosexual and cisgender. However, the homogenizing nature of these models fails to account for the vast diversity in genders and sexualities that actually exist. After all, if biology naturally determines that everyone should be heterosexual masculine men and feminine women, or if socialization artificially brainwashes all of us into becoming heterosexual masculine men and feminine women, then how do you explain the existence of fabulous bisexual femme-tomboy transsexual women such as myself? I can most certainly assure you I was not socialized to become a bisexual femme-tomboy transsexual woman. And as a biologist, I feel confident in saying that there is no such thing as a bisexual–femme-tomboy–transsexual-woman gene that made me this way.

Because gender artifactualism and determinism are homogenizing models, they both have an "exception problem"—i.e., they fail to provide a reasonable explanation for why so many of us gravitate toward various sorts of exceptional genders and sexualities. Indeed, the explanations that determinists and artifactualists most commonly offer are nothing more than handwaving. For example, gender determinists often try to preserve their model by arguing that exceptional genders and sexualities arise as a result of biological errors. However, this cannot be the case, as statistically LGBTQIA+ people occur at a frequency several orders of magnitude higher than one would predict if we simply represented biological "mistakes" of some kind.[10] Furthermore, if LGBTQIA+ folks were simply the result of some "mistake" (e.g., a mutant gene, or hormonal dysfunction), then the matter of finding this supposed cause should be pretty straightforward. Yet, after decades of searching, a number of biological correlations have been identified, but no definitive cause of same-sex attraction or gender non-conformity has been found.[11] Gender artifactualists also struggle to explain how exceptional genders and sexualities come to exist. Psychologists of the Sigmund Freud school of gender artifactualism have long assumed that LGBTQIA+ people are the products of parent-child interactions gone awry, yet many decades of research has failed to provide any reproducible evidence to support this.[12]

In the feminist and queer activist circles that I travel in, there is a strong tendency to try to explain exceptional genders and sexualities in terms of choice. Indeed, this notion of choice is what drives the perversion of "the personal is political," where people claim that they are purposefully choosing to be gender or sexually non-conforming in order to subvert the gender system. In addition to addressing the "exception problem" in a manner that is consistent with gender artifactualist logic, this assertion does have a ring of truth to it: We all consciously choose who we will sexually partner with, what clothes we will wear, what identity labels we will embrace, and so on. Furthermore, the idea that we have actively chosen to behave exceptionally sounds infinitely more empowering than the idea that we are the result of "wrong turns" during biological or childhood development. However, the choice explanation fails to account for many of our formative experiences back when our exceptional genders and sexualities first became apparent. For example, gender non-conforming children often express their gender differences from the earliest of ages, and in an apparently spontaneous manner. Given that these young children are relatively oblivious to gender expectations during that time in their lives, and have little to no knowledge of gender politics or queer identities, it seems disingenuous to assert that they are somehow consciously choosing to be gender non-conforming. Furthermore, many of us have the experience of being initially surprised, and sometimes even disturbed, by our same-sex attractions or cross-gender identities when we first became aware of them.

In fact, many of us go through significant periods of denying, disavowing, or repressing our exceptional genders and sexualities for fear of the potential social stigma we might face. Such experiences are completely at odds with the choice explanation.

In my own case, prior to becoming consciously aware of my desire to be female at the age of eleven, I had a series of experiences over the course of my early childhood (e.g., in my dreams, fantasies, and play, and in my reactions to gender-segregated spaces and to my own body) that in retrospect seem to be manifestations of an unconscious self-understanding that I should be female rather than male.[13] In *Whipping Girl*, I coined the phrase *subconscious sex* to describe this unconscious self-understanding that (for many trans people) precedes any conscious or deliberate grappling with questions of gender identity.[14] Analogously, many people find that their exceptional gender expression or sexual orientation has a similar unconscious component—that is, they experience indications of it before becoming consciously aware of that aspect of themselves. So in other words, when we discuss specific manifestations of gender and sexuality, we often are conflating two things: an unconscious urge or self-understanding that impels us toward a particular gender or sexuality, and the conscious way that we make sense of that urge or self-understanding (e.g., through identity labels, narratives, and meanings). While the latter is heavily influenced by language, culture, and ideology, the former appears to exist somewhat independent of one's culture and socialization.

I can imagine readers who favor gender artifactualism decrying my claim that these unconscious underlying urges might somehow supersede social forces. They would likely point out that we are social beings, and that no aspect of ourselves can ever exist outside of society and culture. Of course, this is true. But it is also true that we are biological beings, and that nothing can exist outside of biology either. And the idea that the unconscious underlying urges or self-understandings that I have described are shaped to a certain degree by non-social (i.e., biological) forces is supported by the fact that many of us gravitate toward exceptional genders and sexualities despite being socialized to the contrary, and despite our own conscious attempts to repress or disavow those tendencies. Furthermore, exceptional gender identities, expressions, and sexual orientations seem to exist across cultures and throughout history, and analogous behaviors have been observed in nonhuman animals—this suggests that they are at least somewhat intrinsic to bodies rather than societies.[15]

Gender artifactualists might still insist that these unconscious urges can somehow be explained entirely by social forces, and that our biology does not contribute one iota to our genders and sexualities. If this were true, then one would expect that if you took a male child and raised them as female from birth, and if they were not aware of having been gender reassigned, then they would most likely grow up to identify as female, to be feminine in gender expression, and to be attracted to men (just as most people who are socialized female do). Unfortunately, this is not a hypothetical scenario—there are quite a number of cases where doctors have gender reassigned genetically male children and instructed their parents to socialize them as girls. The most well-known case is that of David Reimer, who was surgically reassigned to female after his penis was inadvertently destroyed during circumcision.[16] Despite being socialized female, having a body that appeared female, and being unaware of having been born male, David was always very masculine in gender expression, was attracted to girls but not boys, and throughout his childhood experienced difficult-to-articulate feelings that he should be male rather than female. Upon learning his history, he began to outwardly identify and live as a man. His unconscious self-understanding that he should be male (what I would describe as his subconscious sex) bares similarities to the experiences of transsexuals and of some intersex individuals who have been subjected to nonconsensual genital surgeries and raised as female because doctors considered them to have "ambiguous" genitals.

Similar experiences seem to occur in male children born with cloacal exstrophy, a non-intersex medical condition in which an infant's pelvic region has not completely developed and abdominal organs are exposed. Because male children with this condition are often partially or completely lacking penises, they are sometimes surgically reassigned to female and raised as girls, despite being genetically male and having been exposed to male-typical fetal hormone levels. A follow-up study of fourteen of such children revealed that by adolescence or early adulthood, eight of them had declared themselves male, often spontaneously, without any previous knowledge of their sex reassignment.[17] And all fourteen children, including those that did not reject a female identity, were described as "male-typical" with regards to their characteristics and interests. Since their sex reassignments took place almost immediately after birth, these children were never socialized male. It should be noted that most of their parents had previously raised girls, and there is no evidence that the gender-reassigned children were socialized any differently than their sisters. Also, genetically female children who have cloacal exstrophy are also raised female, but they generally do not show any of the aforementioned stereotypically masculine traits.

The fact that genetic males who are reassigned and socialized female from birth tend to be masculine, attracted to women, and outright male-identified demonstrates that biology does play a significant role in shaping our genders and sexualities, despite gender artifactualist claims to the contrary.[18] Granted, the precise role or extent of this biological influence is up for debate, but the one thing that is clear is that this biological influence does not occur in a determinist manner. After all, there are many instances of genetically identical twins in which one child grows up to be gay or trans, and the other does not.[19] And, of course, if being genetically male automatically led to a male identity, masculine gender expression, and exclusive attraction to women, than how did I become a bisexual femme-tomboy transsexual woman? Those of us who are chromosomally XY differ significantly in our gender identities, expressions, sexual orientations, and in many other aspects of our genders and sexualities (as do people of other chromosomal combinations). Even among the heterosexual cisgender majority, there is still a lot of diversity in gender-associated behaviors (i.e., behaviors that people tend to associate with femininity or masculinity), in the physical and personality traits that individuals are attracted to in their partners, in other sexual interests and preferences, and so on. Sure, there may be certain trends with regard to gender and sexuality—some traits may be more typical and others more exceptional. But in the end, like snowflakes or fingerprints, no two people share the exact same gender and sexuality.

This is why I believe that it is so important to embrace a holistic (rather than homogenizing) model of gender and sexuality, one that attempts to accommodate difference rather than focusing narrowly on sameness. The holistic model that I am forwarding here begins with the recognition that while we may be biologically similar to one another in many ways, we are also the products of biological variation—nobody shares our unique genetic and physiological makeup. And while we may share the same culture, or may be subjected to the same social expectations and norms, we are also each uniquely socially situated—nobody shares our specific set of life experiences or environment. Therefore, while our shared biology and culture may create certain trends (e.g., a preponderance of typical genders and sexualities), we should also expect the variation in our biology and life experiences to help generate diversity in our genders and sexualities (just as there is a great deal of diversity in our bodies, personalities, interests, and abilities more generally).

A second tenet of this holistic model is that all human behaviors, including those associated with sex, gender, and sexuality, are complex traits—that is, they arise through an intricate interplay of countless biological, social, and environmental factors. Because there are many different inputs that may influence our sexes, genders, and sexualities, there will always be a wide range of variation in potential outcomes, rather than one or a few discrete outcomes. Here is an example of how this might work: Given the fact that the majority of people are heterosexual, we might predict that certain sex-specific factors (e.g., sex chromosomes or hormones) might influence sexual orientation on some level. But there also might be other biological factors that are not sex-specific that are involved as well. And most, if not all, of these biological factors (whether sex-specific or not) would be expected to exhibit some variation in the population. When you combine all this with numerous potential social inputs—some of which may be homogenizing (e.g., gender/sexual norms) and others diversifying (e.g., an individual's unique environment and experiences)—then we might expect certain sex-specific trends (due to both biology and socialization), but we would also expect there to be a lot of variation within each sex, as well as overlap between the sexes. Indeed, this is precisely what is observed for sexual orientation, as well as for all other gender and sexual behaviors.

A third tenet of this holistic model is that one can never truly peel away the biological from the social or environmental. The most profound example of how these phenomena are inexorably intertwined is brain development. While our brains share a certain underlying architecture—they are made up of neurons (i.e., nerve cells) organized into subregions that specialize in different tasks—they are also extraordinarily plastic.[20] Learning, socialization, and experience all lead to structural changes in our brains—this can include increases or decreases in the strength of neuron signaling, the number and types of connections made between individual neurons, and even in the number of neurons themselves. Numerous studies have shown that exposure to our culture, as well as certain activities and experiences, can lead to visible, anatomical changes in the brain itself.[21] So in other words, as a result of our unique environment, experiences, and biological variation, our brains become quite individualized to a certain degree. And it is through our individualized brains that we experience and respond to the world around us. So the notion that one can point to a specific behavior or preference (e.g., some aspect of gender or sexuality) and claim that it stems entirely from biology, or entirely from socialization, is flat out incorrect.

While our brains are shaped by learning and socialization, they are not infinitely plastic—that is, they are not completely blank slates. Some traits have a strong intrinsic component. One example of this is handedness. Preferences for left- or right-handedness can be observed *in utero*, and seem to precede socialization.[22] A majority of people are right-handed for reasons that remain elusive. (Humans are not the only animal that displays "handedness"; for instance, most parrots are left-footed.) While handedness appears to be innate, it does not occur in an overly simplistic biologically-determinist fashion, as genetically identical twins are often discordant in handedness (e.g., one is left-handed and the other right-handed), and several potential environmental factors appear to influence handedness.[23] Given our right hand–centric culture, many left-handed individuals have been socialized to write and do other tasks with their right hands. Interestingly, being socialized right-handed has been shown to result in visible changes in left-handed individuals' brains, yet despite these changes, these individuals often still retain a preference for using their left hands for many tasks.[24] So socialization does have a significant impact on our brains and behaviors, even if it cannot fully override certain intrinsic inclinations we may have. This handedness example may have some import in thinking about some aspects of gender and sexuality. For instance, we may have some intrinsic inclinations (such as the unconscious components of gender expression, sexual orientation, and subconscious sex that I discussed earlier). But that does not mean that they arise entirely as a result of biology, as the specific ways in which these traits manifest, and how we experience, interpret, and act on these urges, is no doubt going to be shaped by social norms, expectations, and ideology as well.

Other traits might not exhibit such strong intrinsic components, yet that does not mean that they are entirely social or completely abiological. An example of this is our taste in food.[25] Taste is a biological process: We have taste receptors organized on our tongue into taste buds that are capable of discriminating between different tastes. For this reason, most of us would agree that salt tastes salty, sugar tastes sweet, and lemons taste sour. But taste is also cultural: Our palates and preferences for certain foods are shaped to a large degree by the foods that are most common and available to us in our communities, especially during our formative years. There are also cultural meanings that are sometimes associated with food: In our culture a particular food may be considered to be gross, or a delicacy, and that may influence how it tastes to us. Taste can also be influenced by biological variation. For example, scientists have discovered a genetic variant in one taste receptor that causes some people to experience a strong bitter taste from cruciferous vegetables (such as broccoli, cauliflower, and cabbage), while people who do not have this genetic variant do not experience a bitter taste.[26] Furthermore, people can have different numbers or ratios of specific taste receptors than other people, and this may influence how certain foods taste to us. And finally, taste can be influenced by individual experience: Sometimes people do not like the taste of certain foods because they once got very sick just after eating that food. Or perhaps they might especially like a particular food because it evokes fond memories of eating it as a child. All of these factors—culture, individual experience, shared biology, and biological variation—come together in an unfathomably intricate manner to create our highly individualized palates.

Of course, if we wanted to, we could take a homogenizing approach and reduce the unfathomable complexity of taste down to a matter of simple trends, and make sweeping claims such as "most people like the taste of fatty foods." Determinists might then hunt for the "fatty food gene" and make evolutionary arguments about how our ancestors must have been evolutionarily selected for their preference for fatty food, perhaps because it gave them increased sustenance or encouraged them to hunt for high-protein meat. And artifactualists might argue instead that it is clearly the rise of the fast food industry and the globalization of the American-style diet that has socialized us all toward a preference for fatty foods. But as with all nature-versus-nurture style debates, this obsession with explaining the especially common masks a complete inability to explain the exceptional. For instance, why is my very favorite food uni (i.e., sea urchin roe), given that I was not socialized to eat it (I was thirty when I first tried it), and about half of the people that I have introduced it to here in the United States do not like the taste of it at all? Why is it that I used to abhor asparagus and spinach as a child, but now they are two of my favorite vegetables? Why is it that I cannot stand the taste of mustard and pickles? It does not seem to be obviously genetic, as all my relatives enjoy mustard and pickles. And I cannot blame it on socialization, as I grew up in the United States, where it is standard fare for sandwiches to automatically be served with mustard and a pickle on the side.

As with heterogeneity in taste, the full spectrum of gender and sexual variation can only be adequately explained through a holistic (rather than homogenizing) perspective. Because gender and sexuality have many biological, social, and environmental inputs, they are not particularly malleable—in other words, changing one or a couple inputs would not likely result in a huge overall effect. This explains why most of us find that we cannot easily or purposefully change our genders and sexualities at the drop of a hat (despite some people's claims that "gender is just performance" or that one can simply "pray away the gay"). Like our tastes in food, most of us experience our genders and sexualities to be profound, deeply felt, and resistant to change. Sure, sometimes people experience shifts in their gender or sexuality, just as our taste for certain foods may change over time. But when these shifts do occur, they are almost always inexplicable, unexpected, and sometimes even downright unwanted (at least at first). Such shifts might occur as a result of changes in some combination of our physiology, environment, and/or life experiences.

We may also, at certain points in our lives, purposefully try to fit into societal gender norms, or into certain ready-made identities. When I was growing up, I tried to fit into masculine male stereotypes, but I rejected them because they did not resonate with me. And when I was first experimenting with moving through the world as female, I admittedly put on a somewhat more feminine gender presentation than I do nowadays. But once again, I eventually rejected that because it felt like an act, it did not feel true to me. If you were to ask me why I turned out to be a bisexual femme-tomboy transsexual woman, I could not point to any one cause. And I most definitely did not become this way to fit into the gender binary or anybody else's gender norms—lord knows, my identity tends to confuse a lot of people in both the straight and queer worlds. But what I can say—the only real truth as far as I am concerned—is that being a bisexual femme-tomboy transsexual woman feels right to me; it resonates with me at a deep, profound, visceral level that defies words.

So in conclusion, homogenizing views dwell on either the biological or social forces that supposedly strong-arm us all into conforming to certain norms of human behavior. A holistic view instead focuses on the variation that arises due to the fact that human behaviors are complex traits with a vast array of biological, social, and environmental inputs. As individuals, we fall all over the map with regards to our personalities, senses of humor, how we use language, the art and entertainment we appreciate, our abilities, and the interests, hobbies, and recreational activities we pursue. Similarly, certain ways of being gendered or sexual will inexplicably resonate with us more than others, and this may lead us to gravitate toward certain gender or sexual identities and expressions rather than others. Sometimes, ways of being that resonate with us fit well within societal norms, while other times they may defy such norms.

While societal norms, expectations, and ideals may certainly influence us, they do not wholly determine us.

A HOLISTIC MODEL OF GENDER AND SEXUALITY IS NEITHER REDUCTIONIST, NOR DETERMINIST, NOR ESSENTIALIST, NOR PATHOLOGIZING, NOR DOES IT "REINFORCE" SEXISM IN ANY WAY

So far in this chapter, I have demonstrated that gender artifactualism fails to adequately explain many facets of human gender and sexuality. Furthermore, this ideology is often cited as justification for sexist double standards (whether by psychologists like Freud, Money, and Zucker, or by those who promote the perversion of "the personal is political"). For these reasons, I believe that we should abandon gender artifactualism altogether, and instead embrace a holistic model of gender and sexuality. The holistic model that I have outlined here is capable of accounting for the entirety of gender and sexual variation (both in humans and other animals) and explaining why some facets of gender and sexuality are irrepressible, not freely chosen nor readily changed. Furthermore, this model is consistent with a broad range of research showing 1) that almost all human traits are complex traits; 2) that gender and sexuality are influenced by biology, albeit not in a simple or straightforward manner; and 3) that social and environmental factors also help shape gender and sexuality.

Having spent the last decade in feminist and queer circles (where people often conflate biology with gender determinism), I know that many people will be skeptical of the holistic model that I am forwarding solely because it invokes biology. And based on my past experience forwarding a similar (albeit more rudimentary) model in *Whipping Girl*, I know that some will make the same accusations of my model that they typically make regarding gender determinism—claiming that it is reductionist, determinist, or essentialist, that it naturalizes heter-onormative gender and sexual roles, pathologizes gender and sexual minorities, and so on. While somewhat different in form, these claims all imply that biological perspectives invariably "reinforce" sexism in one way or another. While this laundry list of criticisms may be appli-cable to many gender determinist theories, they are misplaced when it comes to the holistic view I have forwarded here. So in this last section, I will preemptively respond to some of the criticisms that I expect this model will encounter.

A word of warning: To fully explain why my holistic model is not determinist, nor essentialist, and so on, I will need to discuss a few con-cepts in biology that fall outside of the "Biology 101" realm. Since most readers do not have advance training in biology, I will introduce these concepts in plain language, and may oversimplify them a bit for the sake of clarity. Often, I will mention the biological jargon term (in italics) associated with these concepts, so that interested readers can learn more about them elsewhere. Some folks may find some of the arguments in this last section to be esoteric or overly technical—if this is the case for you, feel free to skip ahead to the next chapter, as understanding these concepts is certainly not a prerequisite for understanding and appreciat-ing the rest of the book.

A common critique of the field of biology is that it is reduction-ist—i.e., it focuses on studying small, isolated parts of a system in order to extrapolate how the system as a whole operates. It is true that, for much of the late twentieth century, biology had been in an especially reductionist phase, as researchers focused on identifying and under-standing the functions of specific molecules, genes, proteins, hormones, and neurons. This approach has sometimes led researchers to view these individual components as "master switches" that simply turn certain developmental pathways "on" or "off" in a deterministic manner. How-ever, recent technological advances over the last couple of decades have allowed biologists to focus more on how biological systems function as a whole (an approach that is sometimes called *systems biology*).[27] This work has revealed that biological systems are far more plastic, dynamic, and shaped by environmental influences than previously thought. It has also shown that, rather than functioning like master switches, individual biological components (e.g., specific genes, proteins, hormones, neurons) function through complex interactions with countless other components and therefore act in a more contextual manner, rather than a deterministic one (discussed more below).

I suppose that some critics might argue that, despite the rise of systems biology, biologists still remain reductionist because they tend to search for biological influences, while ignoring social ones. This is a fair criticism, but it is one that can also be made of gender artifactualists who focus solely on social or psychological influences, while ignoring biological ones. In any case, the model that I am forwarding acknowledges that both social and biological forces shape our genders and sexualities, and therefore it avoids the reductionist trappings on both sides of the nature-versus-nurture debate.

To address more general accusations that this holistic view is determinist, we must first lay out what determinism actually entails. As I alluded to earlier, a determinist view of biology generally treats biological factors (e.g., specific genes or hormones) as though they are on/off switches: If a particular biological factor is present, then it will automatically lead to certain predetermined outcomes. Examples include the claim that having two X chromosomes makes a person female, or that the presence of testosterone during a particular stage of fetal brain development will make a child masculine in gender expression. There are several assumptions built into these biological determinist views. The first is that outcomes (e.g., female or male, feminine or masculine) are discrete, rather than display variation within the population. The second is that outcomes are reproducible—that is, a specific trait or behavior will be reliably produced whenever that biological factor is present. The third assumption is that other variables, whether biological, social, or environmental in origin, will not affect the outcome. Finally, this biological determinist view presumes that if the expected outcome does not occur, that must mean that something has interfered with, or disrupted, what is otherwise a normal and natural biological process.

While textbooks, pop-science articles, and news reports often portray biology in this straightforward deterministic way, this is not how biology actually works. Genes and hormones do not act all by themselves, and therefore, do not function like on/off switches. The human genome has roughly 20,000-25,000 genes, and the products of thousands of these genes may be expressed and functioning within any given cell at the same time.[28] And there are numerous different hormones and other chemicals that are produced and modified and whose signals are interpreted by various other gene products. So in other words, the function of any given gene or hormone is dependent on the functions of, and interactions between, countless other different factors. In genetics, the term *epistasis* is often used to describe how different gene products can interact with, and modify the function of, one another.[29] This plethora of different interactions is one of the reasons why virtually all human traits are complex traits, which are dependent upon numerous factors, and therefore always result in a variety of possible outcomes.

Because genes and other biological factors act within intricate networks (rather than as isolated agents), their function is probabilistic rather than deterministic. In other words, any given biological factor may push the system in a particular direction, or predispose one toward a particular outcome, but they do not single-handedly determine that outcome.[30] The probability that a specific biological factor might influence a particular trait is also highly dependent on biological variation.[31] For instance, many genes have multiple variants—that is, slightly different versions of the same gene. These variants may function in a slightly differently way, or one may be more or less active than the other. Humans also display a significant amount of physiological variation—that is, differences in the organs, cells, and chemicals within our bodies. Because we are genetically and physiologically unique, any individual biological factor (e.g., a specific hormone, or gene variant) may have a somewhat different effect from person to person—in fact, in some cases, it has been shown that a single gene variant can have completely opposite effects in two genetically different individuals.[32] Once again, this reality is incompatible with biological determinism.

There are other phenomena that may alter the effect that any specific biological factor has within a given individual. First, there is *noise*— that is, a certain element of randomness or chance that is always at play during molecular interactions.[33] This noise creates differences between otherwise similar cells or organisms, and thus contributes to overall variation. Second, biological systems always exist within environments that may have an impact on them. For instance, we may be exposed to certain chemicals, or food sources, or conditions, or stresses, and so on, and these may impact us physiologically. As I described earlier, our environment (including socialization and culture) plays a huge role in shaping our brains and behaviors. Furthermore, revived interest in a field within biology called *epigenetics* has revealed how environmental or experiential factors can permanently alter gene expression and function within an individual.[34] As a result of all these different environmental effects, many traits display *phenotypic plasticity*—that is, genetically identical individuals will show a range of *phenotypes* (i.e., traits or outcomes) in response to different environments.[35] In many species, sex-related traits display phenotypic plasticity, and such plasticity likely plays a beneficial role in allowing that species to prosper in a variety of different environments.[36]

So to sum up, biological factors do not act deterministically, but rather they contribute to a wide range of outcomes depending upon the genetic, physiological, and environmental background of an individual.

Furthermore, this variation and plasticity means that all traits (including those related to sex, gender, and sexuality) show a range of outcomes rather than discrete outcomes. From this perspective, specific traits or behaviors are neither inherently bad nor good, but rather they are simply different. Of course, some outcomes may be more common than others. Geneticists often describe typical traits as "wild type" (i.e., the type that is most often found in the wild) and exceptional traits as "variant." It is understood among geneticists that variant traits may be beneficial, or more common in certain populations, and/or may become more prevalent over time. So, like my use of the words "typical" and "exceptional" with regards to genders and sexualities, the distinction between "wild type" and "variant" is meant to be descriptive (i.e., simply denoting an observed difference), rather than categorical (i.e., assuming that wild type and variant traits represent discrete outcomes rather than possibilities along a continuum) or judgmental (i.e., assuming that wild type traits are inherently better than variant ones).

In addition to not being deterministic, biology is also not essentialist. Essentialism is the assumption that objects within a particular category—especially for those categories that are assumed to be "natural" (e.g., dogs, cats, trees, humans)—must share some kind of underlying essence with one another. For example, all dogs must share some underlying "dog-ness" that makes them similar to each other and distinct from all other animals. Children especially rely on essentialism in order to make sense of categories, and often essentialist beliefs remain with us well into adulthood.[37] One can see essentialism rear its head when people presume that there must be essential differences between women and men, between homosexuals and heterosexuals, and between different races or ethnic groups.

It has been my experience that, within feminist and queer circles, people often presume that biology (as a field) is inherently essentialist. This always strikes me as bizarre—if anything, biology is anti-essentialist. After all, the central organizing principle in the field of biology is evolution, which states 1) that all animals share a common ancestor; 2) that all individuals within a given population will genetically vary from one another; and 3) that this variation may ultimately give rise to novel traits, and even entirely new species. In biology, there is no such thing as "dog-ness," as dogs can interbreed with wolves, and both those species share common ancestors with coyotes, foxes, and other animals (including humans if you go far enough back!). Furthermore, essentialist presumptions about sex, gender, and sexuality are not supported by biology—in fact, it has become increasing clear over the last few decades that sex-related traits are far less evolutionarily *conserved* or *constrained* than other important traits.[38] To put this another way, sex-related traits are especially plastic, malleable, and susceptible to change over time. This plasticity may account for some of the sexual and gender diversity we see in human beings.

Another anti-essentialist property of biology is *degeneracy*. In biology, the word "degenerate" means that there are multiple different routes that a molecular pathway, or a cell, or an organism, can take in order to achieve the same end result or trait. Most biological processes display some level of degeneracy—this is especially true for the brain, where an almost infinite variety of nerve cell connections and signaling patterns may give rise to the same resulting behavior.[39] With regards to gender and sexuality, this means that you and I might both be feminine, or bisexual, or transsexual, and yet *not* share any single underlying factor that makes us that way, as we arrived there via different independent paths.

Understanding degeneracy may help clear up one of the most common misinterpretations of the rudimentary holistic model I forwarded in *Whipping Girl*. Specifically, when I introduced the concept of "intrinsic inclinations" (i.e., subconscious sex, as well as unconscious components of gender expression and sexual orientation), some people assumed that I was making an essentialist argument, for instance, as though I had claimed that subconscious sex is determined by a specific gene, hormone, or region of the brain. In fact, I was not making that case. As far as I am concerned, subconscious sex is operationally defined (as a persistent self-understanding or desire to be a particular sex) and is not meant to represent a specific and tangible object or essence—the same holds true for unconscious aspects of gender expression or sexual orientation. Granted, I did mention that scientists have found a few tiny regions of the brain that seem to correlate with gender identity and sexual orientation.[40] While I wouldn't be surprised if these regions played *some* role in shaping our genders and sexualities, I believe that it would be foolish to assume that these small clusters of cells are the only regions of the brain contributing to these very complex phenomena. Furthermore, the fact that our brains are highly degenerate—that there are countless different ways to arrive at the same outcome—suggests that an inclination like subconscious sex may be achieved in numerous different ways.

So far I have explained why biology is neither inherently reductionist, nor deterministic, nor essentialist. But there is one more form of anti-biology sentiment that I have encountered in the past. Specifically, some gender artifactualists will argue that, by admitting that biology plays *any* role in shaping human genders and sexualities, I am giving ammunition to gender determinists who appropriate biology in order to promote sexist agendas. And by doing so, I am in effect reinforcing their sexist agendas.

Here is an example of what I mean: In *Whipping Girl*, when I introduced the idea that intrinsic inclinations arise, in part, through biological processes, a few people claimed that I was somehow contributing to the pathologization of gender and sexual minorities. This surprised me, as I explicitly and repeatedly stated that these intrinsic inclinations arise as a result of natural variation, rather than being biological mistakes or defects. However, even upon clarifying this, some still objected on the grounds that the fact that I invoked biology gives credence to those who wish to portray transness or queerness as being the result of faulty genes, hormones, or brains. So in essence, they were arguing that my model is pathologizing, not because it is *actually* pathologizing, but because other people may misuse or misappropriate it to promote pathologization.

Similarly, some people objected to a chapter in *Whipping Girl* in which I discussed some of the changes that I experienced when I hormonally transitioned. Amongst the things that I said were that my muscle-to-fat ratio and my sex drive were both higher when I was hormonally male, then decreased somewhat after I began taking anti-androgens and estrogen. None of this is especially controversial: Doctors often prescribe androgens (e.g., testosterone) to both men and women who wish to increase their sex drives, and athletes often take androgens to increase their muscle mass (as is evident from Major League Baseball's steroid scandal). In that chapter, I went to great lengths to make clear that, while hormones have very real physical effects, these effects may differ somewhat from person to person.[41] I also pointed out that hormones alone cannot account for all of the variation that exists in human muscle mass and sex drives, as there will always be some women who are stronger than certain men, and some men who have lower sex drives than certain women, despite their hormonal makeup. Notwithstanding these qualifications, I came across a few feminists who criticized what I said about hormones, but not because they believed that what I said was incorrect or sexist *per se*. Rather, they argued that my mentioning that androgens had made me physically stronger reinforces the popular sexist claim that "women are inherently weak." And my mentioning that androgens can increase a person's sex drive reinforces sexist beliefs such as "men can't control their sexual impulses" or that "it is unnatural for women to be promiscuous or overly sexual." These arguments were made despite the fact that, in my chapter, I made it very clear that I do not endorse these sexist views. As with the pathologizing claim, my model was being criticized for being sexist, not because it was *actually* sexist, but because other people might misinterpret or misuse what I said in order to forward sexist agendas of their own.

I often refer to such situations as the "biology-is-bad" mindset: people who are sexist often misappropriate biology in order to justify or "naturalize" their sexist beliefs. Because of this, whenever anyone talks about how gender and sexuality might be influenced by biology, feminists often immediately label that person as sexist. However, if that person then goes out of their way to explain why their specific citation of biology is not sexist—or perhaps even challenges sexism—they will nevertheless be accused of "reinforcing" sexism by virtue of the fact that they have brought up the subject of biology, thereby opening the door for *bona fide* sexists to misappropriate biology.

It is clearly problematic to blame a person for the ways in which other people twist or distort their statements. But what I find even more concerning is that this biology-is-bad mindset essentially censors any and all discussions about biology within feminist and queer circles. Indeed, the only discussions that are allowed to exist are those that monolithically portray biological accounts as being reductionist, essentialist, sexist, and so on. This censoring of well-reasoned discussions about biology is institutionalized within academia: While few subjects are more worthy of an interdisciplinary approach than sex, gender, and sexuality, virtually all Gender Studies and Queer Studies programs are embedded within Humanities departments and do not require their students to take advance classes in biology. This has severely undermined feminists' and queer activists' abilities to counter gender determinism's overly simplistic and distorted biological claims. Rather than rebutting gender determinism by arguing that gender is merely a social construct, we should instead be arguing both that gender is influenced by social forces *and that gender determinists misrepresent how biology actually works!* So long as we feminists and queer activists surrender the field of biology to gender determinists, they will be free to misappropriate it toward sexist ends.

Transcending this biology-is-bad mindset offers new directions to challenge sexist claims. For instance, take the aforementioned claim that women on average are less physically strong, and have lower sex drives, than men. The knee-jerk feminist response to such a claim is to pan it for being rooted in biology, and to offer alternative social explanations, such as boys are encouraged to be athletic, and to act on their sexual urges, while girls are not. While I agree that these social explanations certainly contribute to gender differences, such a response seems to deny the very real effects that androgens can have on muscle mass and sex drive. A holistic feminist such as myself would instead emphasize the large amount of variation within, and overlap between, the sexes with regard to physical strength and sex drive—this variation occurs despite socialization and the effects of androgens. But I would further point out that there is absolutely nothing wrong with having a lower sex drive or being less physically strong! The crux of the problem here is that we live in a male-centric world, where being physically strong and having a high sex drive are lauded because they are associated with maleness, whereas being physically weak and having a low sex drive are viewed as inferior because they are associated with femaleness. In other words, sexism does not stem from simply observing that people have different abilities and attributes, but rather it occurs when we project double standards onto those abilities and attributes—when we presume that some traits are superior, more natural, or more normal than others. As feminists, we should challenge these sexist double standards, rather than spending all our effort futilely denying biological influences on gender and sexuality.

HOW DOUBLE STANDARDS WORK

CHAPTER FOURTEEN

G iven that human beings are naturally diverse with regards to our bodies and behaviors, one might expect us to view gender and sexual variation in a relatively neutral fashion—that is, viewing dissimilar traits as being different yet equally valid—much as we generally accept that people vary in their personalities, interests, and hobbies, in their taste in food, humor, art, and entertainment, and so on. Unfortunately, this is not the case. Whether in the straight mainstream culture, or feminist and queer subcultures, most of us tend to project arbitrary meanings and value judgments onto different gendered and sexual bodies and behaviors. Often, this involves classifying specific bodies and behaviors according to some kind of dichotomous scheme—for instance, certain gender and sexual traits are deemed good, while others are bad; some are deemed natural, while others are unnatural; some are deemed normal, while others are abnormal; some supposedly "reinforce the gender system," while others do not. As discussed in the first chapter in this section, we tend to get bogged down in endless debates about whether some specific gender or sexual trait is good or bad, natural or unnatural, etc., without ever examining the underlying distinction that enables us to project these arbitrary meanings and value judgments onto different traits in the first place. Specifically, this fundamental distinction is between marked and unmarked.[1]

When I say that a trait is "marked," I mean that other people actively notice and pay attention to it. To illustrate the unmarked/marked distinction, imagine the following scenario: I am walking down the street in Oakland, California (where I live), wearing a pink shirt and jeans (as I sometimes do). When I have done this in the past, most people who walk by me do not seem to take any particular notice of what I am wearing, presumably because my outfit does not seem noteworthy to them. If, a few minutes after walking past me, you were to ask these people what I was wearing, I doubt that many of them would even recall. In other words, my pink shirt and jeans are unmarked—deemed unworthy of attention. Now, imagine that I am walking down the same city street, but instead of wearing a pink shirt and jeans, I wear a tie-dyed shirt and bell-bottoms. Or a hijab. Or a bridal gown. Or perhaps I am dressed up like Chewbacca. In these latter cases, people probably would take notice of what I am wearing. In other words, all the latter outfits would stand out and garner attention. They are marked.

It is important to emphasize that being marked or unmarked is not something that is inherent in the object itself. Whether an outfit is considered marked or unmarked is specific to both time and place (as the tie-dyed shirt and bell-bottoms might not have looked so out of place in Oakland in the late 1960s/early 1970s, and the hijab would not stand out today in countries where Islam is the majority religion). If I was at a science fiction convention, or a costume party, I probably wouldn't stand out quite so much if I was dressed as Chewbacca. Similarly, my pink shirt and jeans may render me unmarked on a U.S. city street, but if I were to dress like that for a wedding, or a costume party, I would likely stand out like a sore thumb—I would be viewed as not "dressed up" enough. Whether an item of clothing is deemed marked or not also depends on the context of the person who is wearing it. Back when I was perceived as male, I had a pink T-shirt, and when I would wear it, I would definitely garner excessive attention and comments. So while pink shirts are unmarked when worn by women, they are marked when worn by men.

The most crucial thing to understand is that the determination of whether an object or trait is marked or unmarked originates with the person doing the perceiving, and therefore can vary greatly from perceiver to perceiver. In Oakland (as in many urban settings), there are a lot of people who dress unconventionally—for instance, in a punky or artsy fashion. Because they are fairly common here, such people tend not to receive too much attention from other Oaklanders. However, if a tourist from someplace where people dress very conventionally (e.g., a well-off suburb or a small conservative town) were to visit Oakland, they would likely be shocked by such unconventional styles of dress, and they might end up staring at the person as a result. So whether a trait is marked (or not) is most certainly in the eye of the beholder.

WHY DO WE MARK SOME TRAITS AND NOT OTHERS?

Why do we unconsciously mark certain bodies and behaviors while allowing others to remain unmarked? Well, this tendency may stem in part from a number of more general biases in human perception. For example, a large body of research has shown that we perceive people who belong to our *ingroup* (i.e., a group that we are a member of, and identify with) very differently than members of an *outgroup* (i.e., a group to which we do not belong or identify with). Specifically, we tend to favor members of our ingroup (even in laboratory settings where groups are assigned arbitrarily), and we are inclined to perceive outgroup members more negatively, more extremely, and in a more stereotyped manner than we do members of our ingroup.[2] These biases may lead us to mark people who we do not identify with (and thus view as "other"), whereas people who we identify or feel affiliated with may remain relatively unmarked in our eyes.

Another perceptual bias that likely plays some role in creating the unmarked/marked distinction is that we view unexpected traits very differently than their expected counterparts. A trait or event may be considered unexpected if we presume that it is exceptionally rare, that it defies some kind of norm or law that we feel everyone or everything should follow, and/or if it defies a more specific stereotype or assumption that we harbor about a particular type of person. In any case, we tend to pay more attention to, and spend more thought considering, unexpected traits and events than we do expected ones.[3] Furthermore, when a trait or event is unexpected, we are biased toward viewing it more negatively than we would if the same trait or event was expected.[4] Thus, exceptional or unexpected traits tend to be marked relative to typical or expected traits.

Of course, there is more to the unmarked/marked distinction than simply noticing that which is unexpected or exceptional. For example, women make up slightly over fifty percent of the population, and yet we are marked relative to men. This is evident in how people comment on, and critique, women's bodies and behaviors far more than men's, and how things that are deemed "for women" are often given their own separate categories (e.g., chick lit, women's sports, women's reproductive health), whereas things that are "for men" are seen as universal and unmarked. So women are marked, not because we are rare or unusual (as we are in fact slightly more common than men), but because we, as a culture, deem women to be marked.

Here is another example demonstrating that the unmarked/marked distinction is not necessarily related to how common or rare something is. Approximately 0.2 percent of people in the United States are accountants—this is a relatively small number, in roughly the same ballpark as the number of trans people, or the number of women who are sex work-ers.[5] And yet, if the average person was at a friend's party mingling and met someone who mentioned that they were an accountant, that average person would probably not be surprised or shocked. This is because accountants, despite being relatively rare, are not marked in the eyes of society. In contrast, the average person would likely be quite shocked if the party guest mentioned that they were transsexual, or a sex worker. (Once again, this depends upon the perceiver: I have many friends who are transsexual or who are sex workers, so I personally would not be surprised by such information.)

These examples demonstrate that the unmarked/marked distinction is not solely based on how common or rare a trait is, or whether the person in question belongs to our ingroup or outgroup. Rather, in these latter cases, the distinction appears to stem from an implicit social pact. It is as if we, as a society, have all agreed that women are marked relative to men, and that transsexuals and sex workers are extraordinary things to be, whereas accountants (despite being just about as rare) are ordinary. Of course, we did not all gather together as a society to consciously make these determinations. Rather, each of us learns to make such distinctions through the process of socialization. We are taught that certain types of people and ways of being are normal and respectable (and therefore unmarked), while others are deemed abnormal and unrespectable (and therefore marked). From the earliest of ages through adulthood, we internalize these cultural beliefs and learn to employ them in an unconscious manner.

In summary, unmarked/marked distinctions may arise from our own personal biases and expectations, or they may be culturally ordained. In either case, the process of marking a person or trait often occurs on an unconscious level, and therefore takes on an air of common sense: It just seems "natural" for us to focus our attention on people who we view as exceptional or different from us in some significant way. And it feels "natural" to us to comment upon women's bodies more so than men's, or to be shocked when we hear that someone is transsexual or a sex worker, but not when they are an accountant.

THE CONSEQUENCES OF BEING MARKED

We have established that the determination of whether a trait is marked or unmarked is contextual and arises solely from the beliefs and assumptions held by the person perceiving and interpreting the trait, rather than from the trait itself. The next question that we should be asking is: What are the consequences of being marked versus unmarked? For starters, traits that are marked are highly visible and attract attention, whereas unmarked traits are invisible and are generally taken for granted. Because of this visibility and attention, marked traits are deemed *remarkable* (i.e., people feel entitled to comment on them) and *questionable* (i.e., people tend to ask questions about them). So going back to our earlier scenario, when I wear my pink shirt and jeans, people generally do not comment on what I am wearing, nor do they ever ask me why I have chosen that particular outfit. In contrast, if I was dressed as Chewbacca, people would surely make a lot of remarks ("Look at that person dressed like Chewbacca!") and barrage me with questions ("Julia, why on earth are you dressed like that?"). These remarks and questions often occur even when one's attire is not quite this outrageous. For instance, on those occasions when I wear a dress, I find that people make way more remarks about how I am dressed than when I wear a pink shirt and jeans—sometimes these are compliments on how I look or what I am wearing, other times it is unwanted attention in the form of sexually harassing remarks from strange men on the street. And often when I wear a dress, I find that people ask questions such as, "What's the special occasion?" or, "Are you going out on a date?"

The fact that marked traits are deemed questionable can play out in a couple of different ways. In the example of me wearing a dress, the questions that people ask me (e.g., wanting to know why I have "dressed up") may seem innocent enough on the surface. But in actuality, such questions have the potential to be invalidating for me, because they imply that I must have some hidden motive for dressing that particular way. In a sense, these questions are an attempt to compel me to explain my supposed motives. This opens up the door for people to judge whether my explanation seems authentic to them. If, for example, my response is, "There is no special occasion. I just felt like getting dressed up today," they might choose not to believe me, or perhaps they may even insist that there must be some ulterior motive that I am hiding (e.g., a secret lover). So in other words, when some aspect of my person is deemed questionable, the insinuation is that I am engaging in some sort of artificial or inauthentic behavior. And if my answers do not satisfy my inquisitors, they may additionally accuse me of being insincere or deceptive. In stark contrast, my pink shirt and jeans are not deemed questionable, and therefore do not require any explanation—in essence, I am considered to be free of motives, ulterior or otherwise—and because of this, I am not susceptible to accusations of being inauthentic or deceptive.

Of course, the word "questionable" can also mean debatable, dubious, and suspect. These more negative meanings are evident in the Chewbacca example, where my dressing that way would elicit more than just a passing curiosity; it would likely be considered by some to be beyond the pale, and downright unacceptable. In such cases, people would not merely require an explanation, but they would also express disapproval of my behavior regardless of any possible explanation I might offer them. (This disapproval is implied in the comment "Julia, why on earth are you dressed like that?"). So in other words, because marked traits are deemed questionable, they are often viewed as being inherently illegitimate and invalid (whereas unmarked traits are always viewed as legitimate and valid).

This notion of illegitimacy can be seen in other assumptions that plague marked traits. For example, unmarked traits are often considered to be normal, whereas marked traits are deemed abnormal. While the word "normal" can mean common or typical (something that is often true of unmarked traits), it can also mean "healthy," or "living up to standards." These latter meanings are evident in normal's antonym "abnormal," which implies that the trait in question is not merely rare or exceptional, but also unhealthy and corrupt.

Along similar lines, unmarked traits are considered to be natural, whereas marked traits are often deemed unnatural. So while it could be argued that all items of clothing and accessories are unnatural (in the sense that they are a human invention)[6], we nevertheless get the sense that my pink shirt and jeans are somehow more natural than a Chewbacca outfit, or even a dress, jewelry, and heels. There is synergy between the idea that marked traits are artificial and the tendency for people to depict those who express marked traits as being inauthentic and deceptive. Indeed, marked individuals are often portrayed as "fakes," both because their marked trait is viewed as artificial, and because their motives are deemed questionable.[7]

Finally, unmarked traits are often viewed as mundane, whereas marked traits are viewed as exotic. This can cut two different ways. The word mundane is often used as a synonym for boring, and exotic as a synonym for exciting. Most people would probably consider the word "exciting" to have better connotations than "boring," and this might lead them to think that being marked is a good thing. However, the word mundane also means "relating to matters of this world," which implies that exotic traits are "other-worldly" or "alien." In a world where we face constant pressure to conform to various social norms, being depicted as other-worldly or alien can be very disenfranchising. Furthermore, people tend to mystify things that they view as exotic or alien—that is, they depict them as mysterious, uncertain, and obscure. When a person is mystified by others, it is a dehumanizing act, one that discourages others from identifying with, or relating to, that person. When we do not relate to, or empathize with, a person, we will often fail to extend to them the most basic social courtesies and human rights—we may refuse to view them as autonomous beings capable of making their own life choices, we may refuse to acknowledge their bodily autonomy or privacy, and we may refuse to treat them with the politeness, respect, or decency that we accord to other people. As a result of all this, people who are viewed as exotic are often objectified and viewed as mere specimens that somehow exist solely for the benefit of those who are unmarked.

These two potential takes on mundane versus exotic can be seen in the following example. Let's say that you are at a friend's party and you get into a conversation with someone. And you ask them what they do for a living, expecting them to answer that they are a teacher, or an accountant, or a waiter, or whatever else might be considered unmarked in your particular segment of the world. But instead, much to your surprise, they tell you that they are a U.S. senator, or a Hollywood film producer. Or perhaps they say that they are a sex worker, or a trans-sexual activist. All four of these occupations might seem exotic to you, but in different ways: The senator and film producer might seem exotic (read: exciting) compared to your mundane (read: boring) life, whereas the sex worker and transsexual activist might seem exotic (read: alien) compared to your mundane (read: relating to matters of this world) life. As a result, the values that you assign to these people might vary greatly. For instance, you might be envious of the senator and film producer, whereas you might look down upon the sex worker and transsexual activist. In other words, some marked traits may be *glorified* (e.g., senators and film producers), whereas others are *stigmatized* (e.g., sex workers and transsexual activists).

This example also illustrates another important point: people may project a variety of different meanings and value judgments onto those whom they mark. For example, if I were walking down the street mid-day, and suddenly a drag queen were to walk by me, I would probably be surprised, but in a pleasant way, whereas someone who is homophobic or transphobic might be disturbed. Some passersby might shout, "You're fabulous," at the drag queen, while another might shout, "You're a faggot." And still others may be taken aback by the presence of the drag queen but feel relatively indifferent and not project any meanings or value judgments onto them.

While people's reactions may vary greatly, what remains consistent is that different meanings and value judgments tend to "stick" more to marked traits than to those that are unmarked. So returning to my original example, if I were walking down the street wearing my pink shirt and jeans, and some stranger suddenly began berating me by saying, "Oh my God, I can't believe you're wearing a pink shirt and jeans! How despicable," most people would be rather confused by that outburst, precisely because they would likely consider my particular clothing choice to be unmarked, and therefore unremarkable and unquestionable. In fact, they would be far more likely to view the person berating me as acting bizarre and out of order, and me as an innocent victim of an irrational tirade. However, if that person instead called out a drag queen on how they are dressed, people would not be so surprised. After all, regardless of how we personally feel about drag queens (positively, negatively, or indifferently), most of us view drag queens as marked—as inherently remarkable and questionable—and therefore, we will not be shocked if they garner attention, comments, and controversy. Even those people who appreciate drag queens may harbor feelings such as, "Well, if you dress that way in public, you pretty much have it coming to you."

Essentially, people who are marked are generally viewed as "having something" that unmarked people do not have. That "something" can therefore be subjected to remarks, questions, debate, praise or critique; the unmarked person escapes such critical analysis by virtue of the fact that they are not seen as having that "something."

DOUBLE STANDARDS AND THE UNMARKED/ MARKED DISTINCTION

Understanding the unmarked/marked distinction is vital, as it appears to underlie all forms of sexism, as well as marginalization more generally. This is not to say that being marked is the same thing as, or necessarily leads to, being marginalized—as I alluded to in previous examples, we are just as capable of being indifferent to, or even impressed by, someone who is deemed marked as we are of invalidating them. But what is true is that the act of marking automatically creates a double standard, where certain traits are viewed and treated differently than others. This act of marking essentially divides the world up into two classes: those who have the trait in question (for whom meanings and value judgments will tend to "stick"), and those who do not (and who are therefore beyond reproach). These double standards provide the underlying architecture that enables sexism and marginalization.

For example, in Chapter 12 ("The Perversion of 'The Personal Is Political'"), I discussed how cissexism and heterosexism work by portraying people who are trans or who engage in same-sex relationships, respectively, as being inherently remarkable, questionable, artificial, driven by ulterior motives, and deceptive—all of these assumptions stem directly from the fact that these ways of being are marked, whereas cissexuals and heterosexuals remain unmarked. In Chapter 9 ("Bisexuality and Binaries Revisited") and Chapter 6 ("Reclaiming Femininity"), I showed how bisexuality and femininity are similarly portrayed as being remarkable, questionable, artificial, driven by ulterior motives, and deceptive—once again, this stems from the fact that these traits are marked, whereas monosexuality and masculinity remain unmarked. Indeed, if we were to exhaustively consider every form of marginalization known to exist (a project that exceeds the scope of this chapter), I am confident that we would find some of these telltale signs of the unmarked/marked distinction underlying each and every one of them.

To be clear, I am not suggesting that all forms of sexism and marginalization are identical. Each specific form of marginalization differs in its history, the extent to which it is institutionalized, and in the specific set of expectations, assumptions, and stereotypes that it projects onto its respective marginalized group. But they all rely on double standards that stem from the unmarked/marked distinction. This is why the marginalized group (those who are marked) always garners comments and criticism, while those at the center (who remain unmarked) never come under question. It explains why those of us who are part of the unmarked center tend not to identify as white, or able-bodied, or normatively sized, or heterosexual, or cisgender, or monosexual, and so on, as these aspects of ourselves are typically deemed unremarkable, and therefore become invisible to us.[8] This is why activists who wish to challenge a particular form of marginalization often begin by naming the previously unnamed center (e.g., white, able-bodied, normatively sized, heterosexual, cisgender, monosexual) and outlining the many privileges associated with that unmarked status (many of which are directly related to *not* being seen as remarkable, questionable, abnormal, unnatural, deceptive, exotic, suspect, etc.).

Because the unmarked/marked distinction is the underlying mechanism that enables all forms of sexism and marginalization, those of us who are committed to feminism, queer activism, and social justice more generally must make understanding and raising awareness about this distinction one of our top priorities. This involves learning to recognize whenever a particular trait is garnering undue attention and being subjected to the many hallmarks of being marked (i.e., being deemed to be remarkable, questionable, abnormal, unnatural, deceptive, exotic, and suspect). It also requires us to uncover the unmarked trait that is being taken for granted, and thus escaping critique, in any given situation. But in addition to all this, we must also familiarize ourselves with the numerous double binds that marked individuals often face. Basically, a double bind is a no-win situation, one in which there are two potential responses or courses of action, both of which come with negative consequences. In the rest of this chapter, I will discuss many of these double binds (especially those that are associated with stigmatized traits) and demonstrate how they arise directly from the unmarked/marked distinction.

THE INVISIBLE/VISIBLE DOUBLE BIND

Some traits—particularly those associated with our physical bodies—are almost always visible to other people. Common examples might include our sex, race, size, and age. But other traits, especially those related to our desires and behaviors, may not be readily visible in some or all situations. If we have a marked trait, it might seem that we would be better off if that trait was relatively invisible, as this would allow us to move through the world without facing all the attention, remarks, and potential stigmatization that are associated with the trait. But being invisible does come at a cost. For starters, if our marked trait is not visible, then people will tend to automatically presume that we are a member of the unmarked group. This phenomenon could be called the *unmarked assumption*, as a nod to "heterosexual assumption," "cissexual assumption," and "monosexual assumption," which I discussed in previous chapters. This unmarked assumption puts us in the awkward position of either going along with this false assumption, or else disavowing the assumption by "coming out" to the person, or perhaps even every person, who makes this assumption. Both of these courses of action are fraught (as discussed in more detail below; see The Pass/Reveal Double Bind). A second negative consequence of being invisible is that other people who share our marked trait may not recognize us as being "one of them." The drawbacks of being misperceived as an unmarked outsider are especially acute in support, social, and activist spaces centered on, or exclusive to, members of that marked group. Such misperceptions may lead others to question our identity or authenticity as a group member—in other words, we may become marked among our own kind.

THE CREDIT/DETRIMENT DOUBLE BIND

People commonly assume that if anything bad happens to someone who has a marked trait, that the marked trait must somehow be an underlying factor or cause of that unfortunate circumstance. So in my case, if I were to fail out of school, or have an affair, or get a divorce, or if I developed an addiction, or became incarcerated, or were to murder someone, or what have you, I can assure you that there will be people out there who will assume that the event was somehow related to me being transsexual, or bisexual, or due to some other marked trait that I possess. I can also assure you that if any of those things were to happen to me, nobody would claim that it must be because I am white, or middle-class, or able-bodied, or any other unmarked trait that I might possess.

Why does this happen? In Erving Goffman's classic book *Stigma: Notes on the Management of Spoiled Identity*, he makes the case that stigmatized traits (which he refers to as "stigmas") effectively taint a person's moral character in the eyes of others, although he never explicitly explains why this is.[9] I would argue that, when we are marked, people view us (and the specific marked trait we possess) as inherently suspect. Therefore, it is not surprising that people would literally *suspect* that the marked trait caused the unfortunate situation. In any case, this tendency to blame all of one's failings on the marked trait puts a lot of pressure on marked individuals. After all, if we do make a mistake or fail in any way, it will reflect poorly on other people who share the same marked trait. In effect, we will be viewed as a "detriment" to our kind.

If, however, we are perfect, and lead happy and successful lives untainted by controversy or complications, people will not assume that it must be because of our marked trait(s). Instead, they will likely view our success as occurring despite our marked trait(s), and they may even claim that we are a "credit" to our kind. In effect, we will be viewed as the proverbial "exception that proves the rule" (the rule, of course, being that people who have that marked trait are inherently suspect).[10]

THE DISAVOW/IDENTIFY DOUBLE BIND

When marked traits are highly stigmatized, some people who possess the trait may feel strong societal pressure to disavow it—that is, we may distance ourselves from, or deny having, the trait in question. People who choose this route often refuse to identify or associate with other people who share the same trait. A classic recurring example of this is the gay person who refuses to admit that they are gay, and who may even engage in blatant homophobic behavior as a way of disassociating themselves from other gay folks. As with being invisible more generally, this approach may allow the person to escape the attention and stigmatization associated with that marked trait. But it is very psychologically taxing, as it generally involves repressing, and even directing self-hatred toward, that aspect of one's being. Furthermore, this sort of disavowing typically perpetuates the negative societal meanings and stigma that are routinely projected onto that trait.

A more self-empowering strategy is to identify with the marked trait—that is, to admit to ourselves (if not to others) that we possess that trait. This act of self-acceptance often involves rejecting the negative societal meanings associated with the marked trait, and instead viewing it as a neutral or good trait that is unfairly stigmatized by others. Those of us who identify with our marked trait are likely to seek out others who share the same trait for mutual support—after all, no one else truly knows what it is like to live with the specific stereotypes and stigma associated with that trait, and thus we may learn from one another's experiences. If the identity group in question becomes large enough, we may develop our own culture, language, narratives, and ideology to counter the negative depictions of our members in larger society. In other words, the identity approach has the benefit of strength in numbers, and may lead to activism that challenges the societal stigmatization of the marked trait.

While the benefits of the identity approach are obvious, there remain several drawbacks (many of which are evident in tales of exclusion offered in the first section of this book). Specifically, the culture, language, narratives, and ideology that are created by identity groups often display their own double standards and may favor some people who have the marked trait over others. In other words, some of us who have the marked trait may feel excluded by "our own kind" (i.e., the identity group), and this may lead us to disavow that identity label entirely. Another critique of the identity approach is that it merely produces a "reverse discourse" that reinforces the distinction between the marked and unmarked groups.[11] So, for example, embracing the label "gay," creating gay culture, and fighting for civil rights for gay people may seem to perpetuate the original accusation that gay people are inherently different than heterosexuals. Those who reject the reverse discourse route will often disavow the identity label for fear of reinforcing such a distinction. While it is understandable why people might choose to disavow the identity label for this reason, and/or because they feel excluded from their own identity group, such a move typically does nothing to remedy the marked person's (or group's) situation. After all, I could refuse to identify as transsexual or bisexual, but that will not stop others from marking me as transsexual or bisexual and marginalizing me accordingly. So both the disavowing and identifying approaches seem to have significant drawbacks.

THE ACCOMMODATING/ANGRY DOUBLE BIND

When we are marked, other people feel entitled to pay undue attention to, remark about, and call into question that aspect of our being. Such incidents can range from being slightly annoying to downright invalidating.

When we are constantly being put into question like this, there are two general types of responses we might take. The first is to accommodate these actions. For instance, if people are staring at us, we just put it out of our minds. If people make remarks about us, we do not object. If people ask us questions, we politely answer them. This approach can be highly disempowering, as it places us on the defensive and perpetuates the idea that others are entitled to constantly call our marked trait into question, and that it's our job to accommodate them.

The alternative, of course, is to challenge other people when they mark us. So if they stare at us, we tell them that it's impolite to stare, or stare back at them. If they remark about us, we call them out on their comments. If they ask us questions, we remind them of how invasive it is to be interrogated like that. On the positive side, these are proactive approaches that challenge the double standard. But the problem is, the fact that we've been deemed marked means that they feel entitled to call us into question. So in their minds, it is we who are acting inappropriately, and they will likely interpret our righteous responses as an attack on them. Often they will interpret us as acting "angry," even if we challenge them in a polite manner without ever raising our voice.

THE AFFLICTED/CHOSEN DOUBLE BIND

The fact that marked traits garner questions and require explanations often leads people to want to know how such traits came to be in the first place. When people ask me why I am transsexual or bisexual, I often tell them that there is no clear answer, I just am this way. Those of us who hold a holistic view of gender and sexuality (as I outlined in the previous chapter) may accept the fact that such exceptional traits arise inexplicably, but unfortunately we are in the minority. Most people are not satisfied with the idea that marked traits simply exist—they want an explanation, an origin story. Importantly, origin stories are only ever required when a trait is marked. Returning to an earlier example, if someone at a party mentioned that they were an accountant, it is unlikely that people will feverishly want to know how they came to be an accountant. But if a person mentions that they happen to be a sex worker, or transsexual, people will surely want to know how they got to be that way.

The type of explanations or origin stories that people are looking for tend to fall into either the "chosen" or "not chosen" camps. If we say that we purposefully chose to be a particular way, it may feel personally empowering, as it implies that what we are (in this case, a sex worker or transsexual) is a perfectly valid life choice. However, this does open us up to further rounds of inquiry. For instance, people can critique our morality or mental competency for choosing what they deem to be a dubious life path (see The Dupes/Fakes Double Bind below).

An alternative is to claim that we did not choose to be the way we are. The transsexual might claim that they were simply "born that way," and the sex worker might claim that they were destitute and had no other way to make ends meet. Such explanations may in fact be true (or not), but they are regularly cited because they have the beneficial side effect of alleviating further critique. After all, if I was simply "born" transsexual, then it is hard for anyone to deride that aspect of myself as immoral or mentally unsound, as it was not my choice to begin with. In many cases, such explanations are likely to garner sympathy rather than critique. But therein lies the rub: If people feel pity for me because I was born or forced into a marked trait, then the implication is that the marked trait itself is inherently bad.

I refer to this as the afflicted/chosen double bind. The word "afflicted," of course, implies that the non-chosen trait is inherently negative, something that no one would ever choose of their own accord. As I mentioned earlier, some marked traits are seen as inherently good—for instance, being a multi-millionaire. In that case, the non-chosen path (e.g., being born into money) would likely be viewed as a "blessing" rather than an "affliction."

Obviously, not all marked traits are subjected to the afflicted/chosen double bind. For example, it would be hard to make the case that I was "afflicted" with wearing a Chewbacca outfit, as it is assumed that the clothing and accessories we put on are a conscious decision—hence, it must be a choice. Reciprocally, some marked traits are automatically viewed as not being chosen—for instance, being a woman (transsexuals aside), or intersex, or disabled, or a person of color. In such cases, it is not uncommon for others to feel pity toward us (i.e., we are viewed as afflicted), but not hold us personally responsible for being the way that we are.

THE DUPES/FAKES DOUBLE BIND

In certain cases when our marked trait is viewed by others as inherently suspect and artificial, and as "chosen" rather than an "affliction," an immediate follow-up question tends to arise: Why on earth would we make that particular choice? Those who pose this question often reconcile it by assuming that we must not have made that choice freely, but instead were purposefully misguided or coerced by others into making that decision. They may describe us as being driven by "false consciousness" rather than by legitimate, genuine desires. In other words, because they believe that we have been led down a wayward path, they conceptualize us as "dupes." If, however, we have not been duped into choosing this supposedly artificial fate, then the only other obvious possibility is that we must have consciously decided to engage in the unnatural trait in question of our own accord. In other words, they assume that we have purposefully decided to be "fakes."

Perhaps the most common manifestation of the dupes/fakes double bind in our culture can be found in religious fundamentalist reactions to same-sex relationships, where those who engage in such relationships are described as having been either "duped by the homosexual agenda" (read: dupes) or as having "chosen an alternative lifestyle" (read: fakes). I also discussed the dupes/fakes double bind at great length in *Whipping*

Girl, specifically with regard to cis feminist interpretations of people who are feminine (who are seen as either being duped by the patriarchy into dressing and acting like subservient sexual objects, or as purposefully donning artificial mannerisms and styles of dress in order to assimilate into that patriarchal system) or transsexual (who are seen as either being duped by a patriarchal medical system into changing our sex, or as purposefully choosing to be "fake" women and men).[12]

THE ASHAMED/SHAMELESS DOUBLE BIND

All the undue attention that comes with being marked can understandably make a person self-conscious about the trait in question. There are two general types of responses to this hyper self-awareness. The first is for the person to feel ashamed about their marked trait—this is especially likely if the trait is viewed negatively and associated with stigma. Often, when people feel ashamed of their marked trait, they may attempt to play it down, draw attention away from it, or even hide it. Alternatively, if the person in question does not view their marked trait in a negative way, they will be unashamed of it, and as a result, they will not make any attempt to hide it or play it down. In some cases, individuals may take outright pride in their marked trait, and unabashedly flaunt it in front of others, as can be seen in celebrations of Black Power and Queer Pride, and in the reclaiming of what were once derogatory labels, such as gay, queer, dyke, tranny, crip, and fat, to name a few.

Being unashamed about, or showing pride toward, our own marked traits seems to be a far more healthy response, as internalized shame and hiding oneself can cause a great deal of emotional distress. However, being unashamed does come at a price. For starters, if we wear our marked trait on our sleeve (so to speak), then we will have to deal with all of the attention, questioning, and potential stigma that is associated with that trait. And if we outright flaunt our marked trait, others may take that as evidence that the marked trait really does scream out for attention. In other words, prideful flaunting may inadvertently encourage unmarked individuals to feel justified in their questioning and judging of the trait.

Furthermore, if the marked trait is associated with stigma (such as in the cases of transsexuality or sex work), people will often assume that no one in their right mind would freely admit to such a thing. So when those of us who have the trait are open or even proud about it, people will often view us as being immodest or shameless. The distinction between being unashamed and shameless is crucial: Being unashamed simply means that one does not feel shame about something. Shameless, on the other hand, means "insensible to disgrace."[13] In other words, the word "shameless" suggests that we should feel ashamed, but due to a lack of common sense or modesty, we do not. Those of us who are viewed as shameless are often accused of being impolite, and of lacking the tact to know that we should not air out our "dirty laundry" in front of others. Or we may be mischaracterized as "attention seekers" who are exploiting the supposed tragedy of our lives for personal gain or attention. Furthermore, if something bad happens to us (e.g., if we are bullied, harassed, raped, or ridiculed, or if we receive unwanted attention), people will tend to blame us (rather than the perpetrators) for the incident because after all, "we had it coming to us" (read: because we were shamelessly flaunting our marked traits).

Feminists have long discussed how the ashamed/shameless double bind plays out in the lives of many women. Specifically, in our straight male–centric society, women are highly sexualized. This can be seen in the objectification of women in the media, unwanted sexual remarks and propositions from men, having others freely remark about how attractive (or unattractive) we are, and so on. As a result of all this undue attention, many women understandably become self-conscious about their bodies and play down their sexual desires. The word "modesty" is commonly used as a euphemism for this manifestation of the "ashamed" side of the double bind. Other women may react differently. Some might decide that, despite the unwanted attention they receive, they refuse to feel ashamed about their bodies. So instead of playing down their sexuality and wearing "modest" clothing, they will unabashedly flaunt their bodies and sexual desires in a manner that some might describe as "shameless." Women who are deemed "shameless" with regards to their sexuality are often mischaracterized as indecent and obscene, and/or as attention seekers who are exploiting their sexuality for personal gain. And other people (especially men) may feel even more entitled to sexualize such women under the assumption that, because they are flaunting their bodies and sexuality, they must be "asking for it."

In feminist circles, this dilemma is typically referred to as the virgin/whore double bind, where "virgin" represents those who feel self-conscious about, and play down, their sexuality, and "whore" represents those women who flaunt their bodies and sexuality, and thus are accused of being immodest or shameless. While the virgin/whore paradigm has been important for making sense of sexual politics in women's lives, it is also useful to recognize this as but one of many ways in which the ashamed/shameless double bind plays out in the lives of those who are marked.

The ashamed/shameless double bind has played out in a different, albeit parallel, way for me as transsexual.[14] When I first came out to people in my life as trans, perhaps the most common reaction that I experienced was people offering their sympathies, and treating my transness as though it were a tragedy. Clearly, these were folks who chose to view my transness as an "affliction" (despite the fact that I did not portray it that way myself). I kept hearing the same few phrases over and over again: "I can't imagine what you are going through." "You must be really courageous." These felt like backhanded compliments to me, as they insinuated that being trans was an inherently horrible thing to be. People who viewed me as overcoming an "affliction" often seemed quite uncomfortable or disturbed if I would bring up my transness on subsequent occasions. They acted as though I was somehow burdening them by sharing my "problems" (despite the fact that most times I was discussing my trans experiences in a positive light). The message seemed to be clear: They felt bad for me, were glad that they were not me, and did not want to hear anything more about what it was like to be me. In other words, they viewed me as being "shameless" for not having the common sense to play down, or keep quiet about, my transness.

In the years that followed, I found myself writing a lot about being a woman with a penis—it was an aspect of my body that I was expected to hide and feel shame about, so I set out to reclaim it. Often when performing those pieces at spoken word events, I would disarm audiences with one-liners like, "Here's another poem about my penis." People would always laugh, even though the line itself is not especially funny if you think about it. Upon further reflection, it seems clear that the supposed humor in that line arises directly from the ashamed/shameless double bind. After all, as a pre-op trans woman, most people considered my genitals to be discordant with my female body and identity, and thus expected me to be ashamed of that part of me. So when I mentioned (flaunted even!) my penis, the humor stemmed from the fact that the audience was surprised that I could be so "shameless" as to pronounce my genital status in public. Further, by flaunting the fact that I had a penis, I was essentially giving the audience permission to pay undue attention to (e.g., to laugh at) my marked status. Also, when people believe that you should feel ashamed by something, it tends to make them feel uncomfortable.[15] So by acting shameless—by drawing attention to my own supposed failings—I essentially brought that tension into relief. Generally, whenever marked individuals engage in so-called "self-deprecating humor" regarding their marked trait, the ashamed/shameless double bind always seems to be in play. While being "shameless" in public might elicit laughs in more playful and informal settings (e.g., during a performance), in more serious and formal settings (e.g., in the workplace) these same actions may instead be viewed as inappropriate and disturbing.

I have experienced two major health conditions since my coming out as trans, namely, dealing with skin cancer in 2006, and being diagnosed with psoriasis (an auto-immune condition that affects the skin) in 2010. While having a medical condition is very different from being transsexual[16], I must say that the reactions that I received with regards to the ashamed/shameless double bind were remarkably similar. Upon telling people about my skin cancer and psoriasis, I received lots of "I can't imagine what you are going through; you must be really courageous" sentiments followed by a we-must-never-speak-of-this-again type of attitude. Both my cancer and psoriasis evoked a wide range of thoughts and feelings in me—anger, sadness, humor, insight, fear, patience, anxiety, mindfulness, and so on. So naturally, I wanted to openly discuss my experiences, but I felt a lot of external pressure from other people to keep quiet about these aspects of my life. As with my trans status, others wanted me to hide or play down my marked traits in order to protect them from the supposed tragedy of my life. Basically, they wanted and expected me to be ashamed of being "afflicted" by these conditions.

I believe that the ashamed/shameless double bind explains why our society celebrates people who are "stoic" and who keep quiet about their stigmatized conditions. Of course, if one does not adhere to this self-imposed silence, or if one fails to adequately cover up or hide their condition (whether it be psoriasis outbreaks, scars from cancer-related surgeries, or gender discordant traits), they will likely be depicted as "shameless," and as "unseemly" attention seekers. This double bind also explains why almost all talk about stigmatized conditions is relegated to the realm of support groups, which provide the "afflicted" individuals the rare outlet to share their experiences and feelings with others while simultaneously allowing the "unafflicted" to go merrily on with their lives without having to deal with, or even acknowledge, the existence and experiences of the so-called "afflicted." Furthermore, the external pressure placed on marked individuals to hide and keep quiet about our conditions effectively silences our voices in society. And the resulting lack of visibility creates the false impression that our marked conditions are far more rare than they actually are, thus making them even more susceptible to being viewed as abnormal, unnatural, exotic, and alien.

THE HARMLESS/DANGEROUS DOUBLE BIND

The fact that marked people are assumed to be "afflicted" by, and "ashamed" of, our marked traits sometimes leads to the impression that we are fundamentally "harmless." The assumption that marked individuals are harmless is also implied by the expectation that we will (or at least, should) be "accommodating" of all of the attention, remarks, questioning, and critiques we receive from members of the unmarked group. Furthermore, the assumption of "harmlessness" is exacerbated by the fact that, in most cases, specific marked groups represent a minority of the population, and as such, we cannot effectively stand up to, and challenge, the whims of the majority. These multiple forces all collide to put pressure on us to cooperate with the unmarked powers that be. Essentially, these pressures compel us not to raise a fuss, nor to protest our circumstances.

If we refuse to go along with the assumption that we are harmless, we might instead assert that we are "dangerous." This assertion of dangerousness can be found in activist groups that embrace provocative names such as Radical Feminists, Black Panthers, Femme Mafia, Transexual Menace, and Hermaphrodites With Attitude. The "dangerous" approach is tightly intertwined with the "angry," "chosen," and "shameless" sides of previously mentioned double binds. As with those other double binds, the more conservative approach (in this case, acting "harmless") might reduce the overall level of criticism and disdain that the marked person receives, but it does nothing to challenge the unmarked/marked distinction. And while declaring oneself to be dangerous can be quite self-empowering, the unmarked majority will often cite this supposed dangerous nature in order to justify their own questioning, critiquing, and delegitimizing of the marked group.

One final point must be made here: Marked traits may differ in whether they tend to be read by the unmarked center as "harmless" or "dangerous." For example, women, feminine, and disabled people tend to be read as inherently harmless. In such cases, when we assert ourselves as dangerous, we may not be taken seriously. In contrast, people of color and people who are viewed as "transgressively gendered" or "sexually deviant" tend to be read as inherently dangerous, and as such, we may have difficulty convincing other people that we do not pose a threat, no matter what we do.

THE PASS/REVEAL DOUBLE BIND

Some people are visibly marked in such a way that it is impossible to conceal the trait in question, even if they wanted to. But other traits are less visible, or completely unnoticeable, to other people in most situations. To use a previous example, some people are more visibly transsexual—that is, they are often recognized or "read" as transsexual—while other transsexuals are sometimes, or almost always, perceived as cissexual, even though they are not. In the latter case, one might claim that the transsexual "passes" as cissexual.[17] Indeed, the verb "pass" is routinely applied to anyone who has a marked trait but nevertheless is perceived by others as an unmarked person (e.g., a queer person "passes" as straight, a person of color "passes" as white). As I have discussed extensively elsewhere, this use of the word "pass" is problematic for several reasons.[18] Primarily, it gives the impression that the marked person is the active party (i.e., they are working hard to achieve a false appearance), and that the perceiver is merely a passive and objective observer who is "fooled" by the marked individual. While in some cases, the marked person may actively try to appear unmarked, in many other cases, the marked individual is not actively trying to hide or misrepresent themselves. Rather, it is the perceiver who is actively projecting unmarked assumption onto the marked person (e.g., assuming that the person is cissexual, or heterosexual, or white).

Saying that a person who is marked "passes" as unmarked implies that we are being insincere and inauthentic, or worse, that we are actively engaging in manipulation and deception. It also insinuates that our outward appearance is fake, artificial, and merely a ruse. Hopefully by now, readers will recognize these assumptions—that we are being insincere, inauthentic, manipulative, deceptive, artificial, etc.—as being accusations that regularly plague marked traits. So in other words, the concept of "passing" both relies upon and exacerbates many of the negative assumptions about marked traits and people, while letting the perceiver (who is the one actively misinterpreting the world and projecting their own false beliefs and assumptions onto other people) completely off the hook.

When we are marked, unmarked assumption can be endlessly frustrating, as it seems to place the onerous task on us to "come out" to those who misperceive us. "Coming out" results not only in having to deal with the ramifications of being marked, but also with having to overcome the narrative (which exists in the unmarked person's mind) that we were previously "hiding" or "closeting" ourselves, and are now "revealing" our true identity. Sometimes this narrative holds some truth for the marked person as well—for instance, a gay man who "comes out of the closet" may have felt like he was previously hiding himself but is now revealing the truth that he is gay. But other times, this narrative belies the marked person's actual experience. For example, I may not be actively hiding the fact that I am transsexual, but when I drop it into casual conversation (e.g., "back when I was in little league," or "back when I had a penis"), other people may perceive this as a "coming out moment," rather than recognizing that they were the ones who were projecting cissexual assumption onto me all along. Also, the "revelation" narrative that others project onto me may invalidate my experiences and identity in other ways. For instance, if I tell someone I am transsexual, they may interpret that as me "revealing" that I am "really a man," rather than accurately seeing me as a woman who has shared the fact that I am transsexual rather than cissexual. Similarly, if I mention that I am bisexual, I may be misinterpreted as having "revealed" the fact that I am "really" homosexual or heterosexual.

Even if the so-called "revelation" is interpreted accurately, it still pretty much sucks for the marked person. As I have said ad infinitum by this point, when we "reveal" our marked status, we open ourselves up to attention, remarks, questioning, and so on. Further, we can never predict how any given person will react to these supposed "revelations," so we must always be on guard and prepared for the worst possible negative reaction. Finally, if we are perceived as having just "revealed" our marked status, we may be bombarded by accusations that we have been insincere, inauthentic, manipulative, deceptive, and artificial, even when such allegations are patently untrue.

CHALLENGING DOUBLE STANDARDS AND THEIR DOUBLE BINDS

To summarize, double standards (including sexisms and other forms of marginalization) are generally rooted in the unmarked/marked distinction, and this distinction leads to numerous double binds that can wreak havoc on the lives of minority and marginalized groups. When confronted with a double bind, by definition, there is no "right" choice— each option has some drawbacks for the marked person. Given this, it is not surprising that marked individuals may respond to these situations in a variety of ways depending upon their past experiences navigating their way through the world with that particular marked trait, the specifics of their immediate situation, and other personal or constitutional factors.

Furthermore, while I presented the concept of unmarked-versus-marked by focusing on specific traits in isolation, this is not how the world actually works. The reality is that each of us is a unique conglomeration of traits, some of which are marked and others unmarked. Often, we have very different histories and relationships with our marked traits—e.g., I might flaunt the fact that I am transsexual, but hide the fact that I have psoriasis; I might strongly identify as a cancer survivor, but disavow the label bisexual. Also, as discussed earlier, whether an aspect of our person is marked or unmarked may change dramatically depending upon the social setting. Finally, as we know from intersectionality, the marginalization we face from being marked in multiple ways may lead us to experience our marked traits (and other people's reactions to them) differently than people who experience those traits individually, or in different combinations. These countless disparities will most certainly impact how any given person chooses to react to the double binds they face.

Unfortunately, those of us who are passionate about feminism, queer activism, and social justice often fail to recognize these double binds for what they are (i.e., no-win situations), and sometimes we will stubbornly insist that one particular response will eliminate the marginalization that we face, while the reciprocal choice will "reinforce" that marginalization. For example, feminists have long argued about how best to respond to the virgin/whore double bind—this debate has been so fiercely contested that it has been referred to as the "feminist sex wars."[19] Some feminists believe that women should respond to our societal sexualization by playing down our sexualities—e.g., by refusing to wear especially feminine or revealing clothing and discouraging or eliminating pornography and sex work. Such calls to play down or draw attention away from female bodies and sexualities position these feminists on the "virgin" or "ashamed" side of the double bind.[20] On the other side of this debate are self-identified "sex-positive" feminists who claim that women have been made to feel shame about our bodies and sexualities for too long, and that, instead of trying to hide or repress female sexuality, we should be celebrating and informing people about it. Such feminists may flaunt their bodies without shame, talk explicitly about their sexual desires and experiences, and possibly even produce their own feminist porn—in other words, they fall on the "whore" or "shameless" side of the double bind.

While people on both sides of this debate may have the best of intentions, it seems clear to me that neither of these remedies will significantly reduce the sexualization women face in our society. After all, this sexualization is not initiated by what women do (i.e., whether we choose to act like "virgins" or "whores"), but rather it exists in the minds of the perceivers who mark women and interpret our bodies and behaviors through a sexualizing mindset.[21] The most constructive way to reduce sexualization is by changing the way people view women, not by policing women's behaviors.

Another example of activists failing to appreciate these double binds for what they are can be found in the "reformist versus radical" debate within queer activism. This debate is centered on a number of interrelated double binds: invisible/visible, accommodating/angry, afflicted/chosen, ashamed/shameless, and harmless/dangerous. Reformists tend to choose the more conservative approaches to these double binds—e.g., by claiming that queer people are simply "born that way," patiently answering all the questions and concerns posited by the straight majority, and by playing down, or refusing to flaunt, their queerness (as insinuated in the often-cited phrases: "My sexual orientation is nobody's business but my own," and, "We're just like you (read: straight people) except for our sexual orientation"). Radical queer activists instead proudly shout, "We're here, we're queer, get used to it!" and advocate that all queer people must come out of the closet. They also often assert that being queer is a valid life choice (rather than an "affliction"), and that their genders and sexualities are inherently "transgressive" and "subversive." Both the radical and reformist sides of this debate will insist that their approach will lead to salvation, whereas the reciprocal approach will ultimately lead to doom. (More specifically, reformists will accuse radicals of "holding back the movement," and radicals will accuse reformists of "reinforcing the gender system.")

The problem with both these approaches is that they fail to appreciate that queer people are a heterogeneous group. Each of us faces a unique set of circumstances, and therefore we may respond quite differently to any given situation. But even more importantly, these approaches fail to realize that because queer people are marked, we have been placed in a double bind. Neither prescribed solution gets to the heart of the problem: the fact that other people mark us as queer, and by doing so, they will perceive, interpret, and treat us differently than the straight majority no matter what course of action we take.

The expectation that all members of a particular marked group should react to the double binds they face in the exact same way represents another manifestation of the perversion of "the personal is political." Such approaches deny both human diversity and the fact that we are all uniquely socially situated and have to navigate our way through the world with a different assortment of marked traits. If we truly want to challenge the marginalization we face, then we must move away from obsessing over what marked and marginalized individuals do, and instead turn our attention (and our critiques) toward the act of marking other people, and the subsequent assumptions and meanings that the perceiver projects upon those they have marked.

MYRIAD DOUBLE STANDARDS

CHAPTER FIFTEEN

I n the first chapter of this section, I suggested that we should be wary of viewing gender and sexism in terms of some sort of hegemonic "gender system"—such as the patriarchy, or heteronormativity, or the gender binary, or kyriarchy, and so on. Admittedly, each of these concepts provides a seemingly self-consistent model for how sexism arises and functions, and each has a great deal of explanatory power, in that they account for many people's experiences with sexism. The problem is that each of these models is incomplete, as they all fail to address certain forms of sexism and marginalization. Furthermore, when we single out some force outside ourselves (e.g., a particular hegemonic gender system) as the source of the marginalization we face, it encourages us-versus-them thinking, as we start imagining ourselves as being uniquely oppressed, while everyone who does not share our identity or circumstance is assumed to be our oppressor. This sort of rhetoric often fosters an "oppression Olympics"–type mentality, where people claim that certain forms of marginalization (invariably the ones that they themselves face) are worse than—and therefore, take precedence over—other forms of marginalization. Along the same lines, when we become invested in an us-versus-them narrative, where we are righteous do-gooders who are committed to overturning some kind of external evil force, then we will likely be resistant to the idea that we ourselves may sometimes act in sexist or marginalizing ways toward others.

Rather than relying on one-size-fits-all gender systems that attempt to explain gender and sexism in their entirety, we should instead acknowledge that we live in a world of *myriad double standards*. In any given situation or setting, some double standards may be in play, while others may not. And all of these double standards may intersect with one another, thus leading to a diverse array of experiences with sexism and marginalization.

Thinking about sexism and marginalization in terms of myriad double standards implores us to challenge *all* double standards: those that are prevalent, and those that are rare; those that negatively impact us, and those that negatively impact others; those that we are currently aware of, as well as those that are currently unknown to us. Having such a mindset can make us more open to learning about new double standards when they are first described to us (rather than outright dismissing them because they do not fit into our worldview), and more mindful of the fact that we ourselves are fallible (as we may be unknowingly engaging in, or enforcing, certain double standards ourselves). Perhaps most importantly, thinking in terms of myriad double standards encourages humility, as it forces us to admit that there are many aspects of gender and sexism that we do not personally experience, and therefore cannot fully know about. For this reason, it would be conceited for us to project our fixed and limited perspective of the universe onto other people.

DOUBLE STANDARDS TAKE MANY FORMS

In order to make sense of this notion of myriad double standards, I find it useful to consider double standards as falling into one of three general categories: universal assumptions, hierarchies, and stereotypes. In this section, I will describe and provide examples for each of these types of double standards, and the role that they play in sexism and marginalization. In subsequent chapters, I hope to show how distinguishing between these types of double standards can result in more effective, and less exclusive, activist movements.

The first type of double standard that I'd like to discuss is *universal assumptions*—as the name suggests, these are basically norms or expectations that we make in a general fashion about everyone and everything around us. For instance, we might assume that everyone we meet will be cissexual and gender-normative; that they will experience sexual attraction and that that attraction will be monosexual in nature; that they will be monogamous in their relationships and vanilla in their sexualities. We may also expect (depending upon the setting) that most or all of the people we meet will be white, middle-class, able-bodied, normatively sized, and so on. These universal assumptions represent double standards in that they essentially create two types of people who we will view very differently: Some people (and their actions) will be viewed as typical and expected and therefore will remain unmarked. In contrast, people and actions that defy these universal assumptions will be perceived as exceptional and unexpected, and therefore we tend to mark them.

Of course, many universal assumptions are not truly universal, but rather context-specific. We might expect everyone we meet in everyday life to be heterosexual, but upon entering a gay bar, we might expect everyone we meet to be homosexual. Our personal experiences may also greatly influence which universal assumptions we hold and which we reject. So while most people may presume that everyone they meet will be heterosexual, as a queer woman with many queer people in my life, I no longer make this assumption (although I admittedly did back when I was a young, isolated queer). It should also be said that there can be varying degrees of unexpectedness. For example, when I tell people that

I have a female partner, sometimes they are initially surprised, but then they quickly adjust their expectations and assumptions about me (e.g., by re-categorizing me as queer). However, I have had times when I have come out to people as transsexual (especially a decade ago, when there was far less trans-awareness than there is today) where people absolutely did not believe that such a thing was possible—they were in utter disbelief and dumbfounded. I often describe this latter situation as being considered *beyond the realm of possibilities*, and it often results in a substantial increase in one's markedness (i.e., we become even more remarkable, questionable, exotic, and suspect in the eyes of others).

As I discussed in the previous chapter, we have a tendency to mark people who strike us as exceptional, as unexpected, and who are members of an outgroup (i.e., a group we do not belong to, or identify with). This may lead us to view them as remarkable, questionable, and exotic, but it does not necessarily result in us viewing them as being "better" or "lesser" than us. For instance, when I tell people that I am a scientist, sometimes they find that interesting and unusual, and they will ask me all sorts of questions about it, but they don't generally view me as being superior or inferior to them as a result.[1] In contrast, some marked groups are viewed as being superior or inferior to the unmarked majority in some way, and I will refer to this type of double standard as *hierarchies*. Of course, hierarchies can go in one of two directions. In some cases, the marked group is glorified, and viewed as superior to the unmarked majority, as is often seen with celebrities, professional athletes, and people who hold exceptional power or wealth. In many other cases, the unmarked group is marginalized. Hierarchies that marginalize the marked group provide the foundation for traditional sexism, heterosexism, monosexism, cissexism, racism, classism, ableism, ageism, sizeism, and many other forms of marginalization. Since this book is primarily concerned with sexism and marginalization, from here on out, when I discuss hierarches, I will be exclusively referring to the marginalizing variety.

Marginalizing hierarchies position the marked group as being less legitimate than the unmarked group. This sense of illegitimacy may stem somewhat directly from many of the previously discussed hallmarks of marked traits, such as being viewed as inherently questionable, artificial, abnormal, exotic, alien, and suspect. But other times, this sense of illegitimacy may be enhanced by additional assumptions that are projected onto the particular marked group in question. I will generally refer to these additional assumptions as *stereotypes*. The word "stereotype" has many potential definitions[2], but here I will use it to refer to any possible trait (whether a bodily attribute, a type of behavior or tendency, a motivation or desire, a past experience, etc.) that is not a defining characteristic of a group, but that people nevertheless associate with members of that group. So for example, one might say that the defining characteristic of transsexuals is that we identify as members of the sex other than the one we were assigned at birth—in other words, that is a trait that one must possess in order to be considered transsexual.[3] But in addition to that defining trait, there are numerous additional traits—that is, stereotypes—that people associate with transsexuals: They may presume that we are mentally ill, or over-the-top in our gender expressions, or brave, or dangerous, or immoral, or promiscuous, or unattractive, or attention seekers, or sex workers, or manipulative, or that we have had unhappy childhoods, or have had "sex change operations," or are unaware of feminist politics, and so on. Stereotypes are clearly double standards in that people will tend to make the above assumptions about transsexuals, but not cissexuals.

This particular list of transsexual stereotypes is by no means comprehensive, but it does highlight a few important points. First, while all of these stereotypes exist (as I can attest, having personally experienced them all myself), they can vary significantly from person to person, and place to place. I may meet one person who, knowing that I'm transsexual, assumes that I must be brave, having survived an unhappy childhood.

Then the next person might presume that I am a promiscuous attention seeker who is most likely a sex worker. One person may assume that my female gender identity is the product of mental illness, whereas another may assume that my claiming a female identity stems from a lack of feminist awareness. So basically, there are countless different configurations of stereotypes that people may hold about any given group. And over time, new stereotypes may be invented, or come into vogue, whereas others may slowly disappear from public consciousness.

People tend to think of stereotypes as assumptions that are held by the dominant majority and projected onto the marginalized group. While this is typically the case, what gets less attention is that members of a marginalized group may also project stereotypes onto their own group. Sometimes these stereotypes resemble those held by the dominant majority, whereas other times the group may generate novel stereotypes of themselves.

Another noteworthy point is that the same stereotype may be shared by different groups. So being "over-the-top in gender expression" is a stereotype shared by both transsexuals and people who are feminine; being "promiscuous" is a stereotype shared by transsexuals and bisexuals. Furthermore, one group's stereotype may be the defining characteristic of another stigmatized group. For example, sex workers and people with mental disabilities are both stigmatized groups who face their own hierarchies, as well as a slew of stereotypes specific to them (e.g., people with mental disabilities may be stereotyped as incompetent and dangerous; sex workers may be stereotyped as promiscuous and criminal). So when transsexuals are stereotyped as mentally ill, or as sex workers, many of the stereotypes associated with these groups may rub off on me as well, even if I do not belong to either of these two other groups personally.

While some stereotypes may have positive connotations (e.g., being seen as brave[4]), most of the stereotypes targeting transsexuals and other marginalized groups tend to have blatantly negative connotations. Some are condemning judgments about our character or worth (e.g., claims that we are immoral and unattractive), some impart upon us character traits that are viewed disparagingly by most people (e.g., being promiscuous and manipulative), and still others attempt to link us with other marginalized groups who have their own negative stereotypes to contend with (e.g., people with mental disabilities or sex workers). Together, these negative connotations reinforce the idea that the marginalized group in question (in this case, transsexuals) is inherently illegitimate and suspect, thereby supporting the initial hierarchical double standard (in this case, cissexism).

Another phenomenon that I will consider alongside stereotypes (as it involves assumptions that people make about specific individuals or groups) is *attribution*—this is a term that social psychologists use to refer to the hypothetical reasons that we imagine caused a particular behavior or event.[5] So to use an example from the last chapter, if I were to wear a pink shirt and jeans, you probably wouldn't spend much thought on why I chose that outfit, as such an outfit would be unmarked in your eyes. However, if I was wearing a dress (which garners your attention, and is therefore marked in your eyes), you may spend some time considering why: Is Julia going on a date? Or is she trying to impress someone? Our tendency to invent hypothetical causes and motives to explain the exceptional and unexpected is what creates the impression that marked people and behaviors must somehow be inherently questionable and suspect.

The process of attribution might seem innocent enough on the surface. After all, it makes sense that we would be curious as to why things happen. The problem is that, as with stereotypes, attributions are double standards, in that they are disproportionally projected onto marked groups, but not the unmarked majority. As a transsexual, I am inundated with attributions that attempt to explain why I exist (was it a genetic defect? mental illness? hormones gone awry? bad parenting?), and people regularly project (or attribute) ulterior motives onto me to explain why I identify as female (to assimilate into straight society? for sexual reasons? to infiltrate women-only spaces?). In stark contrast, cissexuality and cissexual gender identities are never questioned or rendered suspect in this way.

There are a number of biases that influence the attributions that people tend to make.[6] One such bias (which social psychologists call *fundamental attribution error*) is that we tend to assume that a person's behaviors stem directly from their disposition or nature, rather than from situational or other factors.[7] This bias helps to explain the human tendency to "naturalize" or "essentialize" other people's behaviors—that is, to assume that my behaviors arise from the type of person that I am (whether it be transsexual, bisexual, woman, etc.). Because of this bias, if I do anything that other people deem to be remarkable (e.g., if I wear a dress), those people are likely to presume that that behavior must somehow have been caused by my transsexuality or "transsexual nature."[8] Notably, fundamental attribution error becomes even more pronounced when we view the person in question as a member of an outgroup rather than our ingroup. Thus, if a cissexual woman wears a dress, other cissexuals will not be inclined to attribute that to her cissexuality, whereas in my case, they would likely attribute it to my transsexuality (e.g., my supposedly "over-the-top gender performance" and/or "desire to assimilate into straight society"). Another way of putting this is that we tend to have more essentialist views of outgroups, and this tendency can wreak havoc on minority populations. This explains why the dominant majority often talks about "the queers," or "the transgenders," or "the blacks" as though they are one uniform group who all share similar characteristics and tendencies. In stark contrast, people rarely (if ever) say "the straights," "the cisgenders," "the whites," because these populations are ingroups for most people in our culture. As such, these groups are seen as relatively heterogeneous, and their actions and life choices are not attributed to the unmarked traits that they share in common (e.g., their straight-ness, cis-ness, white-ness).

As with stereotypes, the attributions people make about marginalized groups often have negative connotations—this is one way in which they strengthen the corresponding hierarchies. But they also support hierarchies in another, less obvious way. Namely, both stereotypes and attributions portray the marginalized group as sharing all sorts of additional traits and tendencies that are not typically exhibited by non-group members. In other words, stereotypes and attributions create the illusion that the marked and unmarked groups are distinct, mutually exclusive, and perhaps even "opposites" of one another. This plays a crucial function in maintaining the hierarchy in question. After all, if you believe that men are superior to women, or that cissexuals are more legitimate than transsexuals, then it is in your interest to create as sharp of a distinction between those groups as you can. Thus, when we project stereotypes onto women that we do not project onto men, or when we attribute motives to transsexuals that we don't attribute to cissexuals, it makes women and transsexuals appear far more dissimilar and disparate from men and cissexuals, respectively, than they actually are.

Furthermore, stereotypes and attributions have a *homogenizing effect* on groups—that is, they give the impression that members of a particular group are more similar to one another than they actually are. For instance, they imply that most or all transsexuals are attention seekers, dangerous, and so on, and that most or all women are nurturing, sexually passive, and so on. Marked groups in particular tend to be misperceived as especially homogeneous for two reasons. First, stereotypes and attributions are more frequently projected onto marked groups, and tend to "stick" to them more than their unmarked counterparts. All these stereotypes and attributions create the impression that members of the marked group are quite similar to one another. Second, as I discussed a moment ago, when a group is marked in our eyes, we are more likely to assume that their behaviors arise directly from their "group nature." In comparison, unmarked groups are assumed to be relatively heterogeneous and are not typically seen as having a "group nature."

There are examples for which this asymmetry (i.e., marked groups being viewed as homogeneous, and unmarked groups viewed as heterogeneous) does not entirely hold true. Specifically, when two groups are viewed as complements, or presumed to be "natural opposites" (as in the case of women and men), the two groups often associate with other binary pairs. Thus, women are stereotyped as soft and men as hard, women are stereotyped as passive and men as active, and so on. This complementation has a homogenizing effect on both groups, as both are now associated with many other additional traits. However, even in such scenarios, the marked group will still tend to be viewed as more homogeneous than the unmarked group, as they have far more stereotypes and attributions associated with them.[9]

Before moving on, there is one further consequence that sometimes arises when groups are seen as relatively homogeneous. Namely, once people begin to view two different groups as being mutually exclusive, or even "opposites," there will inevitably be some individuals who do not fit nicely into either of these two camps. Such individuals may be perceived as falling outside of the two groups, or perhaps inhabiting some sort of limbo or liminal space between the two. The existence of such individuals will seemingly call this particular binary or hierarchy into question, and as a result, they may be viewed with suspicion by members of both groups. Often, this suspicion leads to the creation of a new hierarchy between people who fall neatly into one of the two groups (and who are viewed as legitimate), and those who seem to obscure the distinction between the two groups (and who are thus deemed illegitimate). An obvious example of such a hierarchy is monosexism, where people who fit seamlessly into the hetero/homo binary are viewed as more legitimate than those who do not.[10] As a result of this, it is possible for a particular group (in this case, homosexuals) to be delegitimized by one hierarchy (heterosexism), yet be viewed as relatively legitimate according to another hierarchy (monosexism).

ISMS

When we talk about sexism and marginalization, we often talk about them in terms of some overarching ideology or ism that is prevalent in society. Isms are generally composed of the three types of double standards that I have discussed so far. For instance, traditional sexism (the overarching ideology) consists of a universal assumption (that maleness and masculinity are the norm), a hierarchy (that women are seen as less legitimate and important than men), and a slew of stereotypes and attributions. But, of course, there is more to an ideology than just double standards. Each ism also has its own history and mythology, means by which it is transmitted and by which people are indoctrinated into it (e.g., language, stories, schools, traditions), ways in which it is institutionalized (e.g., through laws, medicine, government bureaucracy), and so on. By focusing primarily on double standards here, I am not in any way denying or dismissing these latter aspects of isms—they are important and need to be addressed in our analyses and activism. But I do think that breaking down an ism and examining its constituent double standards can bring to light how different forms of marginalization function and interact that typically remain obscure—that is what I am trying to do here.

Also, a point of clarification: Sometimes I may use a term like "traditional sexism" to refer rather specifically to the hierarchical double standard, and other times to refer to the overarching ideology or ism. While this may sometimes be confusing, it also has practical applications. For example, I find that people who are unfamiliar with a specific ism often have a hard time grappling with the idea that there is some kind of overarching ideology that is institutionalized in society, especially when they personally do not see it. In contrast, people grasp the idea of double standards on a very basic level, and it is not nearly as intimidating to them. In my own activism, I find that getting people to acknowledge that a marginalized group faces a number of double standards is far easier, and it opens the door for them to subsequently consider that marginalization in terms of an overarching ideology.

INTERSECTIONALITY

To summarize thus far, as a member of a marginalized group, I may be subjected to a plethora of double standards, and some of these double standards may overlap with those faced by other marginalized groups. This complex network of double standards becomes even more elaborate when we consider the heterogeneity that exists within any specific group. For example, in addition to being transsexual, I am also a woman, bisexual, and feminine, to name a few other marked traits that I possess. Each of these other aspects of my being are delegitimized by different hierarchies, and they are subjected to a different set of stereotypes and attributions: Women (like transsexuals) are stereotyped as manipulative; bisexuals (like transsexuals) are stereotyped as promiscuous; and people who are feminine (like transsexuals) are stereotyped as being over-the-top in our gender expressions.

These are obvious examples of *intersectionality*, where different forms of marginalization compound one another. When framed this way, it becomes clear why different forms of marginalization tend to exacerbate one another. For one thing, if I am already viewed as illegitimate and suspect for being transsexual, my supposed illegitimacy and the suspicion that I face will only be enhanced when people also perceive me as belonging to another marked group(s), such as being a woman, or bisexual, or feminine. In addition, because there is some overlap in the stereotypes projected onto me for different aspects of my being, people may perceive me as being doubly manipulative (because I am a woman and transsexual), or doubly promiscuous (because I am bisexual and transsexual), or especially over-the-top in my gender expression (because I am feminine and transsexual).

I also possess numerous traits that are unmarked in our culture: I am white, able-bodied, and normatively sized, to name but a few. Because of their unmarked statuses, these aspects of my person will not negatively compound the marginalization that I face as a transsexual (or as a woman, or bisexual, or feminine person). But other members of my group(s) will differ from me with regards to these traits, and the intersectional marginalization they face will differ significantly from my own experiences. Trans women of color, and bisexual disabled women, and fat queer femmes, all face marginalization in a variety of different configurations, and some of their experiences will overlap with mine, and with one another's. But many of our experiences will also differ significantly.

Sometimes the concept of intersectionality gets reduced to the notion that certain people are doubly oppressed, or triply oppressed, or quadruply oppressed, and as a result, they are worse off than people who only face a single form of marginalization. While this can certainly be true, what often gets overlooked is the fact that each of us lies at the intersection of myriad double standards, some of which marginalize us, and others that do not. Rather than solely using intersectionality to rank everyone according to how much privilege they have, or how much oppression they face, instead intersectionality should encourage us to view each person as being uniquely situated within a multidimensional web of marginalization. We each grapple with a somewhat novel subset of double standards, we each face different obstacles (albeit some far more so than others), and we each have different blind spots—aspects of gender and sexuality, and sexism and marginalization, that we are unable to view from our vantage point. And while it's been said many times before, it bears repeating: There is absolutely no such thing as a universal female, or bisexual, or transsexual experience. All groups are fundamentally heterogeneous, and their individual members will inevitably be extraordinarily varied in their experiences.

IDEALITY

There has been increasing awareness within feminist and queer movements about the importance of intersectionality—the fact that, because marginalized groups are heterogeneous, their individual constituents may differ greatly in whatever additional hierarchies they may also face (e.g., whether they face traditional sexism, and/or heterosexism, and/or racism, and/or ableism, and so on). But this same heterogeneity will also result in individual constituents being impacted differently by the various stereotypes that are projected onto the group as a whole. In the spirit of intersectionality, I call this latter phenomenon *ideality*, because it plays a major role in determining whether an individual is considered by others to be an "ideal" or "legitimate" member of the group.

For example, there are countless stereotypes—that is, assumptions or traits associated with a particular group—that are routinely projected onto women: We are presumed to be feminine in gender expression, nurturing, verbal and communicative, attracted to men and not women, to have female-typical genitals, to have been assigned a female sex at birth, and to have experienced menstruation.[11] As a woman, I conform to some of these double standards (e.g., the first few), but defy others (e.g., particularly the latter ones). Other women will differ from me, as well from other women, with regards to the specific configuration of stereotypically female traits that they happen to possess. In fact, given that every marginalized group is associated with a plethora of stereotypes, and given that every person is to some degree unique in our desires, interests, bodies, behaviors, and histories, then it follows that every single one of us will inevitably conform to some of the stereotypes that are projected onto members of our group, while defying others.[12]

If we just so happen to conform to a particular stereotype that is projected onto our group, then we will remain relatively unmarked in the eyes of others (i.e., we are marked with regards to the hierarchy, but not the stereotype). Because we are not marked by this particular double standard, we will tend not to notice it, nor be concerned by it. Hence, feminine women tend not to be overly concerned by the assumption that all women should be feminine; heterosexual women tend not to be overly concerned with the assumption that all women should be exclusively attracted to men; and so on. On the other hand, if we defy or transgress a particular stereotype, then we will be marked by it—in a sense, we are doubly marked by both the hierarchy and the stereotype.[13] Being doubly marked in this manner often leads people to view us as being an atypical, if not downright illegitimate, member of the group. This is why women who are not feminine, or not nurturing, or infertile, or intersex, or trans, or bisexual, or lesbian, or asexual, are all sometimes accused of not being a "real woman," albeit for different reasons. Of course, the more closely associated a stereotype is with the group, the more likely that a group member will be delegitimized for failing to conform to it.

The fact that members of the same marginalized group will differ in the stereotypes that they face can have a huge impact on determining the course of activism the group will take. For instance, if most women happen to be cissexual and heterosexual, then they probably won't view the assumptions that all women are assigned and socialized female, and are exclusively attracted to men, to be "women's issues," even though these double standards clearly dictate criteria that all women are expected to meet. Furthermore, such activists may even buy into the pervasive rhetoric that trans and/or queer women are not "real women," and they may subsequently take steps to exclude those groups from participating in their movement (as I have chronicled in previous chapters). Such instances of exclusion will only add to the perception that the group in question (in this case, women) is far more homogeneous than they actually are.

CHALLENGING MYRIAD DOUBLE STANDARDS

In past chapters, I have argued that biological, cultural, and experiential variation ensures that each person will differ greatly in the collection of traits that they possess. In this chapter, I have tried to illustrate that because we differ so greatly with regards to such traits, we are each uniquely positioned within an intricate network of myriad double standards. As a result, we each have a very specific (and limited) view of sexism and marginalization. We will each be highly cognizant of, and concerned with, the double standards that directly impact us. But we each also display significant blind spots—aspects of gender and sexuality, and sexism and marginalization, that we cannot readily view because we do not experience them firsthand.

Knowing that there are myriad double standards, how should we as activists approach challenging sexism and other forms of marginalization? In the next chapter, I will compare and contrast two different potential strategies—*fixed* versus *holistic* perspectives—and explain why I believe that the latter provides a more accurate and inclusive approach to feminism and queer activism.

FIXED VERSUS HOLISTIC PERSPECTIVES

CHAPTER SIXTEEN

Women, and gender and sexual minorities, face various forms of sexism, and often we band together to create movements designed to challenge these sexist double standards. Typically, these movements begin with a group of activists who share a particular identity, or grapple with similar circumstances, and who together start to articulate the marginalization they face. Their initial focus will understandably be centered on those double standards that are most relevant to their own lives. Sometimes they will conceptualize this particular set of double standards as forming a singular type of prejudice—an ism or phobia— that people harbor in their minds. And they may focus their activism on raising awareness about the harm that this type of prejudice inflicts in an attempt to convince people in the dominant mainstream to condemn such practices. This approach to fighting double standards is often described as *single-issue activism*.

In other cases, activists will conceptualize the suite of double standards that concerns them in terms of a gender system, one that is hegemonic, omnipresent, and which subjugates the masses in order to benefit the privileged few. Gender systems are often imagined to consist of multiple isms that are inexorably linked in such a way that one cannot effectively challenge them on an individual basis. It is often argued that gender systems are far too institutionalized and far-reaching to be reformed, and therefore they must be subverted or overthrown via mass-scale revolution.

Many debates within feminism and queer activism—especially those regarding the issue of exclusion—pit single-issue activism against the overthrowing-the-gender-system approach, thus creating a false dichotomy: Should we settle for a more moderate, incremental strategy of reducing prejudices on an individual basis, or should we take a more radical strategy of full-scale gender and sexual revolution?

I wish to intervene in this debate to propose an alternative view. I would argue that, while clearly different from one another, both of the above strategies are anchored in a *fixed perspective* of sexism and marginalization, one in which activists are only concerned with a finite subset of double standards. This concern may stem from activists' first-hand experiences being marginalized by the double standards in question. Or, if one does not have direct experience with the double standards in question, the activist nevertheless acknowledges their existence because other activists have previously raised awareness about them. While different fixed perspectives may vary significantly from one another in their analyses of the issue and the specific solutions they propose to challenge sexism and marginalization, they all share a fundamental problem: They fail to consider the countless double standards that remain outside of their purview. And this results in a host of recurring problems that haunt feminist and queer movements.

The most obvious problem that stems from only acknowledging

a limited subset of double standards is that many people's experiences with marginalization will be theorized out of the movement. This can be seen in single-issue activism, where racism and classism have been viewed by some feminists and gay rights activists as falling outside the scope of their organizations' mission statements. This has led to pre-dominantly white- and middle-class–centric movements, where the concerns of the most marginalized members of those groups (i.e., those who lie at the intersection of multiple forms of marginalization) fail to be adequately addressed.[1]

Furthermore, some double standards take longer to articulate than others. While critiques of traditional sexism have existed in various forms for well over a century, the concept of homophobia/heterosexism as we now know it did not really exist until the 1950s and 1960s. And the contemporary bisexual movement (and its critique of biphobia/mono-sexism) and the contemporary transgender movement (and its critique of transphobia/cissexism) emerged in the 1980s and 1990s.[2] The asexual movement (and its critique of asexophobia) is more recent still.[3] When I was writing *Whipping Girl* in 2005-06, I set out to raise attention about trans-misogyny, masculine-centrism, and subversivism (the assumption that some people's genders and sexualities subvert the gender system, and therefore are superior to genders and sexualities that are deemed more conservative) because I felt that these forms of sexism had received little to no attention previously.[4] All of these more recently articulated forms of sexism have been omitted from past (and often present) anti-sexist movements that rely on fixed approaches.

Given this history, it seems reasonable to suspect that there are many other forms of sexism that currently exist, but which have not yet been articulated or garnered public awareness. In addition to this, sexism and marginalization are not static phenomena. As cultures and movements shift, new sexist double standards may arise. As feminists and queer activists, we should always be on the lookout for novel, unarticulated, and underappreciated forms of sexism and marginalization, and our theories and activism should be flexible enough to acclimate to these newer double standards when they arise or become apparent. In contrast, fixed perspectives, with their limited and predetermined sets of relevant double standards, do not readily accommodate newly articulated forms of sexism and marginalization.

When we omit certain forms of sexism or marginalization from our theories and activism, we are not merely excluding those particular marginalized groups from our movements. Rather (more often than not) our lack of consideration for these double standards may lead us to delegitimize those very groups ourselves. For instance, on numerous occasions, I have heard trans activists who are unaware of the disability and sex worker rights movements make ableist, sexualizing, and/or anti-sex worker remarks in their attempts to distance themselves from stereotypes of trans people as being mentally ill or sex workers. Such disparaging claims not only exclude trans people who are sex workers or who have mental disabilities from trans activism, but they also contribute to the societal marginalization of these other groups more generally.

When we base our theories and activism on a pre-selected handful of double standards, while ignoring all others, it limits the number of tools that we have to understand sexism and marginalization, thus leading to a less nuanced, if not outright distorted, view of the world. This is highly evident in the countless cis feminists who are concerned about traditional sexism, but who are oblivious to cissexism, and who therefore relentlessly view trans people, issues, and experiences solely through the lens of "male privilege." Or those gay and lesbian activists who are concerned with heterosexism, but who are oblivious to monosexism, and who are only able to make sense of bisexual lives via the construct of "heterosexual privilege." As the saying goes: "When your only tool is a hammer, every problem looks like a nail." Human beings are way too heterogeneous for us to treat other people's experiences with gender and sexuality, and sexism and marginalization, as though they are proverbial "nails" that can be dealt with in a one-size-fits-all manner. Therefore, we must constantly be seeking to expand our toolkit—in this case, by trying to uncover and understand the heterogeneity in people's experiences, and in the myriad double standards they face.

Limiting our theories and activism to a small subset of double standards often leads to ignorance. But it can also lead to downright arrogance. After all, if we believe that we are fully aware of all the relevant sexist double standards that exist, and that we truly understand how they function, then we will begin to fancy ourselves as some kind of authority on the subjects of gender and sexism, essentially anointing ourselves as omniscient arbiters of what counts as sexism (and what does not), and which gender- and sex-related behaviors are righteous (and which should be condemned). When we become convinced that we have superior knowledge over others, then we will inevitably become entrenched in our views, impervious to new ideas and strategies to combat sexism, and reluctant to engage in constructive dialogue with people whose identities and experiences differ significantly from our own.

A hallmark of this "omniscient arbiter" problem is our tendency to presume that particular gender and sexual expressions, identities, and bodies have fixed meanings built into them that hold true in all situations and contexts. For example, feminists and queer activists who hold fixed perspectives will sometimes claim that the color pink always signifies submissiveness, that feminine dress always turns a person into a sexual object, that heterosexuality is inherently conservative, that BDSM is inherently immoral, that androgyny is the only truly natural form of gender expression, and/or that bisexuals reinforce the gender binary (to name a few that I have heard on multiple occasions).

The notion that these sorts of personal judgments represent universal truths is highly problematic. For one thing, it denies individual and cultural differences. For example, a contemporary cis woman might view the color pink as symbolizing submissiveness because she associates it with the passive and deferential role she was socialized to inhabit as a young girl. But my perspective of the color pink is very different as a trans woman who was socialized male. Rather than being something that was forced upon me, femininity was something that I naturally gravitated toward. And having to endure male socialization, I was taught to repress or hide my femininity, and pink was a color that I was supposed to avoid like the plague. It was downright dangerous. The first time that I dared to wear a pink T-shirt in public as a man was an act of defiance.

Of course, the color pink isn't inherently dangerous or inherently submissive. It is just a color. On its own, it has no inherent meanings. But it begins to take on meanings—completely different meanings—depending upon what context it appears in, and the beliefs and assumptions that are held by the person who is doing the perceiving and interpreting. Indeed, the notion that pink is for girls, or that it symbolizes submissiveness, is a modern Western invention that did not exist before the nineteenth century. And for a time in the early twentieth century, many people associated pink with boys and masculinity because they viewed it as being a "more decided and stronger color," whereas blue was deemed "more delicate and dainty."[5] So while many of us today viscerally experience pink as a profoundly feminine color, that is only because we are viewing it though the prism of our own unconsciously held double standards. Similarly, I would argue that expressions of gender and sexuality more generally—whether feminine dress, heterosexuality, consensual BDSM, androgyny, bisexuality, or what have you—do not have any fixed inherent meanings on their own, but rather they garner meanings based upon whatever cultural, ideological, or personally-held double standards that we project onto them.

If we believe that gender and sexual traits have fixed meanings, then we are likely to feel justified in encouraging or compelling others to only express "good" traits (e.g., those that we deem moral, natural, or normal), and to outright avoid "bad" traits (e.g., those that we deem immoral, unnatural, or abnormal). In other words, fixed perspectives often lead us headlong into the messy business of policing other people's genders and sexualities. Sometimes we police behaviors and traits that are already viewed as suspect and illegitimate in the culture at large (in the above examples, bisexuality and consensual BDSM).[6] When we do this, we are basically contributing to the societal marginalization of people who possess these traits. However, other times we condemn behaviors that are generally praised in our culture (e.g., feminine dress in women, heterosexuality), while simultaneously praising the reciprocal behaviors that are culturally panned (e.g., androgyny, homosexuality). In other words, when we are entrenched in fixed perspectives, we often reverse the double standards that we do not like, rather than eliminating them entirely. While I can certainly understand why a marginalized group might want to flip-flop the hierarchies that oppress them—for instance, by claiming that homosexuality is superior to heterosexuality, or that androgyny is more legitimate than conventional masculinity or femininity—in the end, such approaches only continue to perpetuate sexism and marginalization, albeit in somewhat modified forms.

Often activists who reverse double standards will claim that such maneuvers are necessary in order to subvert some form of societal sexism. For example, a feminist might claim that if all women became lesbian and/or androgynous, then those collective personal endeavors would have the effect of undermining or overturning traditional sexism. (These are the sort of claims that I highlighted in Chapter 12, "The Perversion of 'The Personal Is Political.'") This argument assumes that many currently existing stereotypes about women (e.g., being exclusively attracted to men and feminine in gender expression) are somehow "built into" traditional sexism. In other words, these arguments seem to conflate a hierarchy (in this case, traditional sexism) with the countless stereotypes that are associated with the marginalized group (i.e., women).

As I alluded to in the previous chapter, stereotypes are highly variable, malleable, and often ephemeral. While traditional sexism exists in countless societies and throughout history, the specific stereotypes associated with women and men may differ significantly over time, and from culture to culture. In Western cultures during the late eighteenth century, showing off one's legs was viewed as masculine, whereas covering up one's legs was seen as feminine—nowadays that assumption is reversed.[7] As I previously noted, the notion that the color pink is for girls and blue is for boys may seem second nature for us, but in the early 1900s, many people held the opposite assumption. Even within the last fifty years, common gender stereotypes—such as men must have short hair and women long hair, that men work outside the home and women work within the home, and even that men and women must be exclusively heterosexual—no longer hold as much sway as they used to. In other words, stereotypes may come and go over time, and vary from person to person, without the hierarchy ever waning. Indeed, one can rather easily imagine a world where women are able to engage in same-sex relationships and dress androgynously, yet still be viewed as being less legitimate than men in the eyes of society.

So despite claims to the contrary, reversing stereotypes like this will not automatically dismantle the associated hierarchy. But what it most certainly will achieve is making the corresponding activist movement more exclusive. For instance, there has been a tendency within certain strands of feminism to tout women who shun feminine gender expression and relationships with men as model feminists, while viewing feminine and heterosexual women in a rather condescending manner. So it's no surprise that many contemporary feminine heterosexual women who are all for eliminating traditional sexism nevertheless avoid labeling themselves as feminists.[8] If feminists instead worked to eliminate these stereotypes rather than reverse them—for instance, by emphasizing that women are heterogeneous with regards to their sexual orientation and gender expression—I believe that feminism would be a far more robust movement than it is today.

Because activists who hold fixed perspectives only recognize certain double standards, but not others, they often express wildly inconsistent attitudes toward stereotypes. For instance, many feminists who contend that women should transgress stereotypes like compulsory femininity and heterosexuality, will simultaneously insist that women should conform to other stereotypes, such as that women should have been assigned female at birth, and should be interested in loving committed relationships rather than seeking out promiscuous uncommitted sex.

In the previous chapter, I mentioned ideality—how members of a group will inevitably be heterogeneous with regards to whether they defy or conform to the specific stereotypes that are associated with their group, and how this can lead some individuals to be misconstrued as being illegitimate members of the group. Thus, a woman like myself can be excluded from feminism both for the fact that I transgress certain stereotypes (e.g., by not being assigned female at birth) *and* conform to other stereotypes (e.g., being feminine) associated with women.

This picking and choosing of which stereotypes one should conform to and which should be transgressed is completely arbitrary. As a femme-identified trans woman, I could turn cis feminist double standards on their head, and claim that cissexual assumption is a double standard that all righteous feminists should transgress, whereas compulsory femininity is a double standard to which all righteous feminists should conform. And I could write brilliant manifestos declaring that all people must change their sex, and embrace feminine gender expression, as that is the only way to subvert traditional sexism. My new movement would be super self-empowering (not to mention convenient) for me, but it would disenfranchise countless women. It would also be complete bullshit, as it is based on the fallacies that gender and sexual traits have fixed meanings, that there are a limited number of double standards, and that, therefore, there are straightforward one-size-fits-all solutions that will challenge sexism in all situations and contexts.

A HOLISTIC APPROACH TO FEMINISM

That is a relatively brief summary of the many pitfalls associated with relying on fixed perspectives on sexism and marginalization. Often when I give presentations on this topic, I make the following analogy: Those of us who live on the planet Earth are anchored to a fixed position in the universe. When we look up at the night sky, we see the same familiar set of stars, forming the same constellations we were taught to recognize as children: Orion, the Big Dipper, and so on. It is easy for us to mistakenly presume that we are viewing the universe in its fullest capacity, but that is not actually the case. There are countless other stars and galaxies that we cannot perceive from our position in the universe. And even those stars that we can discern would appear to be in entirely different configurations if we observed them from a different vantage point. The three stars that make up Orion's belt would most likely look like an odd-shaped triangle, rather than a nice and neat straight line, if we were to view it from some distant solar system.

Analogously, each of us is located at somewhat fixed positions within a network of myriad double standards. Most of us go through our lives facing the same sets of double standards over and over again—they seem real and reliable to us, whereas other double standards consistently remain invisible or distorted from our vantage point. Given this, I can understand why most people tend to rely on fixed perspectives to make sense of sexism and marginalization. I suppose that I am a little more attuned to this problem than other people, in part due to my transition from male to female. Upon being perceived as female for the first time, I suddenly experienced all sorts of sexist double standards that I was not privy to before, whereas others double standards that had dogged me for years seemed to vanish before my eyes. And the same behaviors and bodily attributes that I had always exhibited suddenly took on very different meanings in the eyes of other people once I was viewed as a woman rather than a man.[9]

In addition to that experience, as a bisexual femme-tomboy transsexual woman, I exist at the borderlands of a number of different identities, and my body and actions are often interpreted in a variety of ways depending upon whether people read me as trans or cis, as feminine or tomboyish, or whether the partner I am with leads people to presume that I am lesbian or heterosexual (funny how they never correctly guess bisexual).[10] And while I often move through more traditional mainstream settings where patriarchal and heteronormative assumptions dominate, I also spend lots of time in exceptional communities—such as feminist and women-only spaces, gay male–dominated queer spaces, old-school lesbian spaces, contemporary queer women's spaces populated primarily by cis women and trans men, mixed queer spaces populated by people of diverse genders and sexualities, and various kinds of trans majority spaces. And I can tell you that every single one of these different spaces has its own set of beliefs and assumptions, and each tends to develop its own set of norms.

The marginalization that I face cannot be summed up in terms of patriarchy, or the gender binary, or some other fixed and monolithic gender system. Rather, as a unique human being driven by my own interests, tendencies, and desires, I feel like I am constantly juggling an ever-shifting conglomeration of double standards.

To be clear, I am not claiming to have some kind of grand knowledge of all aspects of sexism and marginalization as a result of the multiplicity of identities and settings that I have inhabited throughout my life. My perspective remains relatively fixed in many ways as someone who moves through the world as a white, middle-class, able-bodied U.S. citizen. What I am saying is that my experiences have convinced me that fixed perspectives may offer us certain useful insights, but in many ways they are inaccurate and exclusionary, and will ultimately fail us in the end. Therefore, I will spend the rest of the book forwarding an alternative approach, what I call a *holistic approach to feminism*.

I am not using the term "feminism" here in the narrow sense that some use it (e.g., to focus solely on women's rights or issues), but rather to refer to a wide-ranging movement to challenge all double standards based on sex, gender, and/or sexuality. Furthermore, this approach to feminism remains committed to intersectionality and working to challenge all forms of marginalization, rather than focusing solely on specific forms of sexism.

I am calling this feminist perspective "holistic" for at least two reasons. First, it starts from the premise that biological, cultural, and experiential variation come together in an intricate fashion to produce people who are fundamentally heterogeneous with regards to their sex, gender, sexuality, and countless other traits (as I detailed in Chapter 13). Thus, this approach is holistic in that it attempts to accommodate this diversity, rather than favoring people of a particular body type, identity, or tendency. Second, this approach to feminism is holistic in that it recognizes that there are myriad double standards, and it attempts to forge new strategies that challenge *all* forms of sexism and marginalization, rather than merely those that we personally experience or are already familiar with.

Now one might ask: "How can we possibly challenge *all* double standards, especially when we aren't even aware of many of them?" I believe that there are several general strategies that will make a positive impact in this regard. The first, and perhaps most important, is to thoroughly understand the unmarked/marked distinction and the many hallmarks of double standards (e.g., how marked individuals are deemed to be remarkable, questionable, artificial, abnormal, exotic, alien, and suspect), which I already covered in Chapter 14, "How Double Standards Work." We should also be intimately familiar with the many double binds that marked individuals face. Being able to recognize the telltale signs of double standards represents a vital first step toward challenging all forms of sexism and marginalization.

Another obvious strategy is to ensure that when we are confronted with a double standard, that we work to eliminate it, rather than reverse it. We should dismantle hierarchies rather than inverting them. And instead of insisting that all people live up to our own universal assumptions, or the stereotypes that we project onto their specific group(s), we should recognize that people are fundamentally heterogeneous, and they will inevitably fall all over the map with regards to the traits they possess. I discuss this latter point in more detail in the following chapter, "Expecting Heterogeneity."

There are a few other holistic strategies that I will forward over the rest of the book, and which I believe will help undermine all forms of sexism and marginalization in a general way. They include: challenging gender entitlement, self-examining desire, embracing ambivalence, recognizing invalidations, and acknowledging that activism is a balancing act.

EXPECTING HETEROGENEITY

CHAPTER SEVENTEEN

T wo chapters ago, I discussed three different types of double standards: hierarchies, universal assumptions, and stereotypes. Hierarchies position one group as being superior and/or more legitimate than another. In contrast, the latter two types might be thought of as *homogenizing double standards*, as they create the impression that people are more uniform and homogeneous than they actually are. Universal assumptions are norms that all people within a given setting are expected to meet, while stereotypes are norms or assumptions that members of a particular group are expected to meet. When we defy other people's expectations—whether it be universal assumptions or stereotypes—we will become marked in their eyes, and they may marginalize us as a result. Stereotypes in particular play a major role in marginalization, as they create the impression that members of marginalized groups are particularly homogeneous, and therefore distinct from the dominant unmarked group. In other words, universal assumptions and stereotypes can both give rise to, and further bolster, the hierarchies that delegitimize us.

Given this, it stands to reason that if we wish to challenge all double standards (even those that we may not be currently aware of), then a good place to start would be to reject stereotypes and universal assumptions. In other words, as we move through the world or within a specific setting, we must learn to expect that people will *not* all be the same. We must expect to encounter people who will be exceptional, and whose behaviors and opinions will surprise us. In short, we have to learn to *expect heterogeneity*.

I have purposefully chosen to use the word "heterogeneity" rather than "diversity" here. Within feminist, queer, and social justice movements, diversity is something that is routinely touted, albeit only within certain pre-defined parameters. Usually, when people talk about "striving for diversity," they are rather specifically talking about displaying a mix of people of different races, ethnicities, religions, classes, genders, sexual orientations, ages, and/or abilities. In other words, these are the handful of different traits that "count" toward imparting diversity onto an organization or movement. While I most certainly believe that achieving diversity in these regards is important, what concerns me is that these are not the only traits that exist. People also vary in our childhoods, families, geographies, customs, educations, occupations, personalities, use of language, style of dress, tastes, interests, beliefs, experiences, obstacles, and aspirations. These latter traits are usually not considered as falling under the rubric of diversity. So when people talk about wanting to bring "diversity" to their organizations and movements, it often seems as though they're imagining a nice and neat picture of a group of people who on the surface all look different from one another, but yet all behave in the same manner, hold the same opinions, and share the same mutual experiences and perspectives. That is not diversity, it is merely fantasy.

It is this quest for "diversity," but not true heterogeneity, that leads to the problem of tokenism. For instance, there are many times in which

I am the only trans woman within a given feminist or queer space. In and of itself, this would not be such a bad thing provided that people recognized heterogeneity—both the fact that my experiences and the obstacles I face as a trans woman will lead me to differ from the non-trans-woman majority in certain ways, but also that I will differ from other trans women in many ways as well. Sadly, I am often not seen as different in these ways. In some instances, people will expect me to behave as a "stereotypical" trans woman. Since the stereotypes people harbor about trans women are often quite disparaging, this can create innumerable difficulties for me in the space. Other times, people will be excited to have me in their space because they view my presence as adding "diversity." But then if I bring up trans woman–specific perspectives or issues, my concerns are sometimes deemed as being "outside the scope" of the space or organization, or my opinions may even be mischaracterized as "divisive." In other words, the assumption is that everyone in the space must conform to a homogeneous set of views and perspectives, despite any superficial appearance of "diversity."

In her book *Feminist Theory: From Margin to Center*, bell hooks has written about the experiences she and other black women have faced as tokens in white-dominated feminist spaces:

> *The condescension they directed at black women was one of the means they employed to remind us that the women's movement was "theirs"—that we were able to participate because they allowed it, even encouraged it; after all, we were needed to legitimate the process. They did not see us as equals. They did not treat us as equals. And though they expected us to provide first hand accounts of black experience, they felt it was their role to decide if these experiences were authentic . . . If we dared to criticize the movement or to assume responsibility for reshaping feminist ideas and introducing new ideas, our voices were tuned out, dismissed,*

silenced. We could be heard only if our statements echoed the senti-
ments of the dominant discourse.[1]

I have heard countless similar stories over the years: feminist organizations that want to be inclusive to disabled people, but who don't want
to hear complaints about how their space is not accessible; queer organizations who want to brag about their age diversity, but who don't want to
hear complaints about how the anti-homelessness policies in their local
gay neighborhood impact queer youth living on the streets. We simply
cannot expect people to differ in their gender, sexual orientation, race,
class, ability, and age without also expecting them to differ from us
in countless other ways—especially with regards to their perspectives,
issues, needs, and concerns. Diversity has become a "buzz word," an oversimplified ideal. We should instead embrace heterogeneity—the fact that
people in the population at large, and within our own movements and
communities, will invariably differ with regards to every possible trait.
Heterogeneity is messy and complicated, but we must come to expect it.

Any group or organization can become somewhat homogeneous
over time, but this tendency seems to be amplified in feminist and queer
settings. One likely reason for this is that we envision ourselves as existing in opposition to the dominant mainstream. Because we are constantly
reacting (or perhaps in some cases overreacting) to straight male–centric
norms that are pervasive throughout society, we are especially inclined
to create subcultures with an inverted set of norms.[2] This explains why
we so frequently try to reverse many of the sexist double standards that
we face, rather than simply eliminating them—a troubling tactic that I
critiqued in the previous chapter. As a result, some people within feminist and queer movements actively denounce or look down upon gender
conformity, feminine dress, heterosexual relationships, monogamy, and/
or vanilla sex, while praising contrarian (and supposedly more revolutionary) ways of being. It's as though we are trying to conquer sexism by

creating some kind of Bizarro World, where heteronormative and patri-archal norms have all been reversed.[3]

Sometimes the norms we invent are not necessarily inversions of sexist double standards, but they are norms nevertheless. I've been in particular segments of the queer community where it seemed as though everybody was dressed similarly, sported the same haircut, enjoyed the same genres of music, and found the exact same people attractive. It's almost as if some of us take the word "homo" a little bit too seriously. This sense that we should all dress and act in a rather uniform fashion creates an insider/outsider mindset, where some people are deemed "*bona fide* queers," or "liberated women," while others are deemed less worthy or merely dupes of the hetero-patriarchy. Such norms are not only exclu-sionary, but they represent a brand new set of stereotypes that queer folks and feminists are now expected to live up to, and for which they may be marginalized if they fail to do so.

In feminist and queer movements, we often decry essentialism. We tend to pounce on anyone who claims that women are naturally pro-grammed to behave in particular ways, or that a particular queer sub-group shares the same underlying genetic, hormonal, or neurological condition. Why do we despise essentialism so much? Well, because it creates the false impression that we are one big homogeneous group who all share the same set of traits, and who are entirely distinct from the dominant group. In doing this, essentialism props up the hierarchies that marginalize us, and imparts stigma onto individuals who fail to live up to the homogenizing expectations that have been placed on the group. So it is profoundly ironic that many of the same people who are fast and loose with accusations of "essentialism" routinely create and enforce an entirely new set of stereotypes that they expect other feminists or queer folks to conform to.

Of course, the people who promote these newfangled stereotypes probably don't see things quite this way. They would probably assert that there are pre-existing stereotypes in the culture—e.g., that women must be feminine and exclusively attracted to men. And so by encouraging women to do the contrary—e.g., being gender-non-conforming and homosexual—they are in effect subverting the original stereotype. While this may sound like a promising tactic, it happens to be patently untrue in practice. Social psychologists have examined under what conditions people abandon the stereotypes they hold. It turns out that when only a few members of a group contradict the group's stereotypes in an extreme manner, they tend to be *subtyped*—that is, thrown into a category all of their own.[4] One can see this subtyping in how people who shatter conventional stereotypes of women are often viewed as being "butches" or "dykes" rather than "real women." Or in the tendency people have to view trans women not as legitimate women who differ from other women with regards to one trait (i.e., being trans), but rather as "trannies" or "transwomen" (a single bizarre hybrid word, rather than the adjective "trans" followed by the noun "women"). By subtyping unconventional women into a separate category, others can preserve their belief that women (as a general rule) conform to stereotypes.

In contrast to this tendency to subtype, social psychologists have found that when non-stereotypic traits are spread more evenly throughout a group—that is, if the group appears to be fundamentally heterogeneous—then people do tend to question and abandon their previously held stereotypes.[5] To clarify, I am not suggesting that those of us who are extremely non-stereotypical should stop being that way; as a heterogeneous group, there will always be some of us who defy group-specific stereotypes more so than others. Rather, I am suggesting that we learn to embrace and celebrate the fact that all groups are heterogeneous, that we differ in almost every possible way imaginable. Forwarding this notion of heterogeneity will not only increase the size of our movements (by welcoming people who currently do not conform to Bizarro World stereotypes of women and queer folks), but it may also more effectively convince the dominant mainstream to relinquish the stereotypes they so often project onto us.

Perhaps nowhere is our reluctance toward embracing heterogeneity more evident than in the way that the concept of "safe space" plays out in feminist and queer settings. While I most certainly believe that we can and should create spaces free of sexism and marginalization—that is, double standard–free spaces—I have found that in practice, the idea of "safe space" routinely devolves into a euphemism for "*same* space," one in which we expect all inhabitants to conform to our homogeneous notions about the group. When we believe that people must meet our requirement of uniformity, then we will be more likely to mark any person in the space whose presence surprises or disturbs us. As I have stated numerous times previously, we tend to mark people who we view as unexpected, exceptional, or as members of an outgroup. And we are inclined to view such groups negatively, suspiciously, and stereotypically.[6]

The straight male–centric mainstream polices atypical individuals by deriding them as unnatural, abnormal, or immoral. In feminist and queer circles—where our focus is on challenging sexism and marginalization—we police our borders by accusing atypical individuals of being our oppressors. In her aforementioned book, bell hooks describes how white women who dominate feminist spaces often accuse feminists of color of being too "angry," and will mischaracterize their critiques as attacks.[7] Alice Echols chronicles how during the early 1970s, feminists who brought up issues of class and lesbianism within the movement were often accused of being "male-identified" and of seeking to sabotage feminism.[8] And as I have discussed in the first section of this book, in queer spaces (where cisgender gay and lesbian folks dominate), transgender, bisexual, and femme folks have repeatedly been accused of "reinforcing" the gender system, and of leveraging male, heterosexual, and/or "passing" privilege over others.

It is patently unreasonable and unfair to expect each marginalized subgroup who shows up in a particular feminist or queer space to have to justify their presence, prove that they pose no threat, and petition for their own inclusion. Rather, it should be incumbent upon each of us to expect to experience difference within our organizations, movements, and communities. We must learn to expect the unexpected, to expect the exceptional. We must expect to encounter people who represent our outgroups, and refrain from viewing them as suspicious, or depicting them as being our oppressors. And rather than simply complaining about essentialism, we should look at the broader picture and challenge all stereotypes, all forms of homogenization.

There are some who have argued that this tendency toward homogenization is somehow related to identity. In other words, when we as women, or as some specific queer subgroup, organize ourselves under a particular identity label, then we will automatically gravitate toward uniformity, essentialism, and exclusion. Activists who believe this will usually propose that the solution to this supposed problem is that we should abandon identity labels altogether. While I agree that homogenization is a severe problem, I wholeheartedly disagree with this particular analysis and proposed solution. First of all, identities are merely ways of expressing certain attributes that we possess, and they don't automatically lead to homogenization. I just so happen to identify (to varying degrees) as a writer, a biologist, a guitarist, a baseball fan, a lucid dreamer, a Californian, a cancer survivor, and a bird person. Each of these labels communicates some aspect of my person. And while some of these identities may be associated with a handful of stereotypes, these stereotypes are fairly loosely held, primarily because none of these groups are particularly marginalized in our culture.

In stark contrast, when I describe myself as a woman, or bisexual, or transsexual, those identities *are* associated with a plethora of strictly enforced stereotypes, precisely because these groups are all highly marginalized in our culture. Such stereotypes are especially relentless and unyielding because they are helping to prop up a hierarchy that is pervasive in our culture. As a result, the dominant majority, as well as other members of my own marginalized group, will harshly judge me based upon whether I seem to conform to, or transgress, these particular stereotypes.

When we attempt to compel minority and marginalized groups to relinquish their identity labels, our concern is entirely misplaced, as the tendency towards homogenization lies not with the marginalized group's choice of labels, but with the projecting of stereotypes onto the group in the first place. To this point, I could choose to reject the labels "transsexual," "bisexual," or "woman" if I wanted, but that would not stop other people from perceiving, stereotyping, and marginalizing me for being these very things. The only thing that abandoning these identity labels would accomplish is making it more difficult for me to talk about the marginalization I face at the hands of the dominant majority.

As activists, it is important for us to talk about our experiences and perspectives as women, queers, trans people, and so on. But we must refrain from viewing our groups homogeneously. We should seek to eliminate all stereotypes associated with our groups, rather than compel other group members to either conform to or transgress those stereotypes. And while all groups necessarily have some kind of defining characteristic(s)—guitarists play guitar, cancer survivors have survived cancer—we should seek to make the requirements to be in the group as loose and accommodating as possible. Since our goal is to challenge sexism, I find it useful to consider group labels as umbrella terms for people who share certain forms of marginalization (as I outlined in Chapter 1, "A Word About Words"). According to this scheme, "women" is an umbrella term for people who move through the world as women, and face traditional sexism as a result; "queer" is an umbrella term for people who are deemed by society as "not straight," and who face similar forms of marginalization as a result. Umbrellas can vary in how broad or specific they are. For instance, sometimes it is relevant for me to speak about being transsexual, as certain forms of sexism that transsexuals face are highly specific to us. Other times it is useful to speak more generally about sexisms that are faced by all transgender people, or queer people, and so on.

I think that sometimes we get a little too hung up about the labels themselves, especially in LGBTQIA+ communities. There are constant attempts to rebrand group labels for political, aesthetic, and/or generational reasons: from homosexual to gay, lesbian to dyke, bisexual to pansexual, transgender to trans*, and so on. And there are constant debates about the pros and cons of reclaiming words like queer, fag, tranny, pervert, and the like. Language is important, and certain labels do have different meanings and connotations than others (although those meanings often shift over time as well). But I do think that we would be better served if, rather than obsessing over label choice and who gets to be included under which moniker, we prioritized wrestling marginalized groups (and their associated identity labels) away from the countless stereotypes that weigh them down. In other words, rather than spending all our effort trying to distinguish our group from others (a project that typically creates new stereotypes and norms for group membership), we should instead highlight the fundamental heterogeneity that exists within all groups, as this will lead us to create more inclusive activist movements, and help to undermine the hierarchies that marginalize us.

CHALLENGING GENDER ENTITLEMENT

In describing my holistic approach to feminism thus far, I have argued that we should expect heterogeneity and that we should stop policing other people's genders and sexualities. I believe that these are useful rules of thumb if we want to foster inclusion and reduce sexism. But of course, alone, these axioms are insufficient. Every day, people are undermined or injured in the name of sex, gender, and sexuality. For instance, some people express their genders and sexualities in ways that are nonconsensual or that delegitimize other people. Given this, it is important to ask: Where should we draw the line between valid expressions of gender and sexual variation, and objectionable expressions of sexism and marginalization? How do we decide which expressions of gender and sexuality we should accept and even embrace, and which we should forcibly seek to challenge and eliminate?

I have already discussed the many problems associated with fixed views of gender and sexuality, and their tendency to deem certain bodies and behaviors to be inherently good or bad, natural or unnatural, moral or immoral. Given this, I believe that what we desperately need is not some sort of gender morality—a one-size-fits-all set of rules that attempts to describe all gender- and sexuality-based oppression and that offers simple, straightforward solutions to how we should challenge it (in previous chapters, I explained why such approaches are impossible and inevitably lead to erasure and exclusion). Instead, what we need is a set of *gender ethics* that are flexible, contextual, and applicable in all situations. In working through this problem, I was influenced by strategies that I developed when I was first coming to terms with my personal relationship with religion. While this may seem like a bit of a digression, I want to briefly share some of these insights, as I believe they are germane to this idea of developing a set of gender ethics.

Religiously, I often describe myself as a recovering Catholic. I was raised Catholic, but I rejected that religion at the age of fifteen, mostly because of the shame and guilt I experienced over many years as an isolated trans child grappling with the belief that my desire to be female was tantamount to sin in the eyes of God. Later in my life, I would eventually meet other Catholic trans people who took a different route than me, continuing to identify as Catholic, but rejecting the more conservative human voices in the Catholic church who dismiss transsexuality and gender non-conformity as sin. In all honesty, that route never occurred to me. Anyway, my initial reaction as a teenager was to outright reject religion entirely. I became a very hardcore atheist—Bill Maher would have loved me as a teenager.[1] Not only did I personally reject Catholicism, but I viewed all religions as nefarious hegemonic institutions that set out to convert and subdue people into submission. I saw people who were devoutly religious as dupes who bought into a restrictive oppressive system that I had long ago tossed away.[2]

It can be quite self-reassuring to hold such a hardline, self-righteous, cut-and-dried view of the world. But as time passed, my once dogmatic views were challenged by new friends and acquaintances who were smart, independent critical-thinker types, yet who nevertheless were religious or spiritual in some way. They challenged my assumption that people can only ever be brainwashed into religion, or that it was somehow a sign of lacking intellectual rigor. As a result, I eventually began to call myself agnostic rather than atheist. Part of this transition involved admitting that while I have never personally experienced evidence that a god or some higher power exists, I also have no definitive proof that such things do not exist. This standard agnostic view very much resonates with the scientist in me. But another important part of my agnosticism was leaving myself open to the possibility that perhaps my religious and spiritual friends have very real experiences that I am not privy to.

This latter idea was heavily influenced by my trans experience. I spent my life struggling with an understanding that I should be female rather than male. While this understanding is very real to me, other people who have not had a trans experience tend to dismiss me as merely being confused or delusional. And I find such claims to be extremely invalidating, but also horribly arrogant. Who are they to judge the validity of my own self-knowledge and understanding? Similarly, I realized that for friends of mine who experience a higher power, or a life force, or a god, or gods (as for some reason, I seem to have as many pagan friends as Christian ones these days), who am I to doubt their self-knowledge and understanding? So sometimes when I am asked about my religious beliefs, I will half-jokingly call myself a "trans-agnostic," to acknowledge the fact that I can never truly speak for other people's religious experiences and perspectives any more than they can speak for my trans experiences and perspectives.

My transition from atheist to trans-agnostic left me with a dilemma of sorts. On the one hand, religion can be a unique, rewarding personal experience for many individuals. On the other hand, religion can be misused as a tool for marginalizing other people, such as when LGBTQIA+ folks are denounced as sinners, when people use passages in the Bible to justify keeping women in a subordinate, second-class position where they must defer to the men in their lives, or when religious doctrine is invoked to justify war, torture, slavery, and murder. It seems to me that in these latter cases, the problem isn't religion *per se* (as other non-religious ideologies such as politics and nationalism have been invoked to justify similar atrocities). Rather, the true problem is simply arrogance and entitlement—when other people assume that their ideology somehow trumps other people's life experiences and self-knowledge, or when they feel that somehow they have the right to force all other people to follow their ideology whether it resonates with those individuals or not.

Over the course of my life, I have come to understand that I am not necessarily opposed to any specific religious ideology or belief system, but what I do reject is other people's *entitlement*. If you worship a particular god, or consensually engage in religious rituals with others who share your beliefs, that is totally fine with me. But if you were to call me a sinner, or insist that I follow your religious laws, or if you believe that I need to be converted to your religion, then your ideology has become nonconsensual, and I object to that kind of entitlement!

I believe that this analogy about religion has great import for thinking through many of our shared concerns about gender and sexuality. On the one hand, we each have a unique gender and sexual experience, where certain desires and expressions inexplicably resonate with us on a deep and profound level, while others do not. We should celebrate this heterogeneity. But there is also a "dark side" of gender—what I call *gender entitlement*—where we arrogantly project our worldview, our norms, our expectations and assumptions about sex, gender, and sexuality onto all other people, regardless of whether it resonates with them or not.

When we talk about all of our beefs with the gender binary—that it forces people into one box or another, how it erases those of us who are gender variant in some way, or worse, outright condemns us for not following other people's gender norms—these problems do not stem from maleness and femaleness, or even "twoness," but rather from gender entitlement—the fact that society expects people to identify and express their genders in particular ways and punishes them if they do not. Similarly, in traditional sexism, people presume that women are inferior to men, and that femininity is inferior to masculinity. Once again, the problem here is not women, or men, or femininity, or masculinity *per se*, but rather gender entitlement—the fact that people make assumptions and value judgments about certain bodies and behaviors, and then nonconsensually project those hierarchies and stereotypes onto all other people.

I would argue that gender entitlement plays a foundational role in all forms of sexism. Therefore, rather than trying to challenge the gender binary, or patriarchy, or any other gender system (all of which are incomplete models that omit certain forms of sexism), I would argue that we should work to eliminate all forms of gender entitlement from the world. In addition to being a more thorough approach, focusing our efforts on gender entitlement is also a more ethical approach. It is ethical because this approach does not undermine or malign people for their bodies and what desires resonate with them—whether they are female, or male, or intersex, or transsexual, or genderqueer, or feminine, or masculine, or androgynous, or heterosexual, or homosexual, or bisexual, or pansexual, or asexual, or kinky, or vanilla, or polyamorous, or monogamous, and so on. Rather, it only challenges people when they nonconsensually project their ideology and expectations about gender and sexuality onto all other people.

RECOGNIZING GENDER ENTITLEMENT

Gender entitlement relies on a central assumption: We presume that whatever beliefs, expectations, or preferences that we personally have regarding sex, gender, and/or sexuality must also apply to, or hold true for, other people. In making this assumption, we often invalidate those people's own gender and sexual identities, desires, and experiences. Sometimes we are consciously gender-entitled—for instance, when we denounce other people's bodies, genders, or sexualities on the basis that they do not conform to some kind of overarching theory or ideology that we believe is true and universal. Other times we are unconsciously gender-entitled, such as when we unthinkingly project the double standards that we harbor (e.g., women are weak, bisexuals are promiscuous, transsexuals are confused about their gender) onto other people.

Gender entitlement often takes the form of homogenizing assumptions about who we believe people are and how we expect them to behave in the future. This includes universalizing assumptions, such as expecting everyone we meet to be heterosexual, or cisgender, or monosexual, and so on. Other assumptions will come in the form of stereotypes that we project onto people belonging to a specific group. Sometimes our assumptions may match those commonly made in the culture at large, whereas other times our assumptions may be quite different (e.g., when queer people boast about having "gaydar"—the supposed ability to know for sure whether other people are queer or not without having to ask them). As I have discussed throughout this book, assumptions pretty much suck. Sure, sometimes the assumptions we make are correct, but often they are flat-out incorrect. And unfortunately, the burden always ends up being on the "assumee" (i.e., the person who the assumption is made about) to challenge any incorrect assumptions that are made by the "assumer" (i.e., the person who makes the assumption). Sometimes when I point out the incorrect assumptions that people make about me, it is no big deal. Other times, it can be slightly awkward or time consuming, and in some instances it can be downright awful. Because of horrible negative reactions that I have received in some cases (especially upon coming out to people as trans), I am often hesitant to correct other people's incorrect assumptions about me. But this also has negative consequences: It forces me to keep quiet about that aspect of myself, which can be both difficult and disempowering. Furthermore, if that information ever comes to light at a later date, I may be accused of hiding the truth or deceiving other people. In other words, incorrect assumptions create a damned-if-I-do, damned-if-I-don't situation for me—what I referred to as the pass/reveal double bind several chapters ago.

Another form of gender entitlement occurs when we unduly place fixed meanings and value judgments onto other people's identities, bodies, and behaviors—for example, when we claim that some genders or sexualities are inherently good and others bad; some inherently moral and others immoral; some inherently attractive and others unattractive; some inherently subversive and others conservative; and so on. Anyone who truly accepts heterogeneity will recognize that bodies, genders, and sexualities are not inherently good nor bad, but rather simply different. I am a bisexual femme-tomboy transsexual woman. My gender and sexuality are not inherently any better or any worse than a cisgender heterosexual masculine man, or an androgynous genderqueer pansexual drag performer. We are all merely different from one another.

Because we may experience certain desires, and because certain ways of being gendered or sexual may resonate with us more than others, it is inevitable that we will develop *personal meanings*—i.e., we will personally like, appreciate, or prefer, some aspects of sex, gender, and sexuality more so than others. But in order to be ethically gendered, we must not presume that our own personal meanings represent fixed meanings—i.e., those that are supposedly universal and apply to all other people. Specific identities and bodies, and expressions of gender and sexuality, do not have any fixed values or meanings—their meanings can vary from place to place, and from person to person. Some people might think that it is wonderful when I wear a dress, while others may assume that it is a bad thing. Some may assume that by wearing a dress I am signaling the fact that I am docile and demure, whereas I may personally feel defiant and badass when wearing a dress. In other words, the act of wearing a dress does not have any fixed or inherent meanings built into it—like all aspects of sex, gender, and sexuality, it is essentially a blank screen that other people will often project their own values, meanings, and assumptions upon. It is one thing to acknowledge our own personal likes and dislikes, but that act becomes entitled and nonconsensual once we start believing that our own preferences represent fixed meanings or values that must hold true for all other people.

Another example of the difference between personal meanings and fixed meanings can be found in how people wrap their brain around romantic and sexual attraction. For example, I find some people attractive, and other people not so attractive. The set of people that I find attractive is unique to me—I am sure that no one else in the world precisely shares it. It is a personal set of meanings that I hold. Most of us respect the fact that people differ in their personal meanings regarding attraction—otherwise we would be in absolute shock every time we met someone that we didn't find attractive, yet learned that they have a significant other. However, some people *do* assume that attraction is a fixed set of meanings, and they will claim that certain people are flatout attractive or unattractive, no ifs, ands, or buts about it. Such people may also deride or dismiss individuals who choose these supposedly "unattractive" partners—for example, by assuming that these individuals must have "bad taste" or be "desperate" to have chosen such partners, or perhaps even claiming that the individual must have some kind of "perversion" or "fetish" for that type of person. Such claims are clearly gender-entitled, as they involve projecting one's own personal meanings regarding attraction and desire onto other people.

Here is another manifestation of gender entitlement: Let's say you hold a specific gender ideology and you meet someone who does not conform to your worldview. You seemingly have two potential responses.

First, you could alter your ideology to accommodate or include that person. Unfortunately, most of us tend to be far too invested in our personal worldview to do that. The more convenient option then is to attempt to delegitimize or erase these individuals who threaten your ideology. This tactic might be described as *gender erasure*. For example, some people are convinced that all men are naturally attracted to women, and all women naturally attracted to men. Such people will often try to invalidate the existence of those who experience same-sex attraction by inventing explanations or ulterior motives, such as, "You're not really gay, it's just a phase; you're just looking for an alternative lifestyle; you just haven't met the right person yet; perhaps you were duped by the homosexual agenda." Throughout this book, I have discussed other ulterior motives that are routinely projected onto people who are trans, bisexual, feminine, and so on. While different, all of these accusations share a common thread: They all actively erase the perspectives and life experiences of people who do not easily fit into the assumer's worldview. And as with all assumptions, the burden of proof then falls onto the assumee (in this case, the person whose identity is being erased) to call out the assumption in order to justify their own existence. Those of us who have had aspects of our body, identity, gender, or sexuality erased by other people know first-hand how invalidating this can be, so we should work hard to eliminate such instances of gender erasure both within our feminist and queer movements, as well as in society more generally.

While it is gender-entitled for us to project our own personal worldview regarding sex, gender, and sexuality onto all other people, what is even more arrogant—not to mention potentially destructive—is when we try to force or coerce other people to alter their desires and behaviors in order to better conform to our personal worldview. I refer to this especially blatant manifestation of gender entitlement as *gender policing*. Bullying is perhaps the most obvious example of gender policing, as it involves verbally or physically punishing people who fail to live up to our assumptions and expectations. But gender policing can also occur through small and seemingly innocuous acts, such as complimenting or praising people when they behave in ways that conform to our expectations or ideals, and withholding praise or making discouraging remarks when they do not. These relatively subtle forms of gender policing form the backbone of gender socialization during childhood, as well as the peer pressure we all experience as both children and adults. Basically, it is gender policing that provides the "compulsory" aspect of compulsory heterosexuality, compulsory femininity, and other forms of sexism.

Finally, the most entitled thing that we can possibly do is to assume that somebody's gender, sexuality, body, or person more generally belongs to us—that we are free to do anything we want with them without their consideration. In other words, this is where gender entitlement ventures into the realm of violence, abuse, rape, slavery, and so forth. Admittedly, gender entitlement can (and often does) play a role in these more extreme cases, but so do many other factors. So I am reluctant to refer to such instances as examples of gender entitlement. Rather, I think that it is more useful to imagine gender entitlement (and entitlement more generally) as being a spectrum where, at the far end, lies complete dehumanization.

ERADICATING GENDER ENTITLEMENT

That is a brief overview of gender entitlement and the central role that it plays in all forms of sexism. I first forwarded this concept in *Whipping Girl*, but unlike some other ideas in that book, gender entitlement never really caught on.[3] Maybe I did not articulate it clearly. Or maybe I should have made it a more consistent theme throughout the book. Perhaps these factors played a role. But I also think that part of the lack of enthusiasm stems from the fact that challenging gender entitlement is such a daunting undertaking. After all, it is relatively easy to excite people about the idea that we should shatter the gender binary, or overthrow the patriarchy, because those scenarios have obvious good and bad guys—we're the good guys trying to change the world for the better, and the bad guys are everyone else who supposedly enforces (or reinforces) the status quo. Challenging gender entitlement is far trickier because all of us make assumptions, and we all make value judgments, and sometimes we project these onto other people. Sometimes we expect other people to live up to our worldview, and sometimes we invalidate them if they do not. Challenging gender entitlement is not about us versus them, the righteous versus the oppressors. It is about being committed to challenging all gender assumptions, expectations, norms, and double standards, whether they stem from us or from other people.

So rather than starting with huge questions like, "How do we eradicate all gender entitlement from the face of the planet?" we should instead start locally by asking: "How do we eradicate gender entitlement from within ourselves?" Or another way of putting it: How do we become ethically gendered individuals? I would say that it must start with us becoming more aware of our assumptions—what assumptions are we making, why are we making them, and are we projecting them onto other people? My experiences in certain (albeit not all) trans spaces and mixed queer spaces have been helpful for me in this regard. When you enter a room where you do not necessarily know how any given person identifies—whether they are trans or cis, queer or straight, female or male or non-binary identified, or the specifics of their anatomy—it can be very humbling. Such experiences bring to the forefront the huge role that gender and sexual assumptions normally play in our culture. I have found these sorts of spaces to be way more consensual than most, as they force us to learn how to respectfully ask people about themselves, and to listen to what they tell us about their identities and lives.[4] Such spaces also tend to be way less judgmental than most settings, as it is taken for granted that people will fall all over the map with regards to their genders, sexualities, and embodiments.

I have also gained insight into how to be ethically gendered from BDSM and polyamorous communities, both of which avoid the idea that there is any one correct or ideal way to be sexual. For example, in the world at large, when people are disturbed or grossed out by a particular sexual act, they will often claim that such acts (and the people who engage in them) are "unnatural," "abnormal," "deviant," or "immoral." In other words, these people nonconsensually project their own value judgments and meanings onto such acts. In contrast, in the BDSM community, people will instead say that such acts "squick" them, meaning that they are personally disturbed or grossed out by that particular act, while at the same time recognizing that other people may legitimately find that act to be enjoyable. The fact that the word squick is typically used in the context of "I statements" (e.g., "I am squicked by missionary position penetration sex") forces people to recognize that their reaction is a personal one rather than a universal one that applies to all people. The BDSM community also accommodates diversity by adhering to flexible ethical guidelines rather than some rigidly fixed set of morals. Specifically, a guiding principle in BDSM communities is that all acts are acceptable provided that they are "safe, sane, and consensual." Similarly, in polyamorous communities, the guiding principle is often called "ethical non-monogamy" (which is admittedly where I borrowed the idea of being ethically gendered). According to ethical non-monogamy, all potential relationship configurations are deemed acceptable provided that all of the involved parties are fully informed and consent to the arrangement(s).

Consensuality also lies at the heart of being ethically gendered. Typically, when we think of consent, it is in the context of distinguishing between sexual experiences that we freely choose (and thus are consensual) versus those that are nonconsensually forced upon us, as in the cases of rape and sexual harassment. Nonconsensual acts dehumanize us—they erase our autonomy, our ability to make informed decisions about our own bodies and lives. While on the surface, instances of gender entitlement may not seem to be as traumatic as sexual harassment or rape, I would argue that they are just as nonconsensual, and are similarly invalidating. After all, when I project my own hierarchies, assumptions, meanings, and value judgments regarding sex, gender, and sexuality onto you, I am essentially denying your autonomy—your ability to decide for yourself who you are, and how you relate to your own sex, gender, and sexuality. This is precisely why it can feel so horribly invalidating when people deny our identity or experiences, treat us inferiorly, presume things about us that are not true, or expect us to behave according to their belief systems.

There are a number of ways in which our sexes, genders, and sexualities can become nonconsensual. If my being a woman requires you to be a man, or requires you to identify within the male/female binary, then that is nonconsensual. If my sexuality requires other people to perform their sexualities in similar or reciprocal ways, that is nonconsensual. If my femme, or transsexual, or bisexual identity is predicated on other people behaving in certain ways, inhabiting certain bodies, or living up to certain norms, then my identity becomes nonconsensual, and therefore not ethical. However, if my body and identity, and my expressions of gender and sexuality, do not make any claims or assumptions about you, nor produce any roles or requirements for you to fulfill, nor directly interfere with your life, then my gender is not nonconsensual, and therefore it is ethical.

When I wear a dress simply because it pleases me to do so, I would argue that that is an ethically gendered act, because my clothing choice does not impinge on anyone else's gender or life. But if I were to claim that all women should wear dresses, or that women always look better in dresses, or if I were to insist that you must wear (or not wear) a dress—these are all entitled claims that go beyond my personal preferences, and instead project my value system onto others.

Such claims are nonconsensual, as they invalidate other people's differing experiences and perspectives.

To be clear, when I say that wearing a dress can be an ethically gendered act, I am most certainly not advocating what is sometimes called "choice feminism"—i.e., the belief that, because I have a choice (in this case, between wearing a dress or not), whatever choice I make will necessarily be an expression of feminism.[5] We must remember that feminism is about challenging sexism. And sexism does not stem from how we "perform" our genders or sexualities, but rather from the double standards that we (and others) nonconsensually project onto other people. Therefore, simply acting upon our own gender and sexual desires (e.g., choosing to wear, or not wear, a dress) does nothing to challenge sexism in and of itself. It is similarly naive to believe that we can challenge sexism by simply responding to the double standards we face in one way or another (e.g., assuming that I can undermine masculine-centrism by wearing a dress, or undermine compulsory femininity by not wearing a dress), as these double standards are not contingent upon our reactions to them. Rather, these forms of sexism reside in the minds of the people who hold them, and the only way they can be undermined *is by changing those people's minds*—i.e., convincing them to relinquish the double standard in question.

To clarify, when I say that wearing a dress can be an ethically gendered act, it is not the dress-wearing that makes it ethical, but rather the fact that I do so in a non-entitled manner (i.e., by refusing to project my own opinions about dresses, or gender more generally, onto other people). And being a feminist is not about the personal choices we make about expressing our own genders and sexualities, but rather our commitment to challenging gender entitlement, both within ourselves as well as other people.

Feminists and queer activists who rely on fixed rather than holistic views might balk at the notion that a woman can wear a dress in an ethically gendered manner. For instance, they might argue that, being socialized female, most women have been brainwashed by patriarchy, heteronormativity, compulsory femininity, etc., into internalizing the idea that women should wear dresses, and therefore such women can never freely choose to wear a dress, as they are always under the influence of that gender system. Granted, I understand the desire to complicate the notion of "free choice"—after all, the life decisions we make are always constrained by the situations we encounter, the options that are presented to us, and the ideologies that we have been exposed to and use in order to make sense of the world. But if we suggest that women who wear dresses are merely operating under a "false consciousness," then we are essentially claiming that they are incapable of making informed decisions about their own bodies and lives. In other words, this assertion denies these women's autonomy, and therefore such claims are gender-entitled.

Furthermore, as I noted several chapters ago when discussing the dupes/fakes double bind, the "false consciousness" argument is problematic in that it is generally invoked against people who are marked. So for instance, those feminists who accuse women of operating under some kind of "false consciousness" for wearing dresses or other feminine items of clothing tend not to make reciprocal accusations of men who wear masculine clothing. Further evidence that the "false consciousness" argument is inherently delegitimizing can be found in the fact that gender-entitled heteronormative patriarchal types make the exact same accusation to invalidate women who do *not* wear dresses: In their eyes, women who eschew dresses must have been "indoctrinated by feminist dogma," rather than having made a free, informed personal decision. Clearly, the "false consciousness" argument is horribly entitled and dehumanizing, and as feminists, we should consider it to be anathema.[6]

Another tactic that is often used to police people's personal choices (and therefore deny their autonomy) is to claim that the choice they have made is inherently unhealthy. Now, lots of personal decisions come with some level of health risk. If I eat lots of bacon and ice cream, or if I go skiing, or walk alone at night, or even get into a car, all of these actions come with some risk. But those who view me as an autonomous person will generally acknowledge that, provided that my actions are not harming or impinging on others, I am free to make such informed decisions about my body and life. In contrast, I have on numerous occasions heard feminists decry women who choose to wear high heels, or get breast implants, or who have lots of casual sex, for having made unhealthy choices. The implication here is that because these women have made an inherently unhealthy choice, they must not be responsible or mentally competent enough to make informed decisions about their own lives and bodies. So, like the "false consciousness" claim, the "unhealthy" trope is a common strategy for denying people's autonomy (which is precisely why heteronormative patriarchal types often use the "unhealthy" trope to invalidate same-sex relationships, transsexual transitions, premarital sex, contraception, and women's reproductive health decisions more generally).

Some feminists and queer activists who are wedded to the approach of policing other people's sex- and gender-related life choices might make the following argument: Sexes, genders, and sexualities are not individual experiences, but rather collective categories. And therefore, while I may claim to wear a dress for purely personal reasons, or a woman who gets breast implants may claim that she has done so to feel better in her body rather than doing it for other people, our actions nevertheless "reinforce" (or "uphold," or "reify," or "naturalize") certain ideas about how women should be. Now throughout this book, I have debunked this argument from multiple angles (e.g., it denies sexual and gender variation; only marked traits are ever subjected to the "reinforcing" trope; insisting that women shouldn't behave a particular way essentially creates a new stereotype that women are now expected to conform to). But in the context of this discussion about gender entitlement, can I just say *how absolutely misplaced this accusation is!* This argument essentially blames people who are ethically gendered (e.g., me, wearing my dress in an non-entitled manner) for the gender entitlement expressed by other people (e.g., those who nonconsensually project their beliefs about dress-wearing onto other people). Such arguments are structurally identical to the "asking for it" charge, where women who dress in particular ways are blamed for any nonconsensual acts (e.g., harassment, rape) that are committed against them.

As feminists and queer activists, we unfortunately have limited time and resources to commit toward challenging sexism and marginalization. As such, we must stop wasting so much of our energy critiquing and policing the bodies, identities, desires, and life choices of other people, both within our own movements and beyond. Instead of falsely accusing people of indirectly "reinforcing" sexism, let's focus our efforts on calling out the real culprits: people who *directly enforce* sexism via gender policing and other forms of gender entitlement. And instead of judging people based upon whether they conform to our own feminist- and queer-minded double standards (e.g., subversive genders are good, conservative genders are bad), let's judge all people's actions according to a *single standard*. Namely, nonconsensual ideologies, assumptions, and behaviors deny other people's autonomy and humanity, and thus should be challenged. And whatever people autonomously or consensually wish to do with their own genders or sexualities should be their choice, provided that they are able to give informed consent, and that their actions remain non-entitled (i.e., they do not impinge on other people's lives).

In an earlier chapter, I critiqued common feminist refrains that we must "bring an end to gender" or "move beyond gender." People naturally differ in our anatomies, physiologies, predilections, and desires, and it is inevitable that we will invent language to describe such differences. But I do think that it would be possible to bring about an end to sexism if we were all willing to refrain from projecting our personal assumptions, meanings, and value judgments onto other people's sexes, genders, and sexualities. And I believe that we could bring an end to most, if not all, forms of marginalization if we were willing to forgo entitlement more generally—that is, if we all stopped nonconsensually projecting the double standards that we hold to be true, or are personally invested in, onto other people.

SELF-EXAMINING DESIRE AND EMBRACING AMBIVALENCE

CHAPTER NINETEEN

n the last chapter, I made the case that we should strive to be ethically gendered, which involves challenging gender entitlement both within ourselves and in other people. This strategy is designed, in part, to foster respect for other people's autonomy, and acceptance of their expressions of gender and sexuality. In other words, this approach removes other people's experiences of identity, attraction, and desire from the realm of public criticism (provided that they are not nonconsensual in nature). This was done intentionally. After all, once we start believing that it is our God-given right to critique other people's genders and sexualities, then we will start imagining everyone around us as falling under our personal jurisdiction. That mindset enables us to feel entitled to police other people's bodies and behaviors, and provides us with a justification to freely delegitimize, dehumanize, and exclude others from our communities. In contrast, challenging gender entitlement allows us to critique instances of sexism, while at the same time recognizing the fundamental heterogeneity of human sex, gender, and sexuality.

Admittedly, removing all autonomous and consensual behaviors from the realm of public criticism wouldn't work in a general sense. For instance, you and I could consensually decide to generate lots of pollution, or build a nuclear bomb together, and that would most certainly have a negative impact on other people. However, the vast majority of personal expressions of gender and sexuality do not have that kind of drastic effect on other people's lives. For instance, if I were to embrace a particular identity, or wear a particular type of clothing, or modify my body in some way, or become aroused while reading erotica, or if I had consensual sex, or participated in an orgy, or entered into a relationship with somebody—in all of these instances, it is difficult to make the case that other people would be directly hurt or injured by my actions. However, there are a few ways in which our autonomous or consensual gender and sexual expressions can indirectly hurt others.

We all grow up in a world that is saturated with myriad double standards. This means that certain people are deemed more legitimate than others. But it also means that certain bodies and traits are assumed to be inherently beautiful, sexy, pleasurable, and vulnerable, whereas others are deemed ugly, unattractive, distasteful, and invulnerable. As with all double standards, it is inescapable that some of these assumptions will seep into our psyche and help shape our burgeoning sexualities. While biology and biological variation may also influence our gender and sexual predilections, I most certainly do not believe that we are "biologically programmed" to be outright disgusted by the idea of same-sex relationships, or grossed out by the idea of being sexual with people who happen to be trans, intersex, fat, disabled, or of a different ethnicity or race than us. In other words, we have been taught to view certain bodies and sexual practices as repugnant. And when we outright dismiss them without thinking, our desires conveniently mirror societal hierarchies and privilege dominant majorities.

So if we truly want to create a world free of gender policing—where our genders and sexualities are not constantly critiqued and demeaned by others—then it is incumbent on us to self-examine our own desires. In other words, being ethically gendered involves more than just challenging gender entitlement. It also requires us to engage in personal reflection and questioning.

As I have already suggested, this process might begin by critically examining that which we are not attracted to. If we do not desire a particular type of person or sexual practice, why is that? Does it simply not pique our interest? Or do we have a strong visceral reaction against it? Do we find it abhorrent? Or do we experience some level of attraction, but we are reluctant to act on it because we would be too embarrassed if someone else were to find out?

As the saying goes, the opposite of love isn't hate, it's indifference. So generally speaking, if we feel a strong sense of repulsion toward particular bodies, identities, or sexualities, that is usually a red flag—a sign that we may need to further examine what double standards may be unconsciously driving that. Similarly, if we find someone or something attractive, but avoid it because we are worried about being tainted by the stigma associated with it, that is another sign that our sexuality is being influenced by double standards. But if after honestly examining our lack of desire we merely find indifference, then perhaps that may be an instance of genuine personal preference.

Along similar lines, we should critically examine what we do desire. Are we attracted to the conventional or unconventional? Do we just so happen to like the type of person who is valorized in our culture or subculture? Are we interested in them because we're trying to fit in? Are we hoping their status will rub off on us? If we are attracted to someone or something that is atypical or maligned in our culture, are we simply more open minded than other people? Or are we partly turned on by the taboo nature of the encounter? Do we mystify them, and view them as exotic? Do we appreciate them as a whole person? Or are we sexualizing them—viewing them as a mere sexual or fetish object? What effect might the nature of our desire have on the person we are attracted to?

This list is not meant to be exhaustive, but it does offer a few examples of the types of questions we should be asking. As a bisexual femme-tomboy transsexual woman who was socialized in a straight male–centric society, I often ask myself: What does it mean that I am feminine, or that I tend to be attracted to other feminine people independent of gender? Is it a reflection of our society's sexualization of femininity? Or a personal reaction to the fact that as a trans child I was nonconsensually forced into masculinity? Or is it an expression of my femme activism? Or perhaps I'm just wired that way. In a straight male–centric world, what does it mean for me to wear a dress, or to have a submissive fantasy, or to go on a date with a man, or to be all crushed out when a woman I am dating surprises me with flowers? Often these self-interrogations do not lead to any straightforward answers. But sometimes we will uncover unquestioned assumptions and double standards that we can then work to overcome.

The purpose of this work is not to purge every single vestige of patriarchy from our desire, as some feminists have argued. Sex, gender, and sexuality are fundamentally heterogeneous, and many desires are irrepressible and insusceptible to conscious change. And since we can never fully remove ourselves from the culture or communities that we're immersed in, I don't believe that there is some kind of natural, unspoiled, patriarchy-free gender or sexuality that we can simply revert to. Just because some aspect of our gender or sexuality "resembles" patriarchy or some other societal norm does not necessarily mean that it is inherently bad, or that we should abstain from it. But we should give our desires thoughtful consideration and critically examine them in the context of myriad double standards.

For me personally, this process has helped me appreciate something that is rarely discussed in feminist and queer politics: ambivalence. People often confuse ambivalence with apathy or indifference, but they are very different. Ambivalence is when we simultaneously hold both positive and negative feelings about something. For me, this means being able to feel empowered by my own expressions of femininity, while recognizing the harmful nature of compulsory femininity. It means experiencing dissatisfaction or dissonance with regards to some aspect of my body, yet recognizing that some people may find that trait attractive and/or love my entire body. It means enjoying experiences and ways of being that resonate with me, while recognizing that they are not for everybody.

Feminist discussions of desire used to be dominated by so-called "sex-negative"[1] thought, which condemned any expression of gender or sexuality that in any way resembled patriarchy or hierarchies more generally. This brought on a backlash: the rise of "sex-positive" feminism, which sought to reclaim maligned aspects of sexuality and free us from sexual shame. I have long considered myself to be a sex-positive feminist, but I am increasingly bothered by a watered-down version of it that seems to be garnering mainstream popularity. It is best characterized by uncritical blanket statements like, "Wearing high heels is empowering!" or, "Pornography is empowering!" or, "Kink is empowering!"[2] Of course, these things can be empowering for certain people in certain contexts. But for other people in other situations, not necessarily. A woman may feel empowered wearing heels but feel disempowered by the sexualizing comments she gets from strangers when she does. A sex-positive feminist may feel empowered by the alternative depictions of female sexuality she finds in feminist porn or a queer BDSM anthology, while a fourteen-year-old boy who uncritically watches hardcore porn or reads *Fifty Shades of Grey* may develop really fucked-up ideas about women.[3]

We live in a world where virtually all aspects of sex, gender, and sexuality are either glorified, stigmatized, sensationalized, demonized, or objectified. Perhaps it's time for us to move beyond portraying desire as something that is either wholly positive or negative. Instead, let's embrace ambivalence, and learn how to talk about both the good and the bad, both the empowering and disempowering aspects of being a gendered and sexual person. Let's find ways to discuss both the ecstasy and the difficulties of being embodied, making life choices, finding love, and having sex, all while navigating our way through the minefields of stereotypes, norms, and hierarchies.

RECOGNIZING INVALIDATIONS

CHAPTER TWENTY

We have all been taught to think about sexism and marginalization in terms of specific ideologies or isms that are pervasive and perhaps even institutionalized within a given society. Obvious examples include racism, classism, traditional sexism, heterosexism, and ableism, to name but a few. Once a particular ism has been articulated, activists can then raise awareness about the ways in which these ideologies create obstacles or disadvantages in the lives of marginalized groups. One can also focus on the subsequent advantages or privileges experienced by members of the dominant group—for example, how racism leads to white privilege, how classism leads to upper- and middle-class privilege, how traditional sexism leads to male privilege, how heterosexism leads to heterosexual privilege, and how ableism leads to able-bodied privilege.

The five isms that I have mentioned thus far—racism, classism, traditional sexism, heterosexism, and ableism—are the ones that I find people in progressive and social justice circles tend to be most keenly aware of. Each of these privileges has a fairly long history of being articulated, analyzed, and discussed, and an understanding that these privileges exist has seeped into the culture at large, albeit to varying extents. But of course, these are not the only five forms of marginalization that exist in our culture, not by a long shot. Some forms of marginalization are in the earliest stages of being articulated, and therefore remain unfamiliar to people outside of certain activist circles. And, no doubt, there are many types of marginalization which have not yet been named or articulated, but which exist nevertheless.

In this chapter, I want to briefly touch upon some of the challenges that I and other activists have experienced in trying to raise awareness about an ism that most people—even most progressive and social justice activists—were (and in some cases, still are) unfamiliar with or completely unaware of, namely, cissexism. My intent here is not to explain cissexism, nor justify the use of cis terminology, as I have done so in previous chapters and elsewhere.[1] Rather, I want to share my experiences in order to make a larger point about the shortcomings inherent in thinking about sexism and marginalization solely in terms of specific isms and privileges. After doing that, I will offer an alternative and complementary strategy for framing disparities in power and legitimacy that exist between different groups. This strategy can be taught in parallel with isms, and will help people to more easily recognize and challenge forms of marginalization that they may have been previously unfamiliar with or unaware of.

ARTICULATING A NEW ISM

When I first became involved in trans activism in 2002, trans folks were significantly lacking in terms and concepts to explain the sexism that we faced. The word "transphobia" had already been coined (presumably inspired by "homophobia") to describe anti-trans discrimination. But as with "phobias" more generally, the term seemed to imply that a few bad apples were irrationally afraid of trans people, but it did not communicate the reality that trans people were almost universally viewed as less legitimate than our non-trans counterparts. During this time period, it was still common for trans activists such as myself to do "transgender 101" panels and workshops, where we shared our stories about being trans with non-trans folks. Essentially, we were trying to convince them that trans people are not monstrous delusional sexually deviant serial killers, and that the fact that we are routinely fired from our jobs, publicly harassed, evicted, arrested, and sometimes murdered, is a very very very bad thing that they should be concerned about. Most activist movements begin this way: trying to convince the dominant majority that you are reasonable legitimate human beings who deserve to be treated as such.

At the time, there was no word for the non-trans majority. Even within the trans community, people were still using labels like "biological," "genetic," and "natural" women and men to refer to such people. Activist types like myself would use the state-of-the-art (for the time) term "non-trans." On top of this, there was almost no discussion (outside of trans activist circles) about how non-trans folks experienced various privileges as a result of not having to deal with transphobia on a daily basis like we did.[2]

When I began working on *Whipping Girl*, I wanted to raise some of these issues but felt linguistically challenged. However, that changed in December 2005, when I stumbled upon a blogpost by Emi Koyama that described the terms cissexual, cisgender, and cissexism.[3] While I had not heard these terms up until that point, they seemed perfect for what I was trying to convey. Basically, this cis terminology paralleled vital steps taken by gay and disability activists (among others) decades ago: Name the previously unnamed and unmarked dominant majority (cissexuals, analogous with heterosexuals and able-bodied people), describe the institutionalized hierarchy that marginalizes you (cissexism, analogous with heterosexism and ableism), and discuss how this system creates many taken-for-granted advantages for the dominant majority (cissexual privilege, analogous with heterosexual and able-bodied privilege).

I personally began using cis terminology in 2006, and I remember that every time I did, I would be asked to explain it because people—even dedicated trans activists and allies—were not familiar with it. In fact, cis terminology was so infrequently used that I had some reservations about employing it in *Whipping Girl*, but I went ahead and used it anyway because I felt it was so critical. In the years since, cis terminology has become more widely used in trans and queer circles, and has gained some traction within activist and progressive circles more generally (although it has not quite entered mainstream public consciousness yet). Overall, I feel that this terminology has helped trans activists to better express our situations and obstacles, and has helped cis people better understand and challenge societal cissexism. But there has also been a troubling trend wherein some folks within queer, feminist, and social justice circles—that is, activists who are already intimately familiar with institutionalized marginalization and discussions about privilege—have strongly resisted and even expressed downright hostility toward cis terminology.

One issue that cis terminology has encountered is what I refer to as the "legitimacy problem." For example, most people in our society will acknowledge that racism and traditional sexism are real forms of marginalization, even if their understanding of these concepts is rudimentary and unnuanced. So if you were to describe a particular act as racist or sexist, other people might strongly disagree with your claim, but they won't likely challenge the very idea that racism and sexism do exist and are actual problems. In other words, racism and traditional sexism are viewed as legitimate concepts. In contrast, in some instances when I have described an act as cissexist, I have had people act incredulously and accuse me of making shit up. In other words, the very concept of cissexism is viewed as fake and illegitimate.

This assumption of fakeness and illegitimacy has been evident within the feminist blogosphere, where it is not uncommon to find cis people who outright reject the words cissexual, cisgender, and cis. There are several different rationalizations people offer to justify this rejection: They might claim that cisgender and cissexual sound too jargony or academic (even though cis terminology has activist, rather than academic, roots).[4] Sometimes they will complain that they don't "identify" with the term cis—claims that echo complaints made by other privileged groups who claim that they don't "identify" as white, or heterosexual, or able-bodied. Perhaps the most illuminating complaint that I have heard regarding cis terminology comes from people who have claimed that, when they are called a cis woman or cis man, that it somehow feels like it undermines their femaleness or maleness. When I first heard this complaint, it struck me as bizarre—after all, cis denotes that one's gender is viewed by society as inherently *legitimate*. Furthermore, cis is just an adjective! Would these same people feel that they are seen as less than a woman or man if they were described as a white woman or an able-bodied man? I highly doubt it. The only way that I can make sense out of this misconception is that most people view trans people as "fake" women and men, or as inferior to cis women and men, and as a result they transfer those inferior meanings onto trans's counterpart, cis.

Given that many cis people have objections to the term cis, it should be no surprise that when you point out to someone that they have cis privilege, sometimes they will act downright appalled. In my experience, this is especially true for many cis women, and cis gays and lesbians, who feel so marginalized by traditional sexism and/or heterosexism that they cannot fathom that they might possibly experience any gender-related privileges whatsoever. While it is common for people to become defensive about or to flat-out deny that they are privileged in any way, what is unusual in this case is that many of the people doing the denying—e.g., cis feminists, and cis gays and lesbians—are familiar with discussions of privilege, marginalization, and intersectionality. Their denial seems to stem from an assumption that the privileges that they are familiar with are legitimate and real, whereas newly articulated privileges, such as cis privilege, are illegitimate and fake. In other words, people have a tendency to privilege some privileges over others.

These incidences also highlight another problem: That people who have a thorough understanding of how institutionalized marginalization and privilege work in one context (for example, in traditional sexism) seem unable or unwilling to apply that knowledge to a similar yet less familiar problem, namely, cissexism. There are countless examples of this, but one that particularly struck me occurred in 2004, just after *Bitch* magazine published an essay I wrote called "Skirt Chasers: Why the Media Depicts the Trans Revolution in Lipstick and Heels."[5] In the piece, I discussed how trans women are frequently depicted as hyperfeminine and hypersexual in both the media and in academic texts. I made a point that was blatantly obvious to me—that these depictions do not accurately reflect the diversity of actual trans women, or trans people more generally. But rather, the media's tendency to depict trans women as hyperfeminine and hypersexual, while largely ignoring trans men, is steeped in traditional sexism—that is, the idea that maleness and masculinity are more legitimate than femaleness and femininity.

After the article was published, I received a number of emails from folks who read the article, and they tended to fall in into one of two camps. The first were from trans women who basically said something along the lines of, "Thank you for saying what I have always known, but have never seen written in print before." The second were from cis women who thanked me for offering them a perspective they had not heard before. Some said that while they were aware that the media distorts the images of women in general—often portraying them as far thinner, younger, less bright, and more conventionally attractive than women in real life—it had never occurred to them that images of trans women might be similarly distorted. Some of them told me that they presumed that the images of trans women they saw in the media somehow represented all trans women.

There is something very wrong with how we teach sexism and marginalization when readers of *Bitch* magazine, which focuses primarily on critiquing media depictions of women, do not extend that analysis to other marginalized or minority groups that they know less about. To be clear, this is most certainly not a *Bitch* magazine problem (as they regularly publish articles that address racism, classism, heterosexism, and other isms in pop culture and the media). Rather, it is a problem that is systemic throughout feminism, queer activism, and other social justice movements. I believe that, at its core, this problem stems from our focusing too exclusively on specific isms. We teach others to recognize traditional sexism, or heterosexism, or racism, or classism, and so on, on an individual basis. But we do not do such a good job at encouraging people to recognize the common tactics that these different forms of marginalization use in order to delegitimize particular groups (stereotyping and media depictions, to name just one). Nor do we do an adequate job of teaching people how to apply what they know about one form of marginalization to another, especially when the latter is unfamiliar or previously unarticulated.

So to summarize, describing marginalization in terms of specific isms is important, as it provides a framework that allows marginalized groups to explain their experiences with prejudice and discrimination, and compels dominant groups to recognize the privileges that they benefit from at the marginalized group's expense. Once people become familiar with a specific ism and the privileges associated with it, they become far more likely to recognize and challenge that form of marginalization whenever and wherever it occurs—and this has most certainly been the case for cissexism and cis privilege. However, as my experiences attest to, centering discussions about marginalization on isms sometimes fails us in pretty significant ways. We tend to focus single-mindedly on one or a few forms of marginalization that we are most aware of and educated about. Yet, we are often oblivious to unfamiliar and unarticulated forms of marginalization, and we often blatantly fail to apply what we already know about marginalization and privilege to these new problems. And when we are introduced to a newly articulated form of marginalization, we have a tendency to view it with suspicion, and we may even dismiss it as being fake and illegitimate.

To be clear, this is not simply an intersectionality problem *per se*. While intersectionality is important and often overlooked, it typically only comes into play once we recognize and acknowledge that some form of marginalization exists and is legitimate. The problem that I am outlining here is: How do we apply what we already know about marginalization to help recognize and analyze unfamiliar and unarticulated forms of marginalization?

A "BOTTOM-UP" STRATEGY TO ARTICULATE SEXISM AND MARGINALIZATION

In considering this matter over the last few years, I have come to the conclusion that most, if not all, of the problems with isms that I have described stem from their "top-down" approach. By top-down, I simply mean that we focus primarily on the ideology or ism that is driving this marginalization—for example, racism, classism, traditional sexism, ableism, heterosexism, cissexism, etc. We talk about how that ism is institutionalized in our society, how it has been enforced over the course of history, how it seeps into our language and media imagery. We talk about the everyday obstacles that marginalized groups face in terms of ideology or ism-specific concepts: for example, the male gaze, racial profiling, gay panic, transphobic violence, and so on. Now, to be clear, every ism does have a different history, and they manifest themselves in people's lives in rather different ways, so this approach is certainly warranted. But what if, in addition to this top-down approach, we also engaged in a bottom-up approach, and looked for similarities between the obstacles that different marginalized groups face in their day-to-day lives?

For example, here is a partial list of the ways in which trans people are often delegitimized in our society: We are often excluded from certain spaces or organizations because of our difference; we often have difficulty obtaining legal documents that can legitimize us in the eyes of society; others often characterize or diagnose us as mentally ill or confused; we are often deemed not competent enough to make decisions about our own bodies and lives; we are often denied medical access or treatment; we are often denied privacy with regard to our bodies and personal histories; we are routinely objectified and sexualized; outsiders often find us "fascinating," and tend to mystify or eroticize our bodies and experiences; information about who we are as people—our experiences, lives, and issues—is difficult to find, and is sometimes purposefully restricted or censored; so-called experts who have not shared our experience often feel entitled to speak on our behalf, and society tends to accept what they have to say about us over what we have to say about ourselves; and finally, sometimes we are accused of being a threat to specific individuals and/or to society as a whole.

Now, I can legitimately view these obstacles in terms of cissexism— that is, an ideology that targets me specifically because I am trans. But an equally valid way of describing my situation is to say that I face many obstacles that are also shared by other marginalized groups. So while we may be targeted by different isms, the tactics people use to *invalidate* us are quite similar. The definition of the word invalidate is to discredit; to deprive of legal force or efficacy; to destroy the authority of; to nullify. In other words, the methods of invalidation that I have just described are tried-and-true ways of delegitimizing people, of knocking people down a peg, of undermining them.

Activists have long recognized these shared forms of invalidation, and we often cite them when we are trying to teach individuals who are familiar with one ism about another, unfamiliar, ism. (Indeed, this is exactly what I have done in earlier chapters where I drew parallels between heterosexism and cissexism.) But what I am suggesting now is that, instead of merely citing these shared invalidations as a means to explain a specific ism, we develop an alternate approach to viewing marginalization that is centered on these invalidations. The idea here is very simple. In addition to teaching people how to recognize and understand different isms, we should also teach them how to recognize the basic forms of invalidation that are repeatedly used to delegitimize and dehumanize people who belong to marginalized groups. Once a person is well versed in these basic forms of invalidation, they should be able to recognize when marginalization is occurring, even if they are unfamiliar with the ideology or ism that is driving it.

There are many possible ways in which a person might be invalidated—here, I will briefly mention a handful of non-mutually exclusive categories of invalidation that seem to recur most often in the context of marginalization.

One of the most common forms of invalidation is the trope of *mental incompetence*—for instance, claiming or insinuating that somebody is mentally incompetent, mentally inferior, or mentally ill. Historically, claims of mental inferiority have been used to justify the mistreatment, and even enslavement, of racial minorities and the poor, and to render women as second-class citizens who are expected to obediently defer to the men in their lives. Mental incompetence is at work when people dismiss queer people as merely being confused about our genders and sexualities, or claim that we must suffer from some sort of mental illness. It should be mentioned that the concept of mental incompetence seems to be closely associated with physical incompetence in a lot of people's minds. So when a particular group is constructed as being physically weak, fragile, incapable and/or in need of assistance or protection (e.g., in the case of women, disabled people, the elderly, and the young), they are often also assumed to be weak-willed, easily susceptible to manipulation, and incapable of making informed decisions about their own lives. In other words, they may be inappropriately dismissed as being mentally incompetent.

Another way to invalidate someone is by *sexualizing* them. When discussing sexualization, people most often think of how women are sexualized by men in our society, but there are other ways in which people can be sexualized. For example, people of color are often depicted as being exotic, promiscuous, or sexually predatory. And LGBTQIA+ people are routinely reduced to our sexualities and bodies, and often accused of being sexually deviant, predatory, or deceptive. There is an extensive body of psychological research that shows that when people are sexualized, they are not treated with empathy, are not taken as seriously, and are seen as less competent and less intelligent than those who are not sexualized.[6] This is why sexualization is such an effective tool for invalidation.

A third general form of invalidation is to accuse someone of being inherently *immoral*, and therefore constituting a threat. Sometimes this supposed immorality stems from a lack of being "civilized" or "cultured"—this gives rise to portrayals of racial minorities, immigrants, and the poor as "savages" who cannot control their "animal-like impulses." Other times, immorality is presumed to stem from a conscious, elaborate, Machiavellian effort to deceive or manipulate other people. For example, a lot of homophobic, biphobic, and transphobic violence stems from assumptions that gender and sexual minorities are out to purposefully deceive straight people. Similarly, women are often accused of tempting men into sin or manipulating men with their "feminine wiles."

There is a tendency to conflate immorality with the state of being *sick, ill, or unhealthy.* This conflation is evident in the way that sexual and gender minorities (who are often viewed as being immoral) are sometimes treated as though they are "infected," "contagious," and need to be "quarantined"—a misconception that predated, but was exacerbated by, the AIDS epidemic. Similarly, people who have chronic illnesses and disabilities are often treated as though they are contagious. This notion of sickness can also be found in the notorious "one-drop rule" (where in post–Civil War America, a person was considered black if they had any African ancestry whatsoever), and in characterizations of people who are poor, homeless, or immigrants as being "disease-ridden" or a "cancer on society." As I discussed in Chapter 18, "Challenging Gender Entitlement," claiming that a person's behaviors and life choices are "unhealthy" is a common tactic to both invalidate the acts in question and to insinuate that the person making those personal decisions must not be mentally competent.

Another method of invalidation is to claim that some type of body or behavior is *anomalous*. Sometimes, anomalous traits are presumed to be abnormal or unnatural, and the people who display such traits are pathologized as "sick," or treated as though they are abominations. Furthermore, the assumption that certain groups of people are rare—mere exceptions to the rule—allows the majority to ignore their views, pretend that they do not exist, or trample their rights and humanity (after all, the needs of the many outweigh the needs of the few, right?). Often the majority will dismiss the obstacles and issues faced by populations that they consider rare as being "frivolous" and not warranting serious concern. When you are assumed to be rare, other people quickly move in to speak on your behalf, or to appropriate your experiences. Because you are presumed to be anomalous, people may come to find you fascinating, they may mystify or eroticize you, and, if they are of an academic bent, they may even study you, thus making you an object of their inquiry.

The last method of invalidation that I will describe here is to accuse someone of being *inauthentic, unnatural, or downright fake*. For example, people who do not live up to society's gender and sexual norms in

some way are invariably accused of not being "real women" or "real men."
There are currently hordes of "birthers" out there who are convinced that
Barack Obama, our first black president, is literally not a "real" American
(an accusation that no WASP president has ever had to contend with to
the best of my knowledge). A few years back, when actor-turned-activist
Michael J. Fox did a series of political ads in support of stem cell research,
conservative radio host Rush Limbaugh claimed that Fox was purposefully "exaggerating the effects" of his Parkinson's and that it was "purely
an act."[7] Of course, once you have depicted someone as inauthentic, as a
fake, then it becomes easy to project nefarious ulterior motives onto them
(such as transsexuals being accused of trying to deceive innocent straight
people into sleeping with us, or queer people being accused of trying to
convert innocent straight people with our homosexual agendas).

The forms of invalidation that I just described are certainly not
comprehensive, but they do seem to regularly come into play with
regards to marginalization. And while I placed them into convenient
categories, it should be noted that these are not discrete phenomena. For instance, the accusation that someone is inherently "sick"
or "unhealthy" is often invoked when that person is also sexualized,
or deemed to be anomalous, immoral, and/or mentally incompetent.
Elsewhere I have written about how sexualization, and the tropes
of mental incompetence, sickness, fakeness, and deception, all come
together in an especially onerous way in certain psychological theories
that pathologize transsexual women.[8] Similarly, female rape survivors
are routinely invalidated via sexualization (e.g., intense focus on her
past sexual history, whether she was flirting, and any clothing she was
wearing that might be considered sexually revealing) combined with
accusations that she purposely misled the rapist (thus portraying her
as being deceptive, and therefore immoral and inauthentic). In fact,
more often than not, different forms of invalidation are invoked simultaneously, and have the effect of exacerbating one another. After all, if

you invalidate someone, thereby dehumanizing them, they will become more susceptible to further acts of invalidation.

Recognizing invalidations can also lead us to consider the concept of privilege in a more general way. Those of us with a background in activism are probably familiar with "privilege checklists," where the rather specific advantages experienced by people who are male, heterosexual, cisgender, white, middle-class, able-bodied, and so on, are thoroughly compiled.[9] A different, but complementary, approach would be to list the many generic privileges that come from not having to routinely face a particular form of invalidation. For instance, some people have the privilege of being seen as relatively normal (i.e., not anomalous or unhealthy), safe (i.e., not immoral or dangerous), natural and sincere (i.e., not unnatural or deceptive), competent and autonomous (i.e., not mentally or physically incompetent or ill), and non-sexualized. Again, this list of generic privileges is not meant to be comprehensive, but it does offer a more generalized way of thinking about the concept of privilege.

Now, any form of invalidation can be used to target practically anybody. One only needs to consider negative political ads, which heavily rely on invalidations—politician X is not a real patriot, or not who they claim to be, or is deceiving voters, or holds some anomalous or extreme view, or is crazy, or lacking in intelligence, or confused about some issue, or has been involved in some unseemly sexual scandal, and so on. However, while invalidations, in theory, can be hurled at just about anybody, in practice, they are usually doled out asymmetrically: Members of marginalized groups are targeted via invalidations more so than members of dominant groups. More to the point, invalidations (like stereotypes, attributions, and other assumptions) seem to stick more to people who are marked in some way and thus are already deemed questionable, suspect, and illegitimate. In contrast, dominant groups are unmarked and thus are relatively impervious to invalidating comments or criticism.

Here is how I believe we can use this concept of invalidations in order to recognize and challenge marginalization. First, one familiarizes oneself with the types of invalidation that I have previously mentioned—sexualization and accusations of mental incompetence, immorality, illness, anomaly, and inauthenticity—and how these invalidations are often used to undermine marginalized groups. And whenever an incident occurs that involves one or more of these invalidations, it should serve as a red flag—a sign that something nefarious may be going on. Now, of course, some people are immoral, and some people do misrepresent themselves, so an accusation that an individual represents a threat, or is merely a poser, does not, in and of itself, signify that marginalization is taking place. So in addition to recognizing invalidations, we must also be on the constant lookout for the telltale signs that a double standard is at work behind the scenes. Pertinent questions one might ask include: Does the invalidation seem to implicate not just the person in question, but an entire group of people who share the same trait? Does this trait, and those who possess it, seem to garner undue scrutiny? Do others question the existence and/or the legitimacy of this trait? Are people who exhibit this trait seen as inferior to those who do not possess it? If so, who is the unmarked group of people who do not exhibit the trait? Is their lack of said trait taken for granted and seen as the norm? What interest might they, or society at large, have in creating and enforcing this double standard?

This combination of seeking out invalidations, and recognizing asymmetries in the ways that they are used, has been very useful in my own activism. It has allowed me to recognize and communicate previously underappreciated double standards. Here is one example. When you are transsexual, it is common for others to assume that anyone who is attracted to you must suffer from some sort of "tranny fetish." While I have long found such incidents annoying, I did not really have an overarching analysis or explanation for this phenomenon—I simply chalked it up to cissexism. But then I began noticing fat activists and disabled activists describing similar situations, where people who found them attractive were assumed to have a fetish for fat or disabled people, respectively. It turns out that the word "fetish" is derived from the Portuguese word for artificial—in other words, fetishes are literally supposed to be fake forms of attraction, rather than real ones (there's that invalidation again!). Upon reflection, it seems clear that there is a double standard here between the majority of people who are presumed to be legitimate objects of desire—when someone is attracted to them, or falls in love with them, that attraction is unmarked and assumed to be real. Other people—transsexual, fat, and disabled people, to name a few—are deemed illegitimate objects of desire, and attraction to us is viewed as unnatural, and is marked with the pejorative term "fetish." Furthermore, this double standard asserts that we cannot be loved as whole people, for our personalities and bodies and other attributes, but rather we can only be other people's "fetish objects." So in a sense, this double standard objectifies and sexualizes us. I sometimes call this double standard "fetishism," which is potentially confusing I admit, but I personally like it, as it insinuates that people who view me as inherently undesirable are the true fetishists, whereas people who find me attractive are let off the hook! Thinking of this issue in this way opens up the possibility to create movements that are less about specific identities (as it would include trans, fat, and disabled folks, and potentially other groups), and more about eliminating methods of invalidation that negatively impact people more generally.

The concept of invalidations has also been valuable to me as an activist because it allows me to quickly appreciate forms of marginalization that do not affect me personally. For example, a few years back, I was writing a lot about the aforementioned psychological theories that pathologize and sexualize trans women. I will not go into the details of the specific theory here, but one aspect of it is that it lumps lesbian, bisexual, and asexual trans women under the same category. As I initially worked on a critique of this theory, whenever I mentioned the word asexual, I put it in scare quotes. The reason why I put it in quotes was because I had never met an asexual-identified person before, so I assumed (and we all know what happens when you assume) that asexuality was not a legitimate sexual orientation, but rather something invented by pathologizing psychologists. Shortly thereafter, the latest *Bitch* magazine arrived at my door, and in it was an article about the burgeoning asexual activism movement.[10] As I read it, it immediately struck me that asexuals face some of the same forms of invalidation that transsexuals face. For instance, asexuality (like transsexuality) is listed as a mental illness in the *DSM* (the *Diagnostic and Statistical Manual of Mental Disorders*, often called the "psychiatric Bible" because it lists all of the officially recognized "mental disorders"), and lay people often assume that asexuals are simply confused about their sexuality. Similarly, asexuals (like transsexuals) are often dismissed or shunned by lesbian, gay, and queer communities.

To be honest, there was a time not so long ago when I might have been skeptical about, or resistant to, asexuality or asexual issues. But because I instantly recognized these shared invalidations, I had a very different response. I began to seek out writings by asexual activists. I began to think about how I might challenge societal asexophobia. I began to think about ways in which transsexuals and asexuals might be able to work together on issues that mutually affect us (e.g., challenging the *DSM*).

I share this anecdote not to show off what a great person I am for recognizing asexual people, but rather to highlight the fact that I am human and I make mistakes. I am aware of certain people and problems, but unaware of others. I want to make the world a better place, but sometimes in the course of that work, I inadvertently hurt other people, other marginalized groups, as I did when I put scare quotes around the word asexual. Activism is hard—it is hard to maintain a balance between forcibly fighting for our own rights, to have our voices heard, while at the same time listening to what others have to say about their own experiences and issues. I think that most of us who are drawn to activism, in one way or another, strive for this balance.

Thinking in terms of specific isms is a very powerful tool, one that I have found especially useful for communicating my views and experiences with marginalization as a trans person to the greater cis majority. But their singular focus—the fact that they are centered on one specific ism—makes them especially seductive. Focusing on one or a few specific isms leads to fixed views of sexism and marginalization, which can be conveniently packaged into nice and tidy ideologies—the patriarchy, white supremacy, compulsory heterosexuality, etc.—that explain some people's experiences with marginalization, but not others. When we rest all of our hopes for changing the world on a single ideology, we can become highly suspicious of competing ideologies and the people who forward them. We can become dismissive of any matter that does not fit neatly into our worldview.

This is why I believe that recognizing invalidations has so much potential. It is inherently pluralistic—its starting assumption is that we do not know all there is to know about oppression, that there are forms of marginalization out there that we are not yet privy to. It encourages us to learn more about other people's experiences, to look for connections between their marginalization and our own—not because all forms of marginalization are the same (because they are not), but rather to further our understanding of oppression and to foster alliances with other marginalized groups.

BALANCING ACTS

CHAPTER TWENTY-ONE

O ver the last half-century or so, there has been a lot of amazing feminist and queer theory and analysis. This work has articulated numerous forms of sexism and marginalization, described the ways in which these different isms have become institutionalized and permeate nearly every aspect of our language and culture, examined how different isms intersect and compound one another, and detailed the many ways in which these isms undermine and injure marginalized groups while privileging those in the dominant group. While this work has been vitally important, most of it has stemmed from fixed perspectives that inevitably legitimize certain people's experiences with sexism and marginalization while erasing or excluding the experiences of many other people.

Throughout the second section of this book, I have forwarded a holistic approach to feminism, which is basically a set of strategies that allow us as activists to challenge sexism and marginalization in a general sense without necessarily excluding or erasing other people's experiences. This approach is not meant to replace all feminist and queer theories and analyses that came before it. Rather, it is meant to serve as a corrective: It contemplates myriad double standards whereas other feminisms have focused more on specific isms or monolithic gender systems; it highlights the many commonalities that exist between how different double standards are enforced and function whereas other feminisms have focused more on the very unique histories and consequences associated with each individual ism; it stresses individual differences in how we each experience sex, gender, sexuality, sexism, and marginalization, whereas other feminisms have tended to frame these matters solely in terms of collective categories and shared experiences of oppression.

I believe that the holistic approach that I have described here will provide a desperately needed complementary approach to more traditional fixed perspectives on sexism and marginalization. To be clear, I most certainly think that we should continue talking about specific isms, and I'm even fine with discussing hegemonic gender systems, provided that we recognize that they are only part of a bigger picture, and that we also work to acknowledge the existence of myriad double standards and the fundamental heterogeneity of people.

Some may criticize this holistic approach for being too abstract, as it contemplates double standards in a generic sense but does not directly address more tangible manifestations or consequences of oppression, such as poverty, rape culture, colonialism, the prison industrial complex, domestic violence, bullying in schools, and so on. This is a fair criticism, one that can be made of many feminist theories. Basically, theories are models that attempt to describe how a particular aspect of the world works, but which may not be able to explain all situations or solve all potential problems. Like all theories, this holistic approach is necessarily incomprehensive. I have tailored this approach primarily to challenge sexisms and sexism-based exclusion, and while I believe that it has import for many other social justice issues, I concede that there may be some instances in which this approach may not be particularly insightful or useful.

While this holistic approach to feminism is not meant to be a sub-stitute for hands-on, real-world activism to change people's lived circum-stances, it does provide us with important guidelines to help us build more genuinely inclusive movements to challenge sexism and marginalization. And while this holistic approach will not directly solve our most pressing issues, it does confront a core problem that enables all of them. Namely, a major reason why people tolerate and perpetuate poverty, rape culture, colonialism, the prison industrial complex, domestic violence, bullying in schools, etc., is because they consciously or unconsciously presume that some people are less legitimate than other people, and thus they deserve what they get.[1] Therefore, teaching people how to recognize and challenge double standards and invalidations in a more general sense may dissuade them from viewing certain populations as being less human than others, and encourage them to take action to challenge these injustices.

Undoubtedly, some people will consider this holistic approach to be "not radical enough" because it does not take hardline stances, such as outrightly condemning certain expressions of gender and sex-uality (whether it be feminine dress, gender conformity, heterosexual-ity, BDSM, sex work, pornography, and so on). It confounds me how some people mistake holding inflexible and uncompromising positions as somehow being a sign of radicalism. I am reminded of all those cognitive research studies showing that people who are politically conservative are "more structured and persistent in their judgments," and desire "order, structure, and closure," whereas political progressives display a "higher tolerance of ambiguity and complexity, and greater openness to new experiences."[2] By this criteria, the holistic approach I have forwarded—which is purposefully designed to be contextual and flexible—is far more progressive than the dogmatic, cut-and-dried theories forwarded by cer-tain (but certainly not all) self-identified radicals.[3]

Challenging sexism and marginalization, and trying to build effec-tive alliances and movements, is truly difficult work. It's no wonder that many of us crave "magical" answers that will readily remedy the problem at hand, and that will work in every context or situation in the future. Given my critiques of fixed perspectives and one-size-fits-all solutions, readers will probably not be too surprised to learn that I am rather dubious of supposed simple straightforward fixes. This is not merely an intellectual or abstract matter for me. Most of the erasure and exclusion that I have personally faced within feminist and queer circles has come at the hands of other people's supposedly righteous and unquestionable solutions to combat sexism and marginalization.

If we really want to be good activists and community members, then we must learn to accept the many gray areas that come with interacting with a heterogeneous group of individuals. I personally find it useful to think of activism as being a balancing act, one in which we balance our own needs and desires with those of others, one in which we are sometimes teachers and other times listeners. As activists, we must allow for multiple (and sometimes seemingly contradictory) possibilities.

One area where these multiple possibilities come into play is in considering which direction(s) our activism should take. Sexism and marginalization permeate almost every corner of our lives, and thus there are a seemingly infinite number of different problems that we might wish to address, and different approaches we might take to counter them. We may act alone or within an organization. We may act locally, more regionally, or globally. We may tackle rather specific problems (e.g., a particular issue faced by transsexual women) or broader issues (e.g., obstacles faced more generally by queer folks, women, or all people). We may find ourselves reaching out to different target audiences: folks in the straight male–centric mainstream (e.g., in our communities, schools, workplaces, the media), in academia or in other specialized fields (e.g., medicine, law), or within our own feminist or LGBTQIA+ movements. Different people have different understandings (or misunderstandings) about sexism and marginalization, so certain approaches may be more effective with some audiences than others.

The existence of myriad double standards necessitates a multiplicity of different approaches to activism. But in order for this to work, we must constantly seek out and learn from the work and activism of others, and we must do everything we can to ensure that our particular approach is not inadvertently marginalizing others. We must also be cognizant of the fact that not all of our voices carry to the same extent. Some marginalized individuals and groups are viewed as being more legitimate than others, and thus people may be more inclined to listen to and be concerned about their issues over those of others. Furthermore, some people have more resources to put toward their activism than others. One important resource is time. In my case, for most of the last decade, I have had a full-time job that gave me the financial security so that I could buy a computer and allocate "free time" toward writing about feminist, queer, and trans issues. Having the time to commit toward activism is not a luxury that everyone has. Money also plays a huge factor in amplifying (or invisibilizing) one's voice. For instance, organizations that fight for same-sex marriage or women's reproductive health causes are able to raise considerable amounts of money from middle-class and upper-class queer folks and women, whereas groups that carry out activism focused on queer folks and women who are of low income, or homeless, or without access to healthcare, or incarcerated, will not be able to raise that kind of money or attention to their cause. Thus, it is incumbent upon those of us who do have a voice (however limited) to help garner awareness and resources toward the issues faced by the most marginalized members of our communities.

Often, the need for a multiplicity of different approaches to activism gets overlooked in the "reformist versus radical" debate. Reformists tend to focus on single issues, make appeals to the straight male–centric mainstream, and attempt to work within the system to create positive change for marginalized groups. Radicals, on the other hand, insist that one cannot change the system from within, and instead call for a full-scale revolution, one that completely dismantles the gender system, white/Western supremacy, capitalism, and/or other superstructures that create hierarchies among people. Reformists and radicals often view one another as mutually exclusive, and as potential threats to each other's activism. I personally think this is shortsighted.

While I would personally like to see radical change enacted in the world (such as eliminating all double standards), I think that conceptualizing all forms of activism in terms of a swift overarching revolution is not completely realistic. While it is possible to completely overthrow a government or economic system, the double standards people harbor regarding marginalized groups are often deeply entrenched in their minds, and may take time to undo. Often the process of unlearning double standards goes through stages: seeing the marginalized group as human beings rather than subhumans or monsters; recognizing the most blatant forms of oppression the group faces (e.g., slurs, violence) while remaining oblivious to more systematic and institutionalized aspects of their marginalization; consciously recognizing this system-wide marginalization and doing what allies should do to help challenge that (e.g., calling out instances of marginalization); and finally, overcoming unconscious internalized remnants of that form of marginalization that reside within ourselves.

While admittedly limited in scope, reformist approaches tend to be fairly effective at shepherding the dominant majority through the first couple stages of this process, after which point they may be open to more substantive change. At the same time, reformists need to remember that people who take more radical approaches are generally pushing the envelope of what is possible, and while their goals may not yet be fully achievable at this moment, the groundwork they are laying now may make those possibilities come true in the future.

While sexism and other forms of marginalization still abound, things have significantly improved in a general sense for women and LGBTQIA+ folks over the last half-century or so (although the people who have most benefited from this progress tend to be those of us who are privileged in other areas of our lives). It is hard to imagine this progress happening if it were not for both radical activism—the unwavering manifestos, riots, direct actions, and rallies—as well as for the more modest and mainstream reforms. I think that both can (and should) occur simultaneously. And they need not conflict or contradict one another provided that neither side of the reformist/radical divide believes that their way is the "one and only true way," and provided that both sides refuse to perpetuate existing double standards, or create new double standards, in the course of their activism.

Sometimes marginalized groups create spaces and organizations that are only for "their own kind" (women-only spaces being one example). Many people find such spaces to be empowering and enlightening. I have had some experiences in trans support groups, or at trans and bisexual caucuses at larger conferences, that have been really amazing. Usually these are relatively small gatherings (less than twenty people), and they feel like a refuge where we can swap stories, share concerns, and support one another without having to navigate a mutual double standard that we as members all face outside the space. I have also been in larger trans-, femme-, and women-only settings and have found them to be less rewarding, and often quite contentious. Why does this tend to happen? Personally, I think that it is easy for five people in a room together to see themselves as distinct individuals who just so happen to share a single trait or obstacle. But as the group gets larger, the gravitational force of homogenization starts to garner momentum; essentially, the group starts generating its own stereotypes and norms regarding its members. As these stereotypes and norms begin to gel, some members will imagine the space as "safe" because they adequately conform to the group's self-stereotypes, while other people will find the space unwelcoming or exclusionary because they don't live up to these same stereotypes. So while I think that "group-only" spaces and organizations (i.e., specific for members of a particular marginalized group) have some merit, I worry about their tendency to veer toward homogenization and exclusion. Perhaps this can be circumvented if we collectively re-imagined group-only spaces as coalitions of heterogeneous individuals who may share a few relevant experiences, issues, or goals, but who differ in every other possible way.

If we want to enact positive change on the rest of the culture, then we cannot rely solely on these insular group-only coalitions. Rather, we have to build broader coalitions with people who are not members of our own group(s). These broader coalitions are vital: After all, there is strength in numbers, and extensive societal change will not come until we convince a huge swath of society to work with us to challenge myriad double standards. Unfortunately, despite being intentionally intersectional, these broader coalitions can also veer toward homogenization and exclusion in the name of safety. Often this homogenization and exclusion is driven by "call-out culture," a phenomenon that many activists before me have chronicled and critiqued in great detail.[4] I want to spend the rest of this chapter discussing this phenomenon because it is pervasive, and because being able to have constructive cross-community dialogues is absolutely essential if we hope to work together to challenge all forms of sexism and marginalization.

"Call-out culture" stems from a set of unwritten guidelines that have evolved over the years in an attempt to make intentionally intersectional activist spaces safe for all of their participants. First, if somebody says or does anything considered to be sexist or marginalizing, others should call them out on it. After all, if the action is not called out, it can create an atmosphere where marginalizing acts are tolerated, thus making the space inhospitable for many marginalized groups. Sometimes the person who does the calling out is a member of the marginalized group who is targeted by the act. But since it should not fall to members of a particular marginalized group to teach others about the oppression they face[5], allies are encouraged to call out the marginalizing act on their behalf. Indeed, anyone who fails to call out such marginalizing acts is likely to be viewed as not a good ally. Finally, if you are called out as having said or done something sexist or marginalizing, you should take responsibility for your actions rather than try to explain or defend yourself. This last guideline is an attempt to counter the tendency of people in the dominant majority to be unaware or uneducated about the form of marginalization in question, leading them to protest the call-out rather than learning from it and correcting their behaviors.

Now individually, all of these guidelines seem reasonable—in fact, they are all things that I have argued for myself at one time or another. However, taken together, this set of guidelines seems to establish a righteous-activist-versus-evil-oppressor power dynamic, where it is presumed that the action in question is always indefensible and the perpetrator is always clearly in the wrong, while the person doing the calling out is unquestionably correct and justified in their critique. This is certainly true on some occasions, but it is definitely not always the case, as I will detail in the next few paragraphs.

For starters, the aforementioned guidelines work well when the action being called out is direct and blatant. So if someone said "women are no good at math," "homosexuality is gross," or "transsexuals can never be real women or men," it is clear that such statements delegitimize the groups in question, and thus are worthy of being called out. However, in many cases, the action that gets called out is not clearly or directly marginalizing. For instance, I have observed people being called out for being cissexist because they wrote an article about an issue that affects women, but failed to discuss how that issue specifically impacts trans women. Conversely, articles by cis authors that *do* discuss trans women's issues sometimes get called out for "speaking on behalf" of trans women, or "appropriating" trans women's issues. I have observed people being called out for being cissexist because they used terminology (e.g., sex reassignment surgery, or FTM/MTF) that many trans people use, but some reject. I've also seen people get called out for quoting or discussing the work of an author who has said cissexist things in the past, even if the passage or work in question has nothing to do with trans people and issues. In all of these examples, the cissexism that was supposedly perpetrated was *indirect*—that is, seemingly unintentional, not especially obvious or clear-cut, and subjective in nature (as trans activists themselves might disagree about whether these acts truly constitute cissexism).

I myself have been called out as "cissexist" on a number of occasions; for instance, for having coined the term "subconscious sex," and for calling myself bisexual.[6] Once I was even called a "cis supremacist" for citing a trans woman who blogged at a predominantly cis feminist blog instead of citing a trans woman who blogged at a trans feminist blog. So while some call-outs are clearly justified, others fall more into gray areas, and still others are clear overreaches. In other words, call-outs are not infallible.

As a trans person myself, I felt like I could defend myself against the aforementioned accusations of cissexism directed against me, and that most onlookers would view it as a legitimate debate amongst trans people. However, if someone were to call me out for supposedly marginalizing a group that I do *not* belong to, any attempt on my part to explain or justify myself would only compound the problem—I would be viewed as being doubly marginalizing, both because of the initial act, and for subsequently refusing to acknowledge that the act was marginalizing. (Indeed, the reason why I have chosen dubious call-outs of "cissexism" in all of my examples here is because, as a trans activist, I am afforded leeway to critique such call-outs. I have also heard numerous dubious or unjustified call-outs citing other isms, but I honestly don't feel like I can openly discuss them given the current climate without opening myself up to . . . well, call-outs.)

I have heard people say that one should simply let unjustified call-outs be—just apologize and move on. This may be fine in some cases, but other times unjustified call-outs can actually undermine another marginalized group. For instance, on a few occasions, I have heard about cis women being told that when they publicly talk about menstruation, or their clitorises and vaginas, they are exercising cis privilege over trans women. While I understand why trans women might feel discounted or disregarded by such discussions, it is a stretch to imply that such acts are actually cissexist, unless of course they were carried out in a gender-entitled manner.[7] But more to the point, cis women face constant societal pressure to *not* discuss these aspects of their body. These repressive forces lead many women to feel bodily shame, and they contribute to the mystification of women's bodies in the culture at large. This is precisely why many feminists choose to publicly talk about menstruation and clitorises and vaginas in the first place—to reclaim and demystify their own bodies. Yet, according to the guideline that one shalt not explain or defend oneself upon being called out, essentially these women should simply remain quiet about their own bodies in order to be good allies of trans women.

Similarly, several bisexual-identified people have told me that they simply stopped using the label bisexual because trans people had told them that it was cissexist because it supposedly "reinforces the gender binary." While these bisexuals believed that the call-out was unjustified, they felt like they couldn't challenge it because that would simply reinforce the presumption that they were cissexist. (Indeed, I wrote Chapter 9, "Bisexuality and Binaries Revisited," because I knew that, as a trans bisexual, I could challenge that accusation, whereas cis bisexual folks would not have been able to do so without being further dismissed as cissexist.)

The notion that call-outs are always infallible, and that the person who is called out has no right to explain or defend themselves, is not merely wrong, but it utterly ignores history. For decades, trans woman exclusion within feminist and queer spaces has been propagated largely via unjustified call-outs: trans women supposedly "express male energy," "possess male privilege," "transition to attain heterosexual privilege," "appropriate women's bodies and experiences," "parody women's oppression," "reinforce patriarchal and heteronormative stereotypes of women," "infiltrate women's spaces," "trigger women who have been raped," and metaphorically "rape women's bodies." Notably, not a single one of these call-outs accuses trans women of actually doing anything directly or blatantly sexist. Yet, they all depict trans women as sexist oppressors on the basis that our bodies, identities, personal expressions, mannerisms, and/or histories are supposedly indirectly sexist.

I would not be here today—participating in feminist and queer movements, writing this book—if it were not for the countless trans women who came before me, and who vigorously challenged unjustified call-outs that were made against them. Similarly, as I have chronicled in previous chapters, lesbian exclusion within feminist settings, and bisexual and femme exclusion within queer communities, have also been predicated on unjustified call-outs—specifically, accusations that these groups are inherently "privileged" and/or "oppressive," and therefore constitute some kind of threat. So while I believe that calling out acts of sexism and marginalization is absolutely necessary for creating safe and inclusive communities, we must also recognize that call-outs can be used as tools for delegitimizing people and outright exclusion.

Furthermore, the idea that we should simply let unjustified call-outs roll off our backs denies the ferocity and mean-spiritedness in which they are sometimes (albeit not always) delivered. Now I am *not* talking about the fact that members of marginalized groups who feel targeted might respond angrily or emotionally to a marginalizing act. Those of us who are marginalized have every right to react strongly to acts that delegitimize us. However, sometimes we go well beyond being angry about the incident, and intentionally smear the person behind it. In other words, rather than trying to simply eliminate sexism and marginalization, we set our sights on invalidating or eliminating *people*. Nowhere is this more evident than in the tendency for call-outs to be framed as "You're being cissexist," or "You're a cissexist," rather than "What you just said (or did) is cissexist."[8] The implication that the person is "a cissexist"—through and through, down to the core—essentially portrays them as irredeemable and unfit to participate in social justice spaces. It also implies that they are "immoral," which we know from the last chapter is a common invalidation used to undermine people, and which is most effective when the person is marked in some way (e.g., individuals who are already marginalized, whom we view as unexpected or exceptional, or who are members of an outgroup).

Feminist, queer, and social justice movements are founded on eliminating oppression. So once we paint a person (fairly or unfairly) as being "an evil oppressor," it becomes rather easy to purge them from our organizations and communities. But there is a flip side to this: Since our collective goal is eliminating oppression, we may also gain perceived credibility within the movement by proving that we are "righteous activists." And what better way to prove that we are righteous activists and allies than to vigorously call out other people whenever they say or do anything that could possibly be construed as marginalizing? I think that this desire to be *seen* as righteous activists and allies helps explain two recurring aspects of this phenomenon: the fact that call-outs are almost always done in public rather than private, and the tendency toward "piling on"—when additional people join the fray after the initial call out, and often long after the person in question has apologized for the incident.[9] If the point of call-outs is truly to make our spaces free of sexism and marginalization, then only one call-out should be necessary, and it can very well be done by taking the person aside after the incident. While public shaming and piling on do not necessarily help to further reduce marginalization, they are ways for us to show others that we are virtuous activists who are on the "right side" of the issue.

There is a negative consequence of public shaming and piling on that is generally overlooked in the heat of the moment: Such incidents can be quite traumatic for the person on the receiving end.[10] I suppose that if the person truly is an "evil oppressor," others may view them as "having it coming to them." But more often than not, the person in question is an activist who is working hard to create positive change, but inadvertently offended or undermined certain individuals. I know quite a few activists who have pulled back from or completely left activism after a particularly nasty piling on. If our goal is to create a stronger and broader coalition, can we really afford to lose committed activists like this? And if we create movements where every perceived infraction garners a barrage of call-outs, how is someone brand new to activism (and who hasn't had the advantage of learning about all the various isms in college or graduate school) ever going to last more than a month or two? Seriously, shouldn't our call-outs encourage the person to improve their knowledge and politics, rather than simply drive them away?

I began the chapter by describing activism as a balancing act. Nowhere is that more true than in how we engage in intersectional activism and cross-community dialogues. Single-issue activists may be able to get away with sporting an us-against-the-world, righteous-activist-versus-evil-oppressor type of attitude, but that mentality is pure poison when it comes to intersectional activism. If we truly want to build broad, intentionally intersectional coalitions (and I believe that we should), then it begins with us recognizing that there is no such thing as a "gold star" activist—that mythical creature who has never once said or done anything inappropriate, offensive, or marginalizing to someone. We have all screwed up at one time or another. Many of us start out relatively uninformed about feminism, queer activism, and social justice, but we learn over time. As activists, we should be judged, not on whether we have all the right answers or say all the right things, but based upon whether we are willing to improve ourselves, learn about and advocate for other people's issues, and work together with others.

Some people are repeat offenders—purposefully and repeatedly marginalizing, and not open to criticism or educating themselves about others' experiences—and by all means they should be held fully accountable. But when this is not the case, we should err on the side of giving people the benefit of doubt: We should presume that if they say or do anything that we perceive to be sexist or marginalizing, that it was likely inadvertent or stemmed from ignorance. This is especially true in social justice settings, where all participants presumably have some interest or investment in challenging marginalization.[11] We should focus any criticism we have on the act, and not the person.

Given that there are myriad double standards, it is impossible for any single person to be aware of and fully understand all of them. Therefore, all of us are ignorant in some ways, yet knowledgeable in others. Keeping this in the forefront of our minds is crucial—it should make us receptive to being called out as well as to the possibility that our call-outs may be somewhat off the mark. It should also encourage us to frame our criticisms in a constructive rather than destructive way—such as, by posing them as "add-ons" rather than "call-outs." For example, if somebody giving a gender-related workshop makes a comment that seems to confuse or conflate trans women with drag queens, rather than saying, "What you said is horribly cissexist," it might be more effective to say, "You seem to be confusing trans women with drag queens, which is something that many trans people find cissexist." The latter remark is less accusatory, more instructive, and therefore more likely to elicit change.

Over the years, I have come to believe that the intensity of our focus as single-issue activists can actually impede progress toward creating broader coalitions. For instance, as a trans activist, I have spent a ton of time rooting out cissexism. This involves critiquing the endless stream of stereotypes and assumptions about trans people, articulating the way our community is affected by particular issues, highlighting how we are often invisibilized in society, discussing how cis people appropriate trans lives and culture, analyzing potentially problematic language, pointing out examples of cis privilege, and so on. All this is important work that should continue. However, the downside is that repeatedly focusing on these specific matters can eventually lead me to see cissexism practically everywhere. Suddenly, if an article I'm reading fails to mention how an issue affects trans folks, I see it as invisibility or erasure. If in a non–trans-related situation, someone uses the word "trap" or "impersonator," it can feel cissexist to me, because those words are often used as slurs against trans folks.[12] When I am at a costume party and see someone who is crossdressed, it can feel like a parody or appropriation of trans people to me, when in fact the person is simply dressed as someone of the other gender.

Sometimes our heightened sense of awareness about a particular form of marginalization can lead us to call out even the slightest potential infractions—hence the many previous examples of call-outs of acts that are indirectly sexist, if sexist at all. In an intentionally intersectional activist setting, this tendency can cause us to myopically view others primarily in terms of how they behave with regards to the particular ism that we are most concerned with, rather than viewing them as different individuals who are marginalized in different ways, and who each brings something different to the table. It can also be quite derailing if every single participant is citing every indirectly sexist or marginalizing comment that they notice. I think that using call-outs more judiciously—for example, in cases when people are clearly projecting sexist or marginalizing double standards onto others—can help reduce the frequency of derailments.

Finally, if we want to create broad intersectional coalitions, we should stop using privilege as a device to undermine others. The concept of privilege is supposed to be a tool designed to make visible the advantages experienced by people who do not face a particular form of marginalization. We can rightly call out people who deny their privilege, or who exercise it over others. But it is not okay to dismiss someone solely on the basis that they "have" a particular form of privilege. Simply having privilege does not make one a monster or oppressor. In fact, all of us have some forms of privilege that others do not have. So it is hypocritical for us to insist that a person's experiences, perspectives, or issues are completely invalid solely on the basis that they have (or have had) some form of privilege that we do not.

I believe that the suggestions that I have offered here are all quite reasonable. But I'll be the first to admit that reasonable solutions only work if everyone who participates also happens to be reasonable. Some people are unapologetically sexist and marginalizing, and are unwilling to change their ways, and they should certainly be taken to task for their behavior. Some people are know-it-alls who are convinced that they are always right, and that there is no reason for them to listen to or consider what other people are saying. Such people should be called out for being arrogant and entitled. But sometimes, the thing that thwarts reasonable cross-community dialogues is our own anger.

I could write an entire book about anger. My anger at all the cisgender, heterosexual, and monosexual people who have made me feel so small, or tried to erase my identity. My anger at all the feminists and queer activists who have deemed my perspective irrelevant, or tried to exclude me from their movements. My anger at all the men and masculine folks who have presumed that my body, femininity, and person were theirs to freely comment upon, critique, harass, and touch without my consent. To be honest, it was my anger (rather than my reason) that drove me to activism in the first place. I was pissed off, and I wanted to change everything. Back then, I was scared of men. I was suspicious of cis lesbians (due to the long history of blatant trans-misogyny in lesbian communities). Upon reflection, I probably wouldn't have made a good intersectional activist back then, as I was too concerned with my own fears, wounds, struggles, and sorrows.

I am in a different place now. I still hurt, but I've done a lot of self-healing. And I still feel anger, it's just not my primary motivation anymore. I used to be a singularly focused trans activist, but these days, I am more interested in being a holistic feminist. Don't get me wrong: I am not trying to say that anger is bad, or that it is simply a phase that we need to get over. Some people never get over the anger, and others maybe never feel it so intensely, or let it spill into their activism. As I said in the beginning of this chapter, activism can (and should) occur in a multiplicity of forms: both angry and reasonable, both radical and reformist, both group-only and cross-community, both single-issue and holistic. All are important. If we acknowledge this multiplicity (rather than thinking of activism as being "my way or the highway"), then maybe we can each figure out for ourselves where we are at personally, what we are most passionate about, and what our place in the movement(s) should be. Legitimate anger has its place in activism, provided that we realize that there are other legitimate ways to be.

As I have highlighted throughout this chapter, activism—especially building broad, intentionally intersectional coalitions—is a balancing act that involves speaking as well as listening, teaching, and learning. It requires us to step out of the relative safety of our fixed perspective, and to take a more holistic approach that accommodates a multiplicity of differing perspectives. Certainly, it is crucial for us to have the concepts, language, and tools in order to forcefully call out acts of sexism and marginalization. But it is also important for us to realize that these same tools have been used in the past to marginalize and exclude others, thus creating smaller insular movements that favor people of certain bodies, identities, and tendencies over others. If we are serious about challenging sexism and marginalization, then we should be just as concerned about these hierarchies that arise in our own movements and communities as we are with ones in the dominant culture. A good place for us to start would be grabbing our metaphorical sledgehammers, and to begin shattering the "righteous activist"/"evil oppressor" and the "infallible activist"/"ignorant oppressor" binaries.

NOTES

Introduction

1. For the record, two years ago I found out that I have a chronic autoimmune condition (see Julia Serano, "Skin," http://juliaserano.blogspot.com/2011/08/skin.html). It is mostly in remission now, but it has led me to question my relationship with ability. Many of the essays compiled in this book were written prior to that knowledge, so I have chosen to leave intact references of myself as "able-bodied," even though my identity in this regard is a little more complicated than that.

2. "A-gay" is queer slang for "an affluent, well-connected, upwardly mobile gay man or woman" (http://en.wiktionary.org/wiki/A-gay). Among feminists and social justice activists, people use the word "liberal" as a pejorative to insinuate that a person's politics are too moderate or conservative.

3. Anne Koedt, "Lesbianism and Feminism," in *Radical Feminism*, Anne Koedt, Ellen Levine, and Anita Rapone (eds.). (New York: Quadrangle/The New York Times Book Co., 1980), 255.

1 – A Word About Words

1. In my previous book, *Whipping Girl*, I discuss at great length how men and people on the trans female/feminine spectrum are impacted by traditional sexism. Julia Serano, *Whipping Girl: A Transsexual Woman on Sexism and the Scapegoating of Femininity* (Emeryville, CA: Seal Press, 2007).

2. Specifically, people generally use the "ism" version to describe the assumption that the marginalized group is inferior to, or less legitimate than, the dominant group, as well as the many ways in which that assumption is reinforced or institutionalized in society. In contrast, the "phobia" version is often used to describe personal reactions of anxiety, fear, or hatred that individual members of the dominant group express toward the marginalized group. As a general rule, I prefer to use the "ism" version, as it is broader, and a more accurate conceptualization of how sexism actually works.

However, when a form of sexism is newly articulated, the "phobia" version is often coined first, and it tends to be more frequently used and easily understood outside of activist circles. So I will sometimes talk about "phobias," but I will be using those terms to refer to the broader aspects of sexism typically denoted by "isms."

3. According to some sources, the term *intersectionality* first appeared in Kimberle Crenshaw, "Demarginalizing the Intersection of Race and Sex: A Black Feminist Critique of Antidiscrimination Doctrine, Feminist Theory and Antiracist Politics," *The University of Chicago Legal Forum*, Volume 139, (1989), 139-167. However, the concepts underlying intersectionality had been articulated prior to that—see Cherríe Moraga and Gloria E. Anzaldúa (eds.), *This Bridge Called My Back: Writings by Radical Women of Color* (Berkeley, CA: Third Woman Press, 2002); Patricia Hill Collins, *Black Feminist Thought: Knowledge, Consciousness and the Politics of Empowerment* (New York, Routledge, 2000); bell hooks, *Ain't I a Woman?: Black Women and Feminism* (Boston: South End Press, 1981); Audre Lorde, *Sister Outsider: Essays and Speeches* (Freedom, CA: The Crossing Press Feminist Series, 1984).

4. The reluctance to include these groups under the queer umbrella stems from both heterosexual-identified people within BDSM and polyamorous communities (who don't consider themselves to be queer with regards to sexual orientation) and from the greater queer community (where more vanilla and monogamous queer folks don't want to have their sexualities or identities associated with BDSM or polyamory).

5. For example, see Julia Serano, "A 'Transsexual Versus Transgender' Intervention" (http://juliaserano.blogspot.com/2011/09/transsexual-versus-transgender.html).

6. I favor the *trans female/feminine* and *trans male/masculine* variations, as they rightly denote the person's gender identity and/or gender expression, with "trans" being an adjective indicating how such identities/expressions differ from our birth-assigned sex. *MTF* and *FTM* are more widely used, but they are not optimal because they seem to depict trans people as being perpetually "in between" genders, or constantly transitioning from one to the other. However, I prefer both of these formulations over *MAAB* and *FAAB (male/female assigned at birth)*. While it is sometimes useful (for clarity) to mention the sex a person was assigned at birth, describing trans people as being a "FAAB" or "MAAB" is horribly delegitimizing, as it defines us based on our birth-assigned sex (a nonconsensual act committed against us, and which many of us come to reject), while simultaneously erasing our gender identities and expressions.

7. Serano, *Whipping Girl*. See also Julia Serano, "*Whipping Girl* FAQ on cissexual, cisgender, and cis privilege" (http://juliaserano.blogspot.com/2011/08/whipping-girl-faq-on-cissexual.html).

8. Serano, *Whipping Girl*.

2 – On the Outside Looking In

1. The Michigan Womyn's Music Festival's policy regarding trans women has evolved somewhat over time (see Emi Koyama's "Michigan/Trans Controversy Archive"

http://eminism.org/michigan/documents.html). Their "womyn-born-womyn-only" policy currently remains in effect, and they have formally stated that trans women who enter "disrespect the stated intention of this Festival." However, they no longer forcibly remove trans women from the space, which has resulted in trans women and cis allies advocating together on the land under the banner "Trans Women Belong Here." For more information about the festival's trans woman–exclusion policy and its evolution, see Riki Anne Wilchins, *Read My Lips: Sexual Subversion and the End of Gender* (Ithaca, NY: Firebrand Books, 1997), 109-114; Michelle Tea, "Transmissions from Camp Trans," *The Believer*, November 2003; Serano, *Whipping Girl*, 233-245; Julia Serano, "Not Quite There Yet . . ." August 23, 2006 (www.juliaserano. com/frustration.html#postTWE), Julia Serano, "Rethinking Sexism: How Trans Women Challenge Feminism," *AlterNet.org*, August 4, 2008 (www.alternet.org/ reproductivejustice/93826); Alice Kalafarski, "Just Another Woman at Michfest," *prettyqueer*, September 1, 2011 (www.prettyqueer.com/2011/09/01/just-another-woman-at-michfest).

2. For an overview of feminist anti–trans woman sentiment, see Pat Califia, *Sex Changes: The Politics of Transgenderism* (San Francisco: Cleis Press, 1997), 86–119; Joanne Meyerowitz, *How Sex Changed: A History of Transsexuality in the United States* (Cambridge, MA: Harvard University Press, 2002), 258–262; Deborah Rudacille, *The Riddle of Gender: Science, Activism, and Transgender Rights* (New York: Pantheon Books, 2005), 141-178; Susan Stryker, *Transgender History* (Berkeley: Seal Press, 2008), 91-111. For pertinent examples of lesbian and radical feminist writings that disparage transsexuals, see Mary Daly, *Gyn/Ecology: The Metaethics of Radical Feminism* (Boston: Beacon Press, 1990), 67-72; Andrea Dworkin, *Woman Hating* (New York: E. P. Dutton and Co., 1974), 185–187; Margrit Eichler, *The Double Standard: A Feminist Critique of Feminist Social Science* (London: Croom Helm, 1980), 72–90; Germaine Greer, *The Madwoman's Underclothes: Essays and Occasional Writings* (New York: Atlantic Monthly Press, 1987), 189–191; Germaine Greer, *The Whole Woman* (New York: Alfred A. Knopf, 1999), 70–80; Sheila Jeffreys, *Beauty and Misogyny: Harmful Cultural Practices in the West* (New York: Routledge, 2005), 46–66; Robin Morgan, *Going Too Far* (New York: Random House, 1977), 170–188; Janice G. Raymond, *The Transsexual Empire: The Making of the She-Male* (Boston: Beacon Press, 1979).

3. Several passages of this chapter (which was originally written in 2005) have previously appeared in the chapter "Bending Over Backwards: Traditional Sexism and Trans Woman–Exclusion Policies" of my first book *Whipping Girl*. This particular passage appears in Serano, *Whipping Girl*, 237.

4. Andrea Dworkin was a leading voice of what is often called "anti-pornography feminism," which dominated much of feminist thought and activism during the 1980s. Anti-pornography feminists generally oppose anything that they feel objectifies women—this typically includes porn, sex work, BDSM, and certain aspects of feminine dress. Because they sought to curb or censor many expressions of sexuality, critics often refer to this movement as "sex-negative feminism."

5. Emi Koyama, *A Handbook on Discussing the Michigan Womyn's Music Festival for Trans Activists and Allies* (Portland, OR: Confluere Publications, 2003), 12-13.

6. This sentence also appears in Serano, *Whipping Girl*, 239.

7. This passage also appears in Serano, *Whipping Girl*, 235-6.

8. This passage also appears in Serano, *Whipping Girl*, 245.

9. As mentioned in Note 1, in the last few years, there finally have been trans women (along with cis women) petitioning for their own inclusion inside the festival.

10. Carolyn Connelly, "Fuck You (A Poem for Monty)," *a brooklyn diary* (self-published, 2003).

11. Julia Serano, "Cocky," *Draw Blood* (Oakland: Hot Tranny Action, 2004).

3 – On Being a Woman

1. Alice Echols actually makes this case in her book: Alice Echols, *Daring to Be Bad: Radical Feminism in America, 1967–75* (Minneapolis: University of Minnesota Press, 1989). "Second-wave" feminism refers to feminist thought and activism that commenced during the 1960s and dominated through the 1980s.

2. Especially in the early 2000s, "tranny boi" was an identity that was popular among younger trans male/masculine spectrum folks. It seems to have declined in popularity, perhaps due to controversy regarding whether trans male/masculine spectrum folks can rightfully reclaim the word "tranny"—see Hazel/Cedar Troost, "'Tranny' & Cis Women: Re-Reclaiming Tranny (or not) part 2," January 8, 2009 (http://takesupspace.wordpress.com/2009/01/08/tranny-cis-women-re-reclaiming-tranny-or-not-part-2/).

4 – Margins

1. I have since written more about my experience with skin cancer in Serano, "Skin."

5 – Trans Feminism: There's No Conundrum About It

1. Aviva Dove-Viebahn, "Future of Feminism: Transfeminism and Its Conundrums," March 20, 2012 (http://msmagazine.com/blog/2012/03/20/future-of-feminism-transfeminism-and-its-conundrums).

Note: Many trans feminists prefer spelling "trans feminism" as two separate words, where *trans* is an adjective that modifies *feminism*. The single-word version—"transfeminism"—looks somewhat alien, and seems to suggest that this is not actually a strand of feminism but something else entirely (just as the single word "transwomen" suggests that trans women are something other than women).

2. Julia Serano, "Trans Feminism: There's No Conundrum About It," April 18, 2012 (http://msmagazine.com/blog/2012/04/18/trans-feminism-theres-no-conundrum-about-it).

3. "Third-wave" feminisms refer to several strands of feminism that arose in the 1980s and 1990s, and which, in different ways, challenged beliefs that were prevalent during second-wave feminism.

4. Patricia Hill Collins, *Black Feminist Thought: Knowledge, Consciousness and the Politics of Empowerment*.

5. Serano, *Whipping Girl*.

6. Gender Public Advocacy Coalition, "50 Under 30: Masculinity and the War on America's Youth, A Human Rights Report" (2006); Jaime M. Grant, Lisa A. Mottet, Justin Tanis, Jack Harrison, Jody L. Herman, and Mara Keisling, *Injustice at Every Turn: A Report of the National Transgender Discrimination Survey* (Washington: National Center for Transgender Equality and National Gay and Lesbian Task Force, 2011).

7. Serano, *Whipping Girl*.

8. Daisy Hernandez, "Becoming a Black Man," *ColorLines*, January 7, 2008, (http://colorlines.com/archives/2008/01/becoming_a_black_man.html); Chandra Thomas-Whitfield, "A Transgender Man of Color Shares his Story," Juvenile Justice Information Exchange, July 15, 2011 (http://jjie.org/transgender-man-of-color-shares-his-story); Kortney Ryan Ziegler, "Uses of Black Trans Male Anger," Huffington Post Gay Voices, April 12, 2013 (http://www.huffingtonpost.com/kortney-ryan-ziegler-phd/uses-of-black-trans-male-anger_b_3065450.html).

9. See Chapter 1, Note 3.

10. The phrase "oppression Olympics" refers to the tendency of people to argue that one group of people (typically a group they themselves belong to) is "more oppressed" than some other marginalized group, rather than acknowledging that both groups face different yet equally legitimate forms of marginalization, and that some people exist at the intersection of the two.

6 – Reclaiming Femininity

1. Serano, *Whipping Girl*, 319-343.

2. Raymond, *The Transsexual Empire*, 79; Morgan, *Going Too Far*, 180.

3. More information about *FtF: Female to Femme* can be found at www.imdb.com/title/tt0443515.

4. This chapter is actually a revised version of the keynote talk that I presented at Femme 2008.

5. Serano, *Whipping Girl*, 345-362.

6. Joan Nestle, "The Femme Question," in Joan Nestle (ed.), *The Persistent Desire: A Butch Femme Reader*, (Boston: Alyson Publications, 1992), 138–146. The specific "femme question" that I am referring to here (and one that Nestle discusses in her piece) is the tendency of both the straight mainstream, as well lesbian and feminist

communities, to construct the existence of femmes as a problem, and to project disparaging ulterior motives onto femmes.

7 – Three Strikes and I'm Out

1. For the record, some trans people experience shifts in their sexual orientation post-transition, whereas many trans people do not. By posing these questions, I am by no means suggesting that all trans people experience or react to our transitions in the same way, or that hormone therapy or social transition has some causal effect on sexual orientation that holds true for all people. Everybody's different.

2. I discuss this hardcore, hypersexualization of trans female/feminine folks (and why I think it happens) in Serano, *Whipping Girl*, 253-271.

8 – Dating

1. The Craigslist personal ad category "w4w" refers to "women seeking women."

2. This problem is so pervasive that (subsequent to my writing this piece in 2010), Drew DeVeaux coined the phrase "the cotton ceiling" to describe how many cis queer women who are fine with trans women in their communities nevertheless draw the line when it comes to dating or being sexual with us.

3. The word "squick" is used in BDSM communities to convey that you feel personally disturbed or grossed out by a particular act (usually a sexual one), yet recognize that others may find it legitimately enjoyable.

9 – Bisexuality and Binaries Revisited

1. Julia Serano, "Bisexuality does not reinforce the gender binary," October 10, 2010, *The Scavenger* (www.thescavenger.net/glb/bisexuality-does-not-reinforce-the-gender-binary-39675-467.html).

2. Shiri Eisner, "Words, binary and biphobia, or: why 'bi' is binary but 'FTM' is not." February 22, 2011, *Bi radical* (http://radicalbi.wordpress.com/2011/02/22/words-binary-and-biphobia-or-why-bi-is-binary-but-ftm-is-not). The contents of this post have been republished in Shiri Eisner, *Bi: Notes for a Bisexual Revolution* (Berkeley, CA: Seal Press, 2013).

3. Sexologist Alfred Kinsey developed this numeric scale to describe people's sexual orientations as being on a continuum, where a 0 denotes exclusive heterosexuality, and 6 denotes exclusive homosexuality. According to this scheme, anyone who scores between 0 and 6 would be considered (at least a little bit) bisexual/ BMNOPPQ.

4. I personally first saw the term *monosexual* in Loraine Hutchins and Lani Kaahumanu (eds.), *Bi Any Other Name: Bisexual People Speak Out* (Boston: Alyson Publications, 1991). And I was introduced to *monosexism* upon reading Jonathan Alexander

and Karen Yescavage (eds.), *Bisexuality and Transgenderism: InterSEXions of the Others* (Binghampton, NY: Harrington Park Press, 2003); and Clare Hemmings, *Bisexual Spaces: Geography of Sexuality and Gender* (New York: Routledge, 2002).

5. San Francisco Human Rights Commission, "Bisexual Invisibility: Impacts and Recommendations" (March 2011). See also Eisner, *Bi: Notes for a Bisexual Revolution*, 59-93; Massachusetts Department of Public Health, "The Health of Lesbian, Gay, Bisexual and Transgender (LGBT) Persons in Massachusetts" (July 2009).

6. Serano, *Whipping Girl*.

7. Serano, "*Whipping Girl* FAQ on cissexual, cisgender, and cis privilege."

8. Serano, *Whipping Girl*, 102-106. I also make a similar case in this book, specifically Chapter 13, "Homogenizing Versus Holistic Views of Gender and Sexuality."

9. Serano, "Bisexuality does not reinforce the gender binary."

10. Eisner, "Words, binary and biphobia, or: why 'bi' is binary but 'FTM' is not."

11. Alexander and Yescavage (eds.), *Bisexuality and Transgenderism: InterSEXions of the Others*.

12. Subversivism is the assumption that genders and sexualities that are deemed subversive or transgressive are inherently superior to those that are more conventional. While this form of sexism is not prevalent in mainstream culture, it does proliferate in feminist and queer circles. Asexophobia is the assumption that people who do not experience sexual attraction (i.e., asexuals) are less legitimate than people who do.

13. Jillian Todd Weiss, "GL vs. BT: The Archaeology of Biphobia and Transphobia Within the U.S. Gay and Lesbian Community," in Alexander and Yescavage (eds.), *Bisexuality and Transgenderism: InterSEXions of the Others*, 25-55.

14. As mentioned in Chapter 8, Note 2, Drew DeVeaux coined the phrase "the cotton ceiling." It has since garnered a lot of controversy, especially on the Internet, where some cis radical feminists who hold vehemently anti-trans views misinterpret it to portray trans women as potential rapists. See Tobi Hill-Meyer, "Ceiling Metaphors Are Used For Systemic Change" (http://tobitastic.tumblr.com/post/19916145506/ceiling-metaphors-are-used-for-systemic-change) and Natalie Reed, "Caught Up In Cotton," April 4, 2012 (http://freethoughtblogs.com/nataliereed/2012/04/04/caught-up-in-cotton).

15. Shiri Eisner, "Words, binary and biphobia, or: why 'bi' is binary but 'FTM' is not."

16. Julia Serano, "Baby Talk," March, 2012 (http://juliaserano.blogspot.com/2013/03/faab-mentality.html).

17. Eisner, *Bi: Notes for a Bisexual Revolution*, 235-259.

10 – How to Be an Ally to Trans Women

1. "Gold star lesbian" is queer slang for a lesbian who has never once been sexual with a man. Within certain circles, "gold star" status is associated with being more "pure"

or authentically lesbian than those who have previously had sexual experiences with men. Needless to say, it is a highly monosexist concept.

11 – Performance Piece

1. The notion that "all gender is performance" or "all gender is drag" is frequently attributed to Judith Butler, and specifically to her book *Gender Trouble* (Judith Butler, *Gender Trouble: Feminism and the Subversion of Identity* [New York: Routledge, 1999]). However, on numerous occasions, Butler has argued that these catchphrases are gross misinterpretations of what she was actually trying to say; see *Gender Trouble*, xxii–xxiv; Judith Butler, *Bodies That Matter: On the Discursive Limits of "Sex"* (New York: Routledge, 1993), 125–126; "Gender as Performance: An Interview with Judith Butler," *Radical Philosophy*, Vol. 67, Summer 1994, 32–39; see also Sara Salih, *Judith Butler* (London: Routledge, 2002), 62–71.

2. The slogans "all gender is performance" and "all gender is drag" are addressed in the previous note. "Gender is just a construct" is another common saying in feminist and queer circles—I debunk it more thoroughly in Chapters 12 and 13.

3. In his television show *The Colbert Report*, Stephen Colbert plays a fictional right-wing political pundit. Satirizing conservatives who insist that racism no longer exists in America, or that we are now living in a "post-racism" world, Stephen's character regularly claims that he doesn't see race, and that "People tell me I'm white, and I believe them . . ."

4. Ze and hir are gender-neutral pronouns favored by many genderqueer people as substitutes for she/he and her/him, respectively. I have nothing against ze and hir *per se*, but I do object to people using them nonconsensually to describe me (I prefer she/her). Indeed, people only seem to use ze/hir when discussing trans people, but never cis people—a tendency that I find to be cissexist.

12 – The Perversion of "The Personal Is Political"

1. A non-comprehensive list of examples: Alexander and Yescavage (eds.), *Bisexuality and Transgenderism;* Pavan Amara, "Feminism: still excluding working class women?" *The F-Word*, March 7, 2012 (www.thefword.org.uk/features/2012/03/feminism_still_); Califia, *Sex Changes*, 86–162; hooks, *Ain't I a Woman?*; bell hooks, *Feminist Theory: From Margin to Center* (Boston: South End Press, 1984); Echols, *Daring to Be Bad*, 203–241; Sharin N. Elkholy, "Feminism and Race in the United States," *Internet Encyclopedia of Philosophy* (www.iep.utm.edu/fem-race); Hutchins and Kaahumanu (eds.), *Bi Any Other Name*; Emi Koyama, "Whose Feminism is it Anyway? The Unspoken Racism of the Trans Inclusion Debate," in Susan Stryker and Stephen Whittle (eds.), *The Transgender Studies Reader*, (New York: Routledge, 2006), 698–705; Lorde, *Sister Outsider*; Robert McRuer, *Crip Theory: Cultural Signs of Queerness and Disability* (New York: New York University Press, 2006); Viviane Namaste, *Sex Change, Social Change: Reflections on Identity, Institutions, and Imperialism* (Toronto: Women's Press, 2005); Nestle (ed.), *The Persistent Desire*; Edward

Ndopu and Darnell L. Moore, "On Ableism within Queer Spaces, or, Queering the 'Normal,'" *prettyqueer*, December 7, 2012 (www.prettyqueer.com/2012/12/07/on-ableism-within-queer-spaces-or-queering-the-normal); Danielle Peers and Lindsay Eales, "'Stand Up' for Exclusion?: Queer Pride, ableism and inequality," in Malinda Smith and Fatima Jaffer (eds.), *Beyond The Queer Alphabet: Conversations on Gender, Sexuality and Intersectionality* (https://the-menace.s3.amazonaws.com/uploads/Beyond_the_Queer_Alphabet_20March2012-F.pdf); Rudacille, *The Riddle of Gender*, 141-178; Serano, *Whipping Girl*, 319-343; Elizabeth V. Spelman, *Inessential Woman: Problem of Exclusion in Feminist Thought* (Boston: Beacon Press, 1988); Stryker, *Transgender History*, 91-111; Wilchins, *Read My Lips*.

2. Whac-A-Mole is an arcade game in which toy moles randomly pop out of different holes. The player tries to knock the moles back into their holes with a hammer. As soon as one is knocked down, another mole pops out of another hole somewhere else. Much like exclusion.

3. Throughout this section, I use "cross-gender–identified" to mean that trans people's gender identities differ from our birth-assigned sex. My intention for this phrasing is not to replace existing terminology. I only use it here because it makes the analogy with "same-sex relationships" more obvious.

4. Reviewed in Vern L. Bullough and Bonnie Bullough, *Cross Dressing: Sex and Gender* (Philadelphia: University of Pennsylvania Press, 1993); Califia, *Sex Changes*, 120–162; Gilbert Herdt, *Same Sex, Different Cultures: Exploring Gay and Lesbian Lives* (Boulder, CO: Westview Press, 1997); Gilbert Herdt (ed.) *Third Sex, Third Gender: Beyond Sexual Dimorphism in Culture and History* (New York: Zone Books, 1996); Leslie Feinberg, *Transgender Warriors: Making History from Joan of Arc to Dennis Rodman* (Boston: Beacon Press, 1996); Serena Nanda, *Gender Diversity: Cross-cultural Variations* (Prospect Heights: Waveland Press, 2000); Joan Roughgarden, *Evolution's Rainbow: Diversity, Gender, and Sexuality in Nature and People* (Berkeley: University of California Press, 2004).

5. As I discussed in Chapter 9, bisexuals face monosexism as well as heterosexism. Sometimes when people lump bisexuals in with lesbian and gay folks, and describe the sexism we face solely in terms of heterosexism, it can erase the societal monosexism we additionally experience (see Eisner, *Bi: Notes for a Bisexual Revolution*, 59-93). That is certainly not my intention here.

6. Serano, *Whipping Girl*, 13, 104-106.

7. Ibid., 170-172.

8. Ibid., 35-64.

9. The patriarchy and gender binary have been explained in previous chapters. The "sex/gender system" is described in Gayle Rubin, "The Traffic in Women: Notes on the 'Political Economy' of Sex," in Linda Nicholson (ed.) *The Second Wave: A Reader in Feminist Theory* (New York and London: Routledge, 1997), 27-62. "Compulsory heterosexuality" is described in Adrienne Rich, "Compulsory Heterosexuality and Lesbian Existence," *Signs* 5, no. 4 (1980), 631-660. The "heterosexual matrix" is

described in Butler, *Gender Trouble*. "Kyriarchy" is described in Elisabeth Schussler Fiorenza, *Wisdom Ways: Introducing Feminist Biblical Interpretation* (New York: Orbis Books, 2001), and encompasses a multitude of intersecting hierarchies, including traditional sexism, racism, classism, colonialism, and potentially others.

10. Sandra Lipsitz Bem, *The Lenses of Gender* (New Haven: Yale University Press, 1993), 111.

11. Dworkin, *Woman Hating*, 174.

12. Ibid., 186-187.

13. Raymond, *The Transsexual Empire*, xviii-xix.

14. Sheila Jeffreys, *Unpacking Queer Politics: A Lesbian Feminist Perspective* (Cambridge: Polity Press, 2003), 44.

15. Judith Lorber, *Paradoxes of Gender* (New Haven: Yale University Press, 1994). Lorber's quote can be found in Greer, *The Whole Woman*, 73.

16. Nanda, *Gender Diversity*, 96-97.

17. Majorie Garber, *Vested Interests: Cross-Dressing and Cultural Anxiety* (New York: HarperPerennial, 1993); Bernice L. Hausman, *Changing Sex: Transsexualism, Technology, and the Idea of Gender* (Durham: Duke University Press, 1995); Carol-Anne Tyler, *Female Impersonation* (New York: Routledge, 2003). I describe these books as portraying transsexuals as "semiotically challenged" because they all argue (in different ways) that transsexuals mistake the supposed trappings of gender (e.g., clothing, gender roles, and other social symbols that signify "woman" or "man" in our culture) as being directly and inexorably linked to natural gender categories (what semioticians would call "the signified" in this example). Garber, Hausman, and Tyler (being gender artifactualists) do not believe that such natural gender categories exist, which leads them to presume that transsexuals are highly misguided in our gender expressions and transitions.

18. Max Wolf Valerio, "'Now That You're a White Man': Changing Sex in a Postmodern World—Being, Becoming, and Borders," in Gloria Anzaldúa and Analouise Keating (eds.), *This Bridge We Call Home: Radical Visions for Transformation* (New York: Routledge, 2002), 245-246.

19. It must be said that cissexuals also emulate the behaviors of cissexual women and men. This is perhaps most obvious in children and teens who are in the process of learning how to act according to societal gender norms. Cissexual gender imitation also occurs in adults—in fact, it's precisely what fashion trends and appearance-oriented advertisements rely upon. Such instances of cissexual gender imitation are typically played down (allowing cissexual genders to appear "real"), in sharp contrast to the hyper-emphasis on transsexual gender imitation (which makes transsexual genders appear "fake").

20. Suzanne J. Kessler and Wendy McKenna, *Gender: An Ethnomethodological Approach* (Chicago: University of Chicago Press, 1978), 112.

21. Ibid., 114.

22. The listed individuals' gender identities, gender expressions, and life choices have all been subjected to intense feminist and academic scrutiny and criticism in the name of forwarding gender artifactualism. Trans critiques of this dehumanizing methodology can be found in Viviane K. Namaste, *Invisible Lives: The Erasure of Transsexual and Transgendered People* (Chicago: University of Chicago Press, 2000), 9-70; Serano, *Whipping Girl*, 195-212.

23. Kate Bornstein, *Gender Outlaw: On Men, Women and the Rest of Us* (New York: Vintage Books, 1994); Feinberg, *Transgender Warriors*; Wilchins, *Read My Lips*.

24. Henry Rubin, "Phenomenology as Method in Trans Studies," *GLQ: A Journal of Lesbian and Gay Studies* 4, no. 2 (1998), 263-281; Serano, *Whipping Girl*, 139-155, 345-349.

25. Bernice L. Hausman, "Review: Recent Transgender Theory," *Feminist Studies* 27, no. 2 (2001), 465-490.

26. Ibid.

27. Janice G. Raymond, "The Politics of Transgender," *Feminism Psychology* 4 (1994), 628-633.

28. Echols, *Daring to Be Bad*, 3-11.

29. Ibid., 211.

30. Ibid.

31. Ibid., 215-216. Radicalesbians, "The Woman Identified Woman," in Koedt, Levine, and Rapone (eds.), *Radical Feminism*, 240-245.

32. Echols, *Daring to Be Bad*, 216.

33. Ibid., 231-232.

34. Ibid., 232.

35. Ibid.

36. Koedt, "Lesbianism and Feminism," 254-255.

37. Ibid.

38. Ibid., 255.

39. The origin of the phrase "the personal is political" is unclear, but it is often attributed to Carol Hanisch, "The Personal Is Political," February 1969 (www.carol-hanisch.org/CHwritings/PIP.html).

40. Koedt, "Lesbianism and Feminism," 255.

41. Echols, *Daring to Be Bad*, 212-213; Karla Jay, *Tales Of The Lavender Menace: A Memoir Of Liberation* (New York: Basic Books, 1999), 137-138.

42. Echols, *Daring to Be Bad*, 212-213, 219-220; Jay, *Tales Of The Lavender Menace*, 137-138.

43. Echols, *Daring to Be Bad*, 212-213.

13 – Homogenizing Versus Holistic Views of Gender and Sexuality

1. Elizabeth Ewen and Stuart Ewen, *Typecasting: On the Arts & Sciences of Human Inequality* (New York: Seven Stories Press, 2006), 357-374; Mara Mayor, "Fears and Fantasies of Anti-Suffragists," *The Connecticut Review*, 7 no. 2 (1974), 64-74; Griet Vandermassen, *Who's Afraid of Charles Darwin?: Debating Feminism and Evolutionary Theory* (Lanham: Rowman and Littlefield Publishers, 2005), 17-23.

2. Reviewed in Rosalind Barnett and Caryl Rivers, *Same Difference: How Gender Myths Are Hurting Our Relationships, Our Children, and Our Jobs* (New York: Basic Books, 2004); Lise Eliot, "The Trouble with Sex Differences," *Neuron* 72 (2011), 895-898; Anne Fausto-Sterling, *Myths of Gender: Biological Theories About Women and Men* (New York: Basic Books, 1985); Anne Fausto-Sterling, *Sexing the Body: Gender Politics and the Construction of Sexuality* (New York: Basic Books, 2002); Cordelia Fine, *Delusions of Gender: How Our Minds, Society, and Neurosexism Create Difference* (New York: W. W. Norton and Company, 2010); Patricia Adair Gowaty (ed.), *Feminism and Evolutionary Biology: Boundaries, Intersections and Frontiers* (New York: Chapman and Hall, 1996); Rebecca M. Jordan-Young, *Brain Storm: The Flaws in the Science of Sex Differences* (Cambridge: Harvard University Press, 2010); Robert N. Lancaster, *The Trouble with Nature: Sex in Science and Popular Culture* (Berkeley: University of California Press, 2003); Serano, *Whipping Girl*, 115-139, 262-271; Edward Stein, *The Mismeasure of Desire: The Science, Theory, and Ethics of Sexual Orientation* (Oxford: University Press, 1999, 119-274; Kelley Winters, *Gender Madness in American Psychiatry: Essays From the Struggle for Dignity* (Dillon: GID Reform Advocates, 2008).

3. Reviewed in Gerald M. Edelman, *Second Nature: Brain Science and Human Knowledge* (New Haven: Yale University Press, 2006); Bruce E. Wexler, *Brain and Culture: Neurobiology, Ideology and Social Change* (Cambridge: The MIT Press, 2006); Margaret Wilson, "The re-tooled mind: how culture re-engineers cognition," *SCAN* 5 (2010), 180-187. See also Notes 20 and 21 for this chapter.

4. David J. Buller, *Adapting Minds: Evolutionary Psychology and the Persistent Quest for Human Nature* (Cambridge: Bradford Books/The MIT Press, 2005); Richard C. Francis, *Why Men Won't Ask for Directions: The Seductions of Sociobiology* (Princeton, NJ: Princeton University Press, 2004); Linda Gannon, "A critique of evolutionary psychology," *Psychology, Evolution & Gender* 4, no. 2 (2002), 173-218; Stephen Jay Gould, "Darwinian Fundamentalism," *New York Review of Books* 44, no. 10 (June 12, 1997); Stephen Jay Gould, "Evolution: The Pleasures of Pluralism," *New York Review of Books* (June 26, 1997). Lancaster, *The Trouble with Nature*; V. S. Ramachandran, *Phantoms in the Brain: Probing the Mysteries of the Human Mind* (New York: Quill, 1998), 183-184, 201-202, 288-291; Robert C. Richardson, *Evolutionary Psychology*

as Maladapted Psychology (Life and Mind: Philosophical Issues in Biology and Psychology) (Cambridge, MA: The MIT Press, 2007).

5. Gabriella Anderson, Haiko Sprott, and Bjorn R Olsen, "Opinion: Publish Negative Results," *The Scientist*, January 15, 2013 (www.the-scientist.com/?articles. view/articleNo/33968/title/Opinion--Publish-Negative-Results/); Daniele Fanelli, "Negative results are disappearing from most disciplines and countries," *Scientometrics* 90 (2012), 891-904.

6. Raymond S. Nickerson, "Confirmation Bias: A Ubiquitous Phenomenon in Many Guises," *Review of General Psychology* 2, no. 2 (1998), 175-220. The overwhelming tendency of science journalists and media outlets to misrepresent and misreport research findings in a manner that depicts biology as deterministic (when it actually is not) is chronicled in Celeste M. Condit, "How geneticists can help reporters get their story right," *Nature Reviews Genetics* 8 (2007), 815-820.

7. Indeed, many of the works cited in Notes 2-4 were penned by biologists and other scientists. For other critiques of biological determinism from a decidedly biological perspective, see Richard Lewontin, *Human Diversity* (New York: Scientific American Library, 1995); Richard Lewontin, *It Ain't Necessarily So: The Dream of the Human Genome and Other Illusions* (New York: New York Review of Books, 2000, 2001).

8. I discussed why this is problematic in Chapter 12. See also Serano, *Whipping Girl*, 195-212.

9. Phyllis Burke, *Gender Shock: Exploding the Myths of Male and Female* (New York: Anchor Books, 1996), 3–136; John Colapinto, *As Nature Made Him: The Boy Who Was Raised as a Girl* (New York: HarperCollins, 2000); Mark Lostracco, "But For Today I Am A Boy," *Torontoist*, May 9, 2008 (http://torontoist.com/2008/05/but_for_today_i_am_a_boy).

10. Roughgarden, *Evolution's Rainbow*, 280–288.

11. Louis Goreen, "The biology of human psychosexual differentiation," *Hormones and Behavior* 50, no. 4 (2006), 589-601; Jordan-Young, *Brain Storm*; Roughgarden, *Evolution's Rainbow*, 185-326; Stein, *The Mismeasure of Desire*, 164-228.

12. P. T. Cohen-Kettenis and L. J. G. Gooren, "Transsexualism: A Review of Etiology, Diagnosis, and Treatment," *Journal of Psychosomatic Research* 46, no. 4 (1999), 315–333; Burke, *Gender Shock*, 54; Stein, *The Mismeasure of Desire*, 229-257.

13. Serano, *Whipping Girl*, 75-93.

14. Ibid. The use of the word "subconscious"—which is rarely used in academic and research settings due to its ambiguous nature—is purposeful here; it is an attempt to relieve the tendency that many have to want to link subconscious sex with a specific gene or region of the brain (I discuss this in more detail later in the chapter). Referring to one's subconscious *sex* (rather than subconscious *gender*) is also intentional, as it reflects many (albeit not all) transsexuals' experience that transitioning is primarily about *sex embodiment* (physical femaleness or maleness) and/or *sex affiliation* (belonging to and being recognized as female or male) than

it is about traits that are more closely associated with the word "gender," such as gender expression and gender roles.

15. See Chapter 12, Note 4, for reviews of how exceptional gender identities, expressions, and sexual orientations are pancultural and transhistorical. Exceptional sexual orientations and sexually dimorphic behaviors in nonhuman animals are chronicled in Bruce Bagemihl, *Biological Exuberance: Animal Homosexuality and Natural Diversity* (New York: St. Martin's Press, 1999); Roughgarden, *Evolution's Rainbow.*

16. Colapinto, *As Nature Made Him.*

17. William G. Reiner and John P. Gearhart, "Discordant Sexual Identity in Some Genetic Males with Cloacal Exstrophy Assigned to Female Sex at Birth," *The New England Journal of Medicine,* Vol. 350 (2004), No. 4, 333–341.

18. Further evidence for this comes from the experiences of intersex people. Specifically, people who are exceptional with regards to sex chromosome complement and/or hormonal makeup are more likely to also be exceptional in their sexual orientations, gender identities, and gender expressions than non-intersex people. This indicates that these biological factors have some influence on these aspects of gender and sexuality, albeit in a limited and non-deterministic manner. Reviewed in Goreen, "The biology of human psychosexual differentiation"; Melissa Hines, Charles Brook, and Gerard S. Conway, "Androgen and Psychosexual Development: Core Gender Identity, Sexual Orientation, and Recalled Childhood Gender Role Behavior in Women and Men With Congenital Adrenal Hyperplasia (CAH)," *The Journal of Sex Research* 41, no. 1 (2004), 75-81; Martina Jürgensen, Olaf Hiort, Paul-Martin Holterhus, and Ute Thyen, "Gender role behavior in children with XY karyotype and disorders of sex development," *Hormones and Behavior* 51 (2007) 443–453.

19. Bella English, "Led by the child who simply knew," *The Boston Globe,* December 11, 2011; Gunter Heylens, Griet De Cuypere, Kenneth J. Zucker, Cleo Schelfaut, Els Elaut, Heidi Vanden Bossche, Elfride De Baere, and Guy T'Sjoen, "Gender Identity Disorder in Twins: A Review of the Case Report Literature," *The Journal of Sexual Medicine* 9, no. 3, (2012), 751–757; Niklas Långström, Qazi Rahman, Eva Carlström, and Paul Lichtenstein, "Genetic and Environmental Effects on Same-sex Sexual Behavior: A Population Study of Twins in Sweden," *Archives of Sexual Behavior* 39, no. 1 (2010), 75-80.

20. Samuel J. Barnes and Gerald T. Finnerty, "Sensory Experience and Cortical Rewiring," *Neuroscientist* 16, no. 2 (2010), 186-198; Heidi Johansen-Berg, "Structural Plasticity: Rewiring the Brain," *Current Biology* 17, no. 4 (2007), R141–R144; Pierre-Marie Lledo, Mariana Alonso and Matthew S. Grubb, "Adult neurogenesis and functional plasticity in neuronal circuits," *Nature Review Neuroscience* 7, no. 3 (2006), 179-193; Arne May, "Experience-dependent structural plasticity in the adult human brain," *Trends in Cognitive Science* 15 no. 10 (2011), 475-482; Ramachandran, *Phantoms in the Brain*; Yaniv Sagi, Ido Tavor, Shir Hofstetter, Shimrit Tzur-Moryosef, Tamar Blumenfeld-Katzir, and Yaniv Assaf, "Learning in the Fast

Lane: New Insights into Neuroplasticity," *Neuron* 73 (2012), 1195-1203; Wexler, *Brain and Culture.*

21. S. Marc Breedlove, "Sex on the Brain," *Nature* 389 (1997), 801; Bogdan Draganski, Christian Gaser, Volker Busch, Gerhard Schuierer, Ulrich Bogdahn, and Arne May, "Changes in Grey Matter Induced by Training," *Nature* 427 (2004), 311-312; Stefan Klöppel, Jean-Francois Mangin, Anna Vongerichten, Richard S. J. Frackowiak, and Hartwig R. Siebner, "Nurture versus Nature: Long-Term Impact of Forced Right-Handedness on Structure of Pericentral Cortex and Basal Ganglia," *The Journal of Neuroscience* 30, no. 9 (2010), 3271-3275; Eleanor A. Maguire, David G. Gadian, Ingrid S. Johnsrude, Catriona D. Good, John Ashburner, Richard S. J. Frackowiak, and Christopher D. Frith, "Navigation-related structural change in the hippocampi of taxi-drivers," *Proceedings of the National Academy of Sciences* 97 (2000), 4398-4403; Thomas F. Münte, Eckart Altenmüller, and Lutz Jäncke, "The musician's brain as a model of neuroplasticity," *Nature Reviews in Neuroscience* 3 (2002), 473-478; Denise C. Park and Chih-Mao Huang, "Culture Wires the Brain: A Cognitive Neuroscience Perspective," *Perspectives on Psychological Science* 5, no. 4 (2010), 391-400; Katherine Woollett, Eleanor A. Maguire, "Acquiring 'the Knowledge' of London's Layout Drives Structural Brain Changes," *Current Biology* 21, no. 24 (2011), 2109-2114.

22. Peter G. Hepper, Sara Shahidullah, and Raymond White, "Handedness in the human fetus," *Neuropsychologia* 29, no. 11 (1991), 1107–1111.

23. Catherine Derom, Evert Thiery, Robert Vlietinck, Ruth Loos, and Robert Derom, "Handedness in twins according to zygosity and chorion type: A preliminary report," *Behavior Genetics* 26, no. 4 (1996), 407-408; Syuichi Ooki, "Nongenetic factors associated with human handedness and footedness in Japanese twin children," *Environmental Health and Preventive Medicine* 11, no. 6 (2006), 304–312.

24. Klöppel et al., "Nurture versus Nature: Long-Term Impact of Forced Right-Handedness on Structure of Pericentral Cortex and Basal Ganglia."

25. Carolyn Korsmeyer, *Making Sense of Taste: Food and Philosophy* (Ithaca, NY: Cornell University Press, 1999).

26. Alexey N Pronin, Hong Xu, Huixian Tang, Lan Zhang, Qing Li, and Xiaodong Li, "Specific Alleles of Bitter Receptor Genes Influence Human Sensitivity to the Bitterness of Aloin and Saccharin," *Current Biology* 17 (2007), 1403-1408.

27. Jonathan Bard, "A systems biology view of evolutionary genetics," *BioEssays* 32 (2010), 559–563; Trey Ideker, Timothy Galitski, and Leroy Hood, "A New Approach to Decoding Life: Systems Biology," *Annual Review of Genomics and Human Genetics* 2 (2001), 343-372; Hiroaki Kitano, "Systems Biology: A Brief Overview," *Science* 295 (2002), 1662-1664.

28. Stein, L. D. 2004. "Human Genome: End of the Beginning," *Nature* 431, 915-916. Note that this view of a finite number of definable genes is overly simplistic; see Thomas R. Gingeras, "Origin of phenotypes: Genes and transcripts," *Genome Research* 17 (2007), 682-690.

29. Jason H. Moore, "The Ubiquitous Nature of Epistasis in Determining Susceptibility to Common Human Diseases," *Human Heredity* 56 (2003), 73–82; Patrick C. Phillips, "Epistasis—the essential role of gene interactions in the structure and evolution of genetic systems," *Nature Reviews Genetics* 9 (2008), 855-867.

30. Gerald E McClearn, "Contextual Genetics," *Trends in Genetics* 22 (2006), 314-319; Robert Plomin, Claire M.A. Haworth, and Oliver S.P. Davis, "Common disorders are quantitative traits," *Nature Reviews Genetics* 10 (2009), 872-878; Anna L. Tyler, Folkert W. Asselbergs, Scott M. Williams, and Jason H. Moore, "Shadows of Complexity: what biological networks reveal about epistasis and pleiotropy," *Bioessays* 31 (2009), 220-227; Michael N. Weedon and Timothy M. Frayling, "Reaching new heights: insights into the genetics of human stature," *Trends in Genetics* 24 (2008), 595-603; Kenneth M. Weiss, "Tilting at Quixotic Trait Loci: An Evolutionary Perspective on Genetic Causation," *Genetics* 179 (2008), 1741-1756.

31. Kelly A. Frazer, Sarah S. Murray, Nicholas J. Schork, and Eric J. Topol, "Human genetic variation and its contribution to complex traits," *Nature Reviews in Genetics* 10 (2009), 241-251; Arnaud Le Rouzic and Orjan Carlborg, "Evolutionary potential of hidden genetic variation," *Trends in Ecology and Evolution* 23 (2007), 33-37.

32. Ralph J. Greenspan, "The Flexible Genome," *Nature Reviews Genetics* 2 (2001), 383-387; Ralph J. Greenspan, "Selection, gene interaction, and flexible gene networks," *Cold Spring Harbor Symposia on Quantitative Biology* 74 (2009), 131-138; Benjamin Houot, Stéphane Fraichard, Ralph J. Greenspan, and Jean-Francois Ferveur, "Genes Involved in Sex Pheromone Discrimination in Drosophila melanogaster and Their Background-Dependent Effect," *PLoS ONE* 7 (2012), e30799; Bruno van Swinderen and Ralph J. Greenspan, "Flexibility in a Gene Network Affecting a Simple Behavior in Drosophila melanogaster," *Genetics* 169 (2005), 2151-2163.

33. Arjun Raj and Alexander van Oudenaarden, "Nature, Nurture, nor Chance: Stochastic Gene Expression and Its Consequences," *Cell* 135 (2008), 216-226; Jonathan M. Raser and Erin K. O'Shea, "Noise in Gene Expression: Origins, Consequences, and Control," *Science* 309 (2005), 2010-2013; Michael S. Samoilov, Gavin Price, and Adam P. Arkin, "From Fluctuations to Phenotypes: The Physiology of Noise," *Science's STKE* 366 (2006), re17.

34. Robin Holliday, "Epigenetics: a historical overview," *Epigenetics* 1 (2006), 76-80; L.J. Johnson and P.J. Tricker, "Epigenomic plasticity within populations: its evolutionary significance and potential," *Heredity* 105 (2010), 113–121; Sui Huang, "The Molecular and mathematical basis of Waddington's epigenetic landscape: A framework for post-Darwinian biology," *Bioessays* 34 (2011), 149-157.

35. Greg Gibson, "The environmental contribution to gene expression profiles," *Nature Reviews Genetics* 9 (2008), 575-581; Massimo Pigliucci, *Phenotypic Plasticity: Beyond Nature and Nurture* (Baltimore: The John Hopkins Press, 2001).

36. Malin Ah-King and Soren Nylin, "Sex in an Evolutionary Perspective: Just another Reaction Norm," *Evolutionary Biology* 37 (2010) 234-246; Amanda Bretman, Matthew J.G. Gage, and Tracey Chapman, "Quick-change artists: male plastic

behavioural responses to rivals," *Trends in Ecology and Evolution* 26 (2011), 467-473; Charlie K. Cornwallis and Tobias Uller, "Towards an evolutionary ecology of sexual traits." *Trends in Ecology and Evolution* 25, no. 3 (2010), 145-152; Roughgarden, *Evolution's Rainbow*.

37. Susan A. Gelman, *The Essential Child: Origins of Essentialism in Everyday Thought* (Oxford: Oxford University Press, 2003).

38. Ah-King and Nylin, "Sex in an Evolutionary Perspective: Just another Reaction Norm"; Eric S. Haag and Alana V. Doty, "Sex Determination across evolution: Connecting the dots," *PLoS Biology* 3 (2005), 21-24; David J. Hosken and Paula Stockley, "Sexual Selection and Genital Evolution," *Trends in Ecology and Evolution* 19 (2004), 87-93;

39. Gerald M. Edelman and Joseph A. Gally, "Degeneracy and complexity in biological systems," *Proceedings of the National Academy of Sciences* 98 (2001), 13763-13768; James M. Whitacre, "Degeneracy: a link between evolvability, robustness, and complexity in biological systems," *Theoretical Biology and Medical Modelling* 7, no. 6 (2010).

40. Serano, *Whipping Girl*, 80-81.

41. Serano, *Whipping Girl*, 65-76.

14 – How Double Standards Work

1. The concept of marked versus unmarked originated in the field of linguistics, but has since been applied to semiotics (the study of signs and symbols), sociology, and related fields. See Wayne Brekhus, "A Sociology of the Unmarked," *Sociological Theory* 16, no. 1 (1998), 34-51; Linda R. Waugh, "Marked and unmarked: A choice between unequals in semiotic structure," *Semiotica* 38 (1982), 299-318. This chapter is my own personal take on the unmarked/marked distinction and how it creates obstacles and double binds for members of marginalized groups.

2. Perry R. Hinton, *Stereotypes, Cognition and Culture* (East Sussex: Psychology Press, 2000), 96-97, 111-115; Lee Jussim, Lerita M. Coleman, and Lauren Lerch, "The nature of stereotypes: A comparison and integration of three theories," *Journal of Personality and Social Psychology* 52, no. 3 (1987), 536-546; David J. Schneider, *The Psychology of Stereotyping* (New York: The Guilford Press, 2004), 229-265.

3. Hinton, *Stereotypes, Cognition and Culture*, 64-66, 77-79, 95-97; Ziva Kunda, *Social Cognition: Making Sense of People* (Cambridge, MA: Bradford Books/The MIT Press, 1999), 92, 127-133, 162-168,

4. Hinton, *Stereotypes, Cognition and Culture*, 95-97; Jussim, Coleman, and Lerch, "The nature of stereotypes: A comparison and integration of three theories"; Kunda, *Social Cognition*, 144-151.

5. In 2006, the number of certified public accountants in the United States was 646,520 (http://ipassthecpaexam.com/number-of-cpa)—that is, approximately 0.22 percent of the population. Gates estimated that the number of transgender people in

the United States is 0.3 percent (Gary J. Gates, "How many people are lesbian, gay, bisexual, and transgender?," The Williams Institute, UCLA School of Law, April 2011) and Olyslager and Conway have estimated that the lower bound on the prevalence of MTF transsexuality (based on reports from Thailand, the U.K., and the United States) is 0.2 percent (Femke Olyslager and Lynn Conway, "On the Calculation of the Prevalence of Transsexualism," paper presented at the WPATH Twentieth International Symposium, September 2007). Older research suggested that 1 percent of U.S. women have worked as prostitutes at some point in their lives (Prostitutes' Education Network, "Prostitution in The United States—The Statistics," www.bayswan.org/stats.html), and McNeill has argued that New Zealand's recent surveys indicating that 0.285 percent of women are active, declared prostitutes (a number assuredly lower than the total number of sex workers) is applicable to the United States (Maggie McNeill, "By the Numbers," April 20, 2011, http://maggiemcneill.wordpress.com/2011/04/20/by-the-numbers). Admittedly, there is no registry or census of transsexuals or sex workers, so these numbers are all estimates, but they are consistent with the general point that these groups are not significantly rarer (and may in fact be more prevalent) than accountants, even though people's reactions to them are often starkly different.

6. To be clear, I am not personally making this point. I have great contempt for the tendency to dismiss things that people do or create as being "unnatural." I find that the natural/unnatural distinction serves little purpose other than to undermine supposedly "artificial" people and ways of being.

7. This was evident in Chapter 12, "The Perversion of 'The Personal Is Political.'"

8. The one obvious exception is that people who are male typically identify as such. This is likely because male and female are viewed as natural complements in a way that does not hold true for most unmarked/marked social distinctions—I discuss this more in the following chapter, "Myriad Double Standards."

9. Erving Goffman, *Stigma: Notes on the Management of Spoiled Identity* (Englewood Cliffs, NJ: Prentice-Hall Inc., 1963).

10. Thomas F. Pettigrew, "The Ultimate Attribution Error: Extending Allport's Cognitive Analysis of Prejudice," *Personality and Social Psychology Bulletin* 5 (1979), 461-476.

11. This idea of a "reverse discourse" originated in Michel Foucault, *The History of Sexuality, Volume I: An Introduction* (New York: Vintage Books, 1990), 101-102.

12. Serano, *Whipping Girl*, 139-140, 337-339.

13. Definition from *Dictionary.com* (http://dictionary.reference.com/browse/shameless).

14. I believe that this difference stems from the fact that transsexuality is typically viewed as a stigmatized trait with no redeemable qualities. In contrast, straight-male-centric culture sends mixed messages about women's bodies, sometimes disregarding or disparaging them, while other times glorifying them as sexual objects.

15. This is discussed in more depth in Goffman, *Stigma*, 16-19, 48-51.

16. Admittedly, some people do view transsexuality as a medical condition and/or mental illness, whereas I view it as part of gender variation.

17. People often say that transsexuals "pass" as women or men, but this is a misnomer. It is more correct to say that we are transsexual women (or men) who "pass" as cissexual women (or men).

18. Serano, *Whipping Girl*, 176-180.

19. Jenna Basiliere, "Political is Personal: Scholarly Manifestations of the Feminist Sex Wars," *Michigan Feminist Studies* 22 (2009), 1-25.

20. To be clear, I am not suggesting that these feminists are "pro-virginity" or somehow "ashamed" of female sexuality. Neither am I suggesting that those who fall on the other side of this double bind are literally "whores" or "shameless."

21. Elsewhere, I have described this as the "predator/prey mindset." Serano, *Whipping Girl*, 253-271; Julia Serano, "Why Nice Guys Finish Last," in Jaclyn Friedman and Jessica Valenti (eds.), *Yes Means Yes: Visions of Female Sexual Power and a World Without Rape* (Berkeley: Seal Press, 2008).

15 – Myriad Double Standards

1. Occasionally people do suddenly view me as being superior ("You must be really smart!") or inferior ("You must be an essentialist!") upon discovering that I am a scientist, but this tends to be the exception rather than the rule.

2. Schneider, *The Psychology of Stereotyping*, 16-26.

3. Of course, people may disagree about what the defining characteristic(s) of a particular group are—I discuss this further in Chapter 17, "Expecting Heterogeneity."

4. While "brave" typically has positive connotations, it is often used as a sort of backhanded complement, the implication being, "Wow, I would never want to be transsexual, you must be so brave for being one."

5. Hinton, *Stereotypes, Cognition and Culture*, 84-95.

6. Ibid.

7. Hinton, *Stereotypes, Cognition and Culture*, 87; Kunda, *Social Cognition*, 103-105, 428-432; Pettigrew, "The Ultimate Attribution Error: Extending Allport's Cognitive Analysis of Prejudice."

8. This helps explain why the credit/detriment double bind (which I discussed last chapter) exists.

9. This can be seen in how many things that are coded "male/masculine" in our culture tend to be seen as universal and are relatively free of meanings and connotations, whereas things that are coded "female/feminine" tend to be seen as highly specific for girls/women, and have strong (and often inferior) meanings and stereotypes associated with them.

10. These secondary hierarchies are prone to form once the group that is marginalized by the initial hierarchy gains a modicum of legitimacy.

11. Some might argue that some of these represent defining characteristics of women rather than stereotypes. I, on the other hand, would say that the defining characteristic of women is that we identify and move through the world as women.

12. Some feminists and queer activists use the word "conform" in a negative sense, to imply that the person in question is actively trying to live up to some assumption or norm. This use of the term is rather presumptuous, as it assumes that the person in question must be driven by ulterior motives such as "passing," or assimilation. In contrast, here I use the word "conform" in a more neutral manner, to convey that other people are constantly projecting assumptions onto us, and by chance, some of the time, some of the assumptions they make about us will just so happen to be correct.

13. Evidence that group members who transgress stereotypes are viewed more negatively than group members who uphold them can be found in Hinton, *Stereotypes, Cognition and Culture*, 95-97; Jussim, Coleman, and Lerch, "The nature of stereotypes: A comparison and integration of three theories"; Kunda, *Social Cognition*, 144-151; Schneider, *The Psychology of Stereotyping*, 442.

16 – Fixed Versus Holistic Perspectives

1. This tendency is discussed in many of the references listed in Chapter 12, Note 1.

2. All of these populations have existed and have fought for recognition, acceptance, and/or equality during earlier time periods. The dates that I list here refer to when these groups first began to articulate their experiences in terms of a society-wide ideology or ism that marginalizes them, and when such critiques started to coalesce into a movement.

3. See "Asexuality: the History of a Definition," (http://asexualexplorations.net/home/documents/asexuality_history_of_a_definition.pdf).

4. Serano, *Whipping Girl*.

5. Jo Paoletti, "Dressing for sexes" (www.gentlebirth.org/archives/pinkblue.html).

6. Granted, we may have different rationales to justify marginalizing these groups, but the end result is the same—such groups are deemed inferior and illegitimate.

7. Susan Brownmiller, *Femininity* (New York: Fawcett Columbine, 1984), 83-84.

8. Admittedly, there are a number of reasons why such women might avoid the "feminist" label, but elsewhere I have made the case that anti-feminine sentiment is part of the problem: Serano, *Whipping Girl*, 319-343. See also Noah Berlatsky, "Katy Perry's Aversion to Feminism Shows Feminism Is Still Radical," *The Atlantic*, December 5, 2012.

9. I describe some of these experiences in Serano, *Whipping Girl*, especially chapters 10 and 17.

10. The idea of existing in the borderlands between two identities stems from Gloria Anzaldúa, *Borderlands/La Frontera: The New Mestiza* (San Francisco: Aunt Lute Books, 1999).

17 – Expecting Heterogeneity

1. hooks, *Feminist Theory*, 11-12.

2. While we certainly reverse some norms, others may closely resemble those of the dominant society. As a result, feminist and queer spaces may display subversivism while at the same time being monosexist, racist, classist, or ableist.

3. Bizarro World is a fictional planet in the Superman comic book series in which all of the rules of Earth are reversed.

4. Hinton, *Stereotypes, Cognition and Culture*, 100-102.

5. Ibid.

6. See Chapter 14, "How Double Standards Work."

7. hooks, *Feminist Theory*, 12-15.

8. Echols, *Daring to Be Bad*, 203-241.

18 – Challenging Gender Entitlement

1. Bill Maher is an American comedian and TV personality who is a very outspoken atheist, and whose critiques of religion often veer into the territory of ridiculing people who are religious for being unintelligent and easily manipulated.

2. This is an example of the dupes/fakes double bind that I described in Chapter 14, "How Double Standards Work."

3. Serano, *Whipping Girl*, 89-93, 165-170, 359-362.

4. Here, I am not talking about invasive questions centered on the inquisitor's own curiosity and anxiety, but rather questions centered on better understanding the person's identity and preferences, such as asking them their preferred pronouns.

5. "Choice feminism" does not appear to be an actual strand of feminist thought, but rather a popular misinterpretation of feminism, one that is perpetuated by the media's obsessive focus on what women do and the life choices we make, rather than on the double standards and double binds we face. In other words, the very notion of "choice feminism"—as well as most debates about it—remains firmly rooted in the fact that women are marked, and thus our behaviors are deemed remarkable, questionable, and suspect. Nothing illustrates this more than the fact that men's life choices are entirely absent from discussions (both pro and con) of "choice feminism."

6. Rather than assuming that some people are operating under a "false consciousness" (which denies their autonomy and their competence to make personal decisions about their own bodies and lives), we should instead consider the following

three possibilities: 1) Perhaps they have made the choice they've made because they lack information or experiences that we possess; 2) Perhaps they've made that choice because they have information or experiences that we are not privy to; or 3) Sometimes people with similar information or experiences nevertheless make different choices. Reframing the matter in this way prevents us from viewing ourselves as omniscient, superior beings.

19 – Self-Examining Desire and Embracing Ambivalence

1. Most feminists who forward such views would not consider their approach to be "sex-negative" (although sex-positive feminists often decry it as such). Lisa Millbank has recently made a case for reclaiming the term "sex-negative" (Lisa Millbank, "The Ethical Prude: Imagining An Authentic Sex-Negative Feminism," *A Radical TransFeminist*, February 29, 2012, http://radtransfem.wordpress.com/2012/02/29/the-ethical-prude-imagining-an-authentic-sex-negative-feminism). While I don't entirely agree with Millbank's analysis on every point, I appreciate her attempt to bridge the gap between sex-positive and sex-negative feminisms, and her writings encouraged me to write this chapter.

2. These claims often dovetail with the popularity of so-called "choice feminism"—see Chapter 18, Note 5. I have no problem with the notion that an individual might find such expressions personally empowering. Rather, it is the way these claims are framed as uncritical blanket statements that concerns me. However, it must be said that the very reason why people feel compelled to offer a justification ("It's empowering!") is because these expressions are marked by others, and thus deemed questionable and suspect. Finally, some radical feminists (who typically fall on the "sex-negative" side of this debate) will cite these everything-sexual-is-empowering claims as evidence that sex-positive feminism (as a whole) is ignorant of, or complicit with, the sexualization of women in our culture. This is patently untrue: Many sex-positive feminists are deeply concerned with this problem—e.g., see Friedman and Valenti (eds.), *Yes Means Yes: Visions of Female Sexual Power and a World Without Rape*. In other words, feminists on both sides of the sex-positive/negative debate want to see an end to sexualization and rape culture. We just have very different ideas of how to get there.

3. *Fifty Shades of Grey* is a novel by E. L. James that depicts a male-dominant, female-submissive BDSM relationship, and which became immensely popular in 2012.

20 – Recognizing Invalidations

1. Serano, *Whipping Girl*; Serano, "*Whipping Girl* FAQ on cissexual, cisgender, and cis privilege."

2. For examples of non-trans/cis privileges, see Hazel/Cedar Troost, "Cis Privilege Checklist," July 10, 2008 (http://takesupspace.wordpress.com/cis-privilege-checklist); Ampersand, "The Non-Trans Privilege Checklist," September 22, 2006 (www.

amptoons.com/blog/2006/09/22/the-non-trans-privilege-checklist). See also Serano, *Whipping Girl*, 161-193.

3. Emi Koyama, "Cissexual/Cisgender: decentralizing the dominant group," June 7, 2002 (www.eminism.org/interchange/2002/20020607-wmstl.html).

4. Queen Emily, "Cis is not an 'academic' term," April 25, 2009 (www.questioning-transphobia.com/?p=1327).

5. Serano, *Whipping Girl*, 35-52. The original article appeared in *Bitch* 26, Fall 2004.

6. Reviewed in American Psychological Association Task Force on the Sexualization of Girls, "Report of the APA Task Force on the Sexualization of Girls" (Washington, D.C.: American Psychological Association, 2007, www.apa.org/pi/women/programs/girls/report-full.pdf).

7. David Montgomery, "Rush Limbaugh On the Offensive Against Ad With Michael J. Fox," *The Washington Post*, October 25, 2006.

8. Julia Serano, "Psychology, Sexualization and Trans-Invalidations," keynote lecture presented at the Eighth Annual Philadelphia Trans-Health Conference, June 12, 2009 (www.juliaserano.com/av/Serano-TransInvalidations.pdf).

9. The idea of "privilege checklists" seems to have originated with Peggy McIntosh's essay "White Privilege: Unpacking the Invisible Knapsack."

10. KL Pereira, "Do Not Want: The asexual revolution gets organized," *Bitch* 37, Fall 2007, 58-63.

21 - Balancing Acts

1. Others will point out that people also tolerate and perpetuate these phenomena because they indirectly or directly benefit from them. While this may be true, people do often engage in undermining and dehumanizing others even when there are no obvious material benefits to be gained from such actions.

2. David M. Amodio, John T. Jost, Sarah L. Master, and Cindy M. Yee, "Neurocognitive correlates of liberalism and conservatism," *Nature Neuroscience* 10, no. 10 (2007), 1246-1247.

3. It seems to me that the word "radical" gets used in two different ways in feminist and queer activism. Sometimes it is used by people who want to address the root causes of sexism rather than merely reduce the many symptoms of sexist oppression. I can identify with this use of the term. Others use it to imply that they (and they alone) are fully committed to the cause and willing to take whatever steps are necessary, and that non–radical-identified activists are either ignorant, wishy-washy, overly compliant, or purposefully selling the movement out. It is this latter segment of self-identified "radicals" that tend to use the label to enforce dogmatic and inflexible points of view.

4. A clearinghouse of articles on the topic of "call-out culture" (from all sides of the issue) can be found at "privilege-checking and call-out culture" (www.metafilter.

com/122432/privilegechecking-and-callout-culture). The articles that I first read on this issue (and which resonated with my own experiences and influenced my writing of this chapter) include Flavia Dzodan, "Come one, come all! Feminist and Social Justice blogging as performance and bloodshed," *Tiger Beatdown*, October 17, 2011 (http://tigerbeatdown.com/2011/10/17/come-one-come-all-bloggers-bear-it-all-out-feminist-and-social-justice-blogging-as-performance-and-bloodshed); Ozy Frantz, "Certain Propositions Concerning Callout Culture (Parts 1-3)," *Ozy Frantz's Blog*, December 2012 (http://ozyfrantz.com/category/callout-culture); Sally Lawton, "The Limits of Social Justice Blogging," *Persephone Magazine*, July 17, 2012 (http://persephonemagazine.com/2012/07/17/the-limits-of-social-justice-blogging); Ariel Meadow Stallings, "Liberal bullying: Privilege-checking and semantics-scolding as Internet sport," *Offbeat Empire*, October 15, 2012 (http://offbeatempire.com/2012/10/liberal-bullying); Hannah Wilder, "The Unicorn Ally," *Pyromaniac Harlot's Blog*, April 3, 2012 (http://pyromaniacharlot.wordpress.com/2012/04/03/the-unicorn-ally).

5. Lorde, *Sister Outsider*, 114-123.

6. I discuss "subconscious sex" in Chapter 13, and the "bisexuals reinforce the gender binary" claim in Chapter 9.

7. For instance, if someone said that "all women menstruate" or "all women have clitorises and vaginas," that claim would clearly be an act of gender entitlement, as it would erase the existence of trans women and many intersex and infertile women. But a woman who simply discusses her own attributes in a non–gender-entitled manner is not exercising cis privilege over trans women as far as I'm concerned. I discuss this more in Serano, "*Whipping Girl* FAQ on cissexual, cisgender, and cis privilege."

8. This notion that a person's cissexist actions stem from some kind of inherent cissexist "nature" or "disposition" may stem from *fundamental attribution error*, which I discuss in Chapter 15, "Myriad Double Standards." As I argued in that chapter, this assumption is quite essentialist.

9. Dzodan, "Come one, come all! Feminist and Social Justice blogging as performance and bloodshed"; Stallings, "Liberal bullying: Privilege-checking and semantics-scolding as Internet sport."

10. Dzodan, "Come one, come all! Feminist and Social Justice blogging as performance and bloodshed"; Joreen, "TRASHING: The Dark Side of Sisterhood," April 1976 (www.jofreeman.com/joreen/trashing.htm).

11. Admittedly, these guidelines may not be as useful in Internet groups and spaces, where people who are not at all interested in social justice causes can purposefully interrupt and disrupt otherwise constructive discussions.

12. Trans people are often disparagingly referred to as male or female "impersonators," which dismisses our gender identities and lived experiences. And on the Internet, some cis men refer to trans women as "traps," the implication being that we deceive them into being attracted to, and sleeping with, us.

CREDITS

Excerpts from "Fuck You (A Poem for Monty)" by Carolyn Connelly appear courtesy of the author.

Excerpts from *Daring to Be Bad: Radical Feminism in America, 1967–75* by Alice Echols appear courtesy of University of Minnesota Press.

Several passages of "On the Outside Looking In" previously appeared in *Whipping Girl: A Transsexual Woman on Sexism and the Scapegoating of Femininity*, by Julia Serano (Emeryville, CA: Seal Press, 2007).

"Reclaiming Femininity" originally appeared in *Transfeminist Perspectives in and beyond Transgender and Gender Studies*, edited by Anne Enke (Philadelphia: Temple University Press, 2012).

ACKNOWLEDGMENTS

First, I want to thank Laura Mazer and Barrett Briske for their editing prowess, and Krista Lyons and everyone else at Seal Press and Perseus Books who helped make this book possible. I also thank Heather Bruce for her help with accessing research materials.

The essays and spoken word pieces compiled in this book were penned at various times over the course of the last eight years. During that period, many people have come in and out of my life, and I have been inspired by countless books, essays, blog posts, events, conferences, organizations, writers, artists, and performers. I cannot possibly mention all of them. Many of the people and organizations that were most influential for me early on are mentioned in the Acknowledgments section of *Whipping Girl*, so I won't reiterate them here. This time around, I especially want to thank the following folks for their friendship and many fruitful discussions about community and exclusion: D. Rita Alfonso, Danielle Askini, Talia Bettcher, Gina de Vries, Maddie Deutsch, Susan Forrest, Rebecca Hammond, Lily Shahar

Kunning, Oberyn Kunning, Katherine Mancuso, Sara Moore, Caitlyn Pascal, Elena Rose, Rachel Ruben, and Ariel Troster.

Many of the chapters in the first section were originally written for spoken word performance events sponsored by the Queer Cultural Center (QCC), and these events took place as part of QCC's annual National Queer Arts Festival in San Francisco. Michelle Tea invited me to write "On the Outside Looking In" for the 2005 show *Transforming Community*, and "Margins" for the 2008 show *FRINGES, MARGINS & BORDERS*. "Performance Piece" was originally written for *Fresh Meat* in 2007 (curated by Sean Dorsey), and subsequently appeared on the webzine *Gay Utopia* (edited by Noah Berlatsky) and in the anthology *Gender Outlaws: The Next Generation* (edited by Kate Bornstein and S. Bear Bergman). "Three Strikes and I'm Out" was written for the 2008 show *Coming Out . . . Again* (curated by Meliza Bañales). "How to Be an Ally to Trans Women" and "Dating" were originally written for the 2009 and 2010 renditions of *Girl Talk: A Cis and Trans Woman Dialogue*, which I co-curate with Gina de Vries and Elena Rose. In addition to these wonderful curators, I also want to thank all the folks at QCC, especially Pam Penniston, Jeff Jones, Rudy Lemke, Chris Dunaway, and Beth Pickens, who all played a role in making the aforementioned shows happen.

"Reclaiming Femininity" was initially a keynote address that I gave at the Femme 2008 conference, and I thank all the organizers of that event for giving me that opportunity. That chapter has also previously appeared in the anthology *Transfeminist Perspectives in and beyond Transgender and Gender Studies* (Temple University Press, 2012), edited by Anne Enke, whom I thank for her advice on reconfiguring that speech into an essay. "Trans Feminism: There's No Conundrum About It" originally appeared on the *Ms. Magazine* blog, and I thank Michele Kort for that opportunity and her editing of the original piece.

The holistic approach to feminism that I outline in the second section was initially inspired by Erving Goffman's book *Stigma: Notes on the*

Management of Spoiled Identity. In it, Goffman draws from a vast array of examples of people who are marginalized in different ways (e.g., for being disabled, queer, of color, sex workers, and so on) in order to create a synthesis of how people are stigmatized, and how stigmatized individuals react to their situations. It was written in 1963, so much of the language is anachronistic, and there are other aspects of *Stigma* that I find a bit problematic. But it encouraged me to try to make sense of the numerous parallels that exist between diverse forms of sexism and marginalization. Also, Alice Echols's *Daring to Be Bad: Radical Feminism in America, 1967-75* was very influential, as it brought to my attention how many of the debates and instances of exclusion that routinely occur today in feminist and queer circles are almost identical in structure to those that occurred back then.

Finally, I am grateful for my family of origin for giving me love and support throughout the years—especially my Mom, who passed away in 2009, and to whom this book is dedicated. I am also thankful for my current flock: Buddy, Bean-Bean, Chico, and Macbeth (birdies), Flutie M'lar (kitty), and Katherine (human) for keeping me company during the long days of writing.

ABOUT THE AUTHOR

Julia Serano is an Oakland, California–based writer, performer, and activist. She is the author of *Whipping Girl: A Transsexual Woman on Sexism and the Scapegoating of Femininity* (Seal Press, 2007), a collection of personal essays that reveal how misogyny frames popular assumptions about femininity and shapes many of the myths and misconceptions people have about transsexual women. Julia's other writings have appeared in anthologies (including *Gender Outlaws: The Next Generation, Word Warriors: 30 Leaders in the Women's Spoken Word Movement* and *Yes Means Yes: Visions of Female Sexual Power and A World Without Rape*), in feminist, queer, pop culture, and literary magazines and websites (such as *Bitch, AlterNet.org, Ms. Magazine Blog, Out, Feministing.com,* and *make/shift*), and have been used as teaching materials in gender studies, queer studies, psychology, and human sexuality courses in colleges across North America. In addition to her gender-related writing and activism, Julia has a PhD in Biochemistry and Molecular Biophysics from Columbia University, and for seventeen years she worked as a researcher in the fields of genetics and developmental and evolutionary biology at UC Berkeley. For more information about all of her creative endeavors, check out www.juliaserano.com.

SELECTED TITLES FROM SEAL PRESS

By women. For women.

Bi: Notes for a Bisexual Revolution, by Shiri Eisner. $16.00, 978-1-58005-474-4. Feminist bisexual and genderqueer activist Shiri Eisner takes readers on a journey through the many aspects of the meanings and politics of bisexuality, specifically highlighting how bisexuality can open up new and exciting ways of challenging social convention.

Whipping Girl: A Transsexual Woman on Sexism and the Scapegoating of Femininity, by Julia Serano. $15.95, 978-1-58005-154-5. Biologist and trans woman Julia Serano reveals a unique perspective on femininity, masculinity, and gender identity.

Gender Outlaws: The Next Generation, edited by Kate Bornstein and S. Bear Bergman. $16.95, 978-1-58005-308-2. Collects and contextualizes the work of this generation's trans and genderqueer forward-thinkers—new voices from the stage, on the streets, in the workplace, in the bedroom, and on the pages and websites of the world's most respected news sources.

Nobody Passes: Rejecting the Rules of Gender and Conformity, edited by Mattilda a.k.a Matt Bernstein Sycamore. $15.95, 978-1-58005-184-2. A timely and thought-provoking collection of essays that confronts and challenges the notion of belonging by examining the perilous intersections of identity, categorization, and community.

Full Frontal Feminism: A Young Woman's Guide to Why Feminism Matters, by Jessica Valenti. $15.95, 978-1-58005-201-6. A sassy and in-your-face look at contemporary feminism for women of all ages.

Transgender History: Seal Studies, by Susan Stryker. $14.95, 978-1-58005-224-5. An introduction to transgender and queer theory from the mid–19th century through today.

FIND SEAL PRESS ONLINE
www.SealPress.com
www.Facebook.com/SealPress
Twitter: @SealPress